ONE FLEW OVER THE KOSOVO THEATER

ONE FLEW OVER THE KOSOVO THEATER

AN ANTHOLOGY OF CONTEMPORARY DRAMA FROM KOSOVO

Edited by Saša Ilić and Jeton Neziraj

Egret

Chapel Hill, North Carolina

2018

PUBLISHER CATALOGING-IN-PUBLICATION DATA
Names: Ilić, Saša, 1972 — editor. | Neziraj, Jeton, 1977 — editor.
Title: One flew over the Kosovo Theater : an anthology of contemporary drama from Kosovo / edited by Saša Ilić and Jeton Neziraj.
Description: Chapel Hill : Egret Imprint, Laertes Press, 2018.
Identifiers : LCCN : 2018933142 | ISBN : 978-1-942281-04-7.
Subjects : LCSH : Albanian drama — Kosovo (Republic) — Translations into English.
Classification : LCC PG9638.K67 O54 2018 | DDC 891.991—dc 23

Originally published in Serbian in 2014 by Radnička komuna Links, Belgrade, as *Let Iznad Kosovskog Pozorišta, antologija savremene kosovske drame.*
A portion of *The Finger* first appeared in *Extract from* The Finger : *a play, Doruntina Basha,*
Wasafiri, © 2014 by Wasafiri, reprinted by permission of Taylor & Francis Ltd, on behalf of Wasafiri.

Egret is an imprint of Laertes Press, Incorporated | www.laertesbooks.org

A NOTE FROM
ARIEL DORFMAN

For many artists and citizens around the world, the tragedy and cause of Kosovo was of great concern and, for my part, I welcomed the possibility of the people of that land to express themselves and their identity freely . . . For a country like Kosovo, the theater is undoubtedly one of the arts that most needs to be able to tell stories — just like the people of Kosovo — without fear — also like the people of Kosovo. Indeed, the freedom that should be represented on the stage of the National Theater is symbolic of the freedom that all those who live and create in Kosovo deserve. The plays in this book are proof that vibrant ideas, subversive laughter, and deeply portrayed characters cannot be silenced.

CONTENTS

A FOREWORD BY ANNA DI LELLIO

This collection of contemporary plays from Kosovo, spanning almost a decade, is deeply influenced by a dramatic historical context. As we examine this period, we must remember that the war began in Kosovo well before 1998 as a low intensity conflict, following Slobodan Milošević's rise to power in Yugoslavia ten years earlier. In 1989, as the Berlin Wall fell and the entire Eastern Bloc moved towards Western Europe and liberal democracy, Yugoslavia remained in the grip of the old Communist apparatus. To seize power and maintain it, Milošević exploited the destructive passion of Serbian nationalist circles and forced the recentralization of Federal Yugoslavia. But first he revoked the constitutional autonomy of Kosovo, which was Serbia's province. Then he went to war in Slovenia, Croatia, and Bosnia to stop these republics from seceding from Yugoslavia, aiming to forcibly annex the areas where Serbs lived, after having ethnically cleansed them.

The comedy, *The Crossroads Café*, is situated during the (Kosovo) Albanians' war of secession from Serbia, which culminated with NATO intervention to stop an anticipated ethnic cleansing by Serbian President Slobodan Milošević. *The Basement* develops during the mass expulsions of Albanians from Pristina in April 1999 and includes the disappearance of the protagonist's son. A missing husband and son casts his shadow on *The Finger* ten years after the conflict, while the monologue *Slaying the Mosquito* belongs entirely to a man exiled by the war, who in exile is missing a part of himself. The 2008 declaration of independence provides the backdrop for *One Flew over the Kosovo Theater,* where the newly won independence is spoiled by a loss of agency.

In the 1990s, as the Yugoslav wars raged elsewhere, Albanians in Kosovo were stripped of their jobs, schools, and all other services and had to cope with a diminished life. They organized as a self-help society without a state. An organic leadership emerged, making an uncompromising choice in favor of peaceful resistance. Albanians lived in poverty, supported by contributions from the diaspora along with some foreign aid, and in fear, under the thumb of Serbian security forces, but avoided a full-blown war until 1998. It was then that the armed guerrillas of the Kosovo Liberation Army (KLA) escalated their actions, provoking a bloody state counterinsurgency that degenerated into a campaign of ethnic cleansing and drove nearly half of Kosovo's Albanian population into neighboring countries.

The war brought to light the long-simmering chasm in Albanian society between the party of accommodation within the Yugoslav state and the party of open rebellion. As the KLA took center stage during the conflict, upping the ante with its successful lobbying for NATO intervention against Milošević, the war also flipped the domestic political power structure on its head. In postwar Kosovo, KLA commanders-turned-politicians asserted themselves over the prewar leadership, which included educated urban elites, as well as state bureaucrats released from the Yugoslav system. The former combatants tried to impose the renewal of a heroic national tradition of resistance against foreign oppressors, but their adoption of national history as dogma — and as a claim to power — faced sharp resistance.

No character in this collection of plays embodies the heroic, martial virtues promoted by the KLA national narrative. Even when Enver, the protagonist of *The Basement*, reminds his frightened young son Gent of the Albanian warrior tradition, it is clear that he is talking in abstractions. The men in the play are defenseless against the Serbian security forces bent on killing them and must either hide or flee. Thus Enver, a professor, waxes uselessly over an epic past. There is hidden irony in his invocation of Mic Sokoli, a nineteenth-century guerrilla leader celebrated for having pressed his chest against the muzzle of an Ottoman cannon, one in a line of heroes making a

Pyrrhic last stand. There could be no sharper contrast between Enver's proud words and his impotence as a patriot, as an intellectual, and literally, as a man, as we learn from a conversation with his wife Pranvera.

The Kosovo secessionist war was typically asymmetric, and the KLA, fighting an overwhelmingly more powerful enemy, followed Mao Tse-Tung's maxim: "The guerrilla must move amongst the people as a fish swims in the sea." And while it began as a small force based on tightknit rural networks and the nationalist underground, the KLA developed a broader popular base in the midst of Milošević's war against civilians. *The Crossroads Café*, in large part, shows how the militants of an unnamed movement, which is clearly the KLA, were supported by an array of different people with an overarching shared national goal, but for a variety of reasons, from conviction to personal connections, opportunism, money, or some other force of circumstance.

Most Albanians lionized the KLA during the war, but many criticized it afterwards, explicitly or not. Sokol, the café owner, finds himself performing difficult missions and misfires — not so much because of his lack of martial qualities, as because of the guerrillas' amateurism. Here the fighters are never present when the action occurs — in particular when the enemy, the Serbian police, must be confronted. Sokol, the Everyman of the play, must suffer all the consequences of his undefended exposure to them.

The Humanitarian Law Center has produced the most accurate available database of human loss during the 1998-2000 period, including the immediate aftermath of the war. Of the 10,415 Albanians, 2,197 Serbs and 528 Roma, Bosniaks and other non-Albanians killed or missing over that period, 8,661 Albanians, 1,797 Serbs and 447 Roma, Bosniaks and other non-Albanians were civilians. The number of missing persons — originally 3,200 — has been halved to 1,666 over the past ten years. Of the latter, about 1,000 Albanians are presumed dead, but without a final resolution of their status.

Enver's son, as well as Zoja's son / Shkurta's husband in *The Finger*, are killed as they step out of their houses — the first to search for food, and the other to reconnoiter. Both are civilians uninvolved in the war, but they are killed nevertheless. Because their bodies are not found, their families live in the hopeless dream of finding them alive, years later. There are many such cases in real life.

In these plays, the absence of physical remains condemns survivors to search relentlessly for more tangible representations of their dead. They see ghostly apparitions, or rummage through the old clothes of the disappeared, trying to conjure up images. There is no normal life in the families of the missing, and both *The Basement* and *The Finger* dramatize the devastation caused by the disappearance of family members. This loss seems also to have broken a previously existing equilibrium and revealed a deep, personal unhappiness with family life.

To borrow a classic feminist argument that has more than one application, the personal is political in Kosovo society. For example, Enver's desperate refuge in an imaginary life of letters and pride, in contrast to his marginal and impotent real life, can be understood in the context of the dramatic loss of status many intellectuals suffered after 1981. That year, they were expelled en masse from the University because of nationalist protests and were never able to regain their position, since Milošević closed Albanian schools altogether in 1990.

Zoja and Shkurta are both trapped in a cycle of subordination and domination, which they hate but have been unable to overcome. In the traditional Albanian home, the son's bride doesn't just join a new family; she becomes that family's possession. As a second fiddle to the mother-in-law, she must obey the older woman until death or age turns the tables. The power thus gained by women in the latter part of their lives compensates for the pain of arranged marriages, unhappy relationships, and domestic violence, as well as their own years of servitude to the older woman of the house. It is a tradition that does not allow for sentiments to be expressed. In *The*

Finger, like the men and women who cannot reveal their love for each other, mother and daughter-in-law cannot show their mutual compassion.

Almost all the characters in these plays suffer from a lackluster love life. Quarrels, betrayals, or estrangement are ubiquitous against a background of violence from outside and within the society. This violence either forces or encourages individuals to choose emigration, and then follows them, uprooting them both physically and spiritually. In *Slaying the Mosquito*, what appears at first to be a semi-comical incident due to the drunkenness of the protagonist later suggests domestic violence. Only at the end do we learn of a mutual victimization, as the object of this violence is brazenly cheating on her husband, a poet exiled to Mexico, where he feels soulless, far from a home he dreams of but can no longer reach.

Following the war, Kosovo became a special type of country. Its already overwhelming Albanian majority increased further, despite population loss due to mass killing and migration, as Serbs left in large numbers. The United Nations suspended Serbia's sovereignty over Kosovo and established an international administration — the United Nations Interim Mission in Kosovo (UNMIK), which governed Kosovo like contemporary Ottoman rulers from June 1999 through February 2008, when independence was declared. For almost ten years, all the vital functions of the country were entrusted to outsiders, diplomats, and consultants affiliated with international institutions such as the UN, the Organization for Security and Cooperation in Europe (OSCE), and the European Union (EU). Security, in the absence of a domestic armed force (which is still substantially lacking), was and is the responsibility of a NATO mission, KFOR. A new vocabulary emerged for this form of governance: It was composed of a plethora of acronyms designating international institutions and agencies, as well as foreign donors.

Tasked with building a state in Kosovo, UNMIK was strongly constrained by the fact that there was no defined state to be built because for years there was no international agreement on what status Kosovo would be granted. What was built instead was an Albanian political and social elite that operated in an environment that was more sensitive to international bureaucratic and political demands than to citizens' needs and aspirations. But citizens had very high expectations for a country they had dreamed of for so long but did not yet possess.

Kosovo, the poorest province of Yugoslavia, went through ten years of complete desertion by Yugoslav state institutions, followed by two years of a devastating war. It emerged from this tragedy quickly, though the merit for the recovery was not due to foreign aid, which went mostly to support a huge international bureaucracy and to create a very small urban civil society. In large part, Kosovo bounced back on the strength of a people accustomed to surviving. Contemporary Kosovo is naturally a mixed bag. Critics are very vocal, citing high unemployment, the lack of good services, and a self-serving political class that can also be threatening through its domestic surveillance, as the fundamental ills of the country. The disappointment with this reality vis-à-vis the dream is palpable in the biting monologue of *Slaying the Mosquito*; but it is also played on a broader scale by the ensemble of *One Flew over the Kosovo Theater.*

Surviving is what the characters of *One Flew* do best. In this play within a play, the National Theater Company partakes, with all other Albanians, in the dreams of a good life and an independent country. Independence is achieved, but at the cost of freedom. The company is asked to produce a celebratory play for an unspecified date, and censorship as well as self-censorship weigh heavily on the outcome. The good life, which is the realization of one's vocation whatever that might be, is defined down because there are no conditions for success.

Kosovo independence was declared on February 17, 2008, and after years of longing, it came as a surprise to the nation because only a very small number of people knew it would be declared on that date. It was a negotiated independence, debated over two long years by an array of actors — among them, in a dominant role, the United States government and other western governments, together with the United Nations. The Kosovo political elite played a secondary role. After declaring independence, Kosovo remained a hybrid state with the lingering institutional presence of the EU and NATO, which enjoy strong powers and are able to override the government's authority. Lacking a seat at the UN because it is not recognized by almost half the member countries, Kosovo still heavily depends on members, such as the United States, which were the first to support its right to exist.

Like the new Kosovo state, most characters in *One Flew*, no matter their status — whether the Secretary of the Ministry of Sport, the Director, or the young actress Rosie — enjoy only very limited freedom. Their choices are already compromised, while they parade their most idealistic ambitions. Thus, they fail the grand celebration of independence as they opportunistically acquiesce to political interference. Individual rebellions are haphazard and futile, whether they are inspired by desperation as in the case of Dilo, the unhappy and drunk actor who reads his wife's humiliating farewell letter rather than his lines, or by quixotic idealism such as James's plan to turn a pile of scrap metal into a functioning airplane.

All the characters in these plays think, talk, and move in a physical space that is both local and confined, and swept by broader events. Whether they are in the city, in a village, or in exile, their immediate environment suffocates them, paradoxically not because of its closeness, but because of its lack of intimacy. Estrangement, lack of freedom, and a sense of loss dominate the comedies as well as the dramas, projecting a critical and somber image of the life of Kosovars.

Naturally, these characters are first of all individuals, displaying individual happiness, sorrow, fear, courage, self-pity, dishonesty, and ambitions. They will provoke individual reactions from readers or theater audiences. What I have suggested in this foreword is to view them against a broader political and social backdrop. It is on that broader stage that a collective drama is being played out: The story of a nation that has a tragic history but sees it as epic and in conflict with the uninspired reality of contemporary life; that is proud of its unique tradition but begins to regard it as a straitjacket; and finally, that survives against all odds.

By Ilir Gjocaj
Translated by Fadil Bajraj

THE BASEMENT

CHARACTERS

ENVER — a professor

PRANVERA — his wife

GENT — their 18-year-old son

FRED — an American humanitarian worker

MERITA — a neighbor

XHEMAJL — Merita's husband

AGRON — Enver's political opponent

ANITA — Agron's 17-year-old daughter

ACT ONE
Scene One

[*The living room. Enver, Pranvera, Gent, and Fred are seated. A clearly visible ID/work permit hangs from a cord around Fred's neck. He wears glasses and winter shoes. A duffle bag is beside him. They sit with their heads bowed, like people who have nothing left to say, or as if they are waiting for something.*]

FRED. [*With the slight formality of a non-native speaker.*] All the international organizations are withdrawing, and ours is calling for us to leave too. The mission is suspended . . . for the time being at least. The situation is considered volatile.

ENVER. Yes, it's understandable.

FRED. But that doesn't actually mean there will be bombing. It's not certain. It's just what they're predicting.

ENVER. We know, of course.

FRED. I just want to say that I still have the hope that everything might be resolved by peaceful means at the last moment. And then . . . But . . . in any case, for now we're leaving.

ENVER. Yes, yes! Of course! The work you've done here has been so important for us, Mr. Fred!

FRED. Now that the time has come to go, I realize how much I've depended on you.

ENVER. It was nothing, Mr. Fred, don't mention it. I considered it my duty. It was nothing.

FRED. I'm happy to have met you, sir, and your wonderful family.

ENVER. Thank you, Mr. Fred.

PRANVERA. Thank you, Mr. Fred. It's been an honor for us.

FRED. Now I must go.

ENVER. Stay, Mr. Fred. Why don't you stay a while? Have something to eat.

FRED. I need to get started . . . I'm just a bit worried, but I hope and pray to God that this will be over quickly. Before I go . . . have you had a chance to think about what I said?

[*Fred takes off his glasses, puts them into their case, and then into his bag.*]

ENVER. Thank you very much, Mr. Fred, for caring about us. But I don't believe it's necessary for us to go anywhere right now. Someday, perhaps, but not now. Not at all. Because really, if men like me run away and abandon the people in times like these, then who can we count on to stay?!

FRED. Professor, I invited you to stay with me in America even before all this . . . to be my guest. And I invited Gent. At least for a rest and to leave this stress behind for a while. It would be good for all of you, and I don't think that Gent has anything against the idea of . . . getting an early start on his studies . . .

GENT. I . . .

[*Enver looks at Gent, who lowers his head, shaking it gently.*]

ENVER. Thank you, Mr. Fred. But, no. None of us can go.

FRED. All the same, I'm asking you one more time to consider the idea. Think about it one more time.

ENVER. We thank you, Mr. Fred . . .

FRED. No, no! Please! I just think . . . oh, it's so difficult to say . . . I think it would be better for everyone, for all of you! And especially for Gent.

PRANVERA. [*To Enver.*] Well, I don't know, maybe . . .

ENVER. Thank you, Mr. Fred . . .

FRED. He . . . all of you . . . will . . . especially after all that he went through during those demonstrations . . . I think the experiences he had . . .

ENVER. Mr. Fred, please . . . ! Please don't question our abilities as parents . . .

FRED. Oh! I'm sorry sir . . . !

ENVER. No, no, I understand you completely. But I just want to say that . . . that . . . this is his home . . . do you understand? And he's a grown man, a real man, aren't you Gent . . . ?

FRED. No, no . . . ! I just meant . . . !

ENVER. We thank you, Mr. Fred, most sincerely. And trust me, I understand you, but there's really no need for you to worry. Not at all. I say that in all honesty.

[Fred tries to say something to clarify his position, but Enver interrupts him again by standing up.]

ENVER. Of course, these are uncertain times, goddamn it! Anything can happen. But we're the same as everyone else, no better and no worse, so what can be done?

FRED. [Sighing.] Okay . . . okay! I believe that this whole thing will be over soon and that it will all be fine. Don't worry. And thank you for everything!

ENVER. We look forward to seeing you soon, Mr. Fred. Very soon, I hope. Think of this as your home.

[He leaves first, stage right, and the others follow. Blackout.]

Scene Two

[Blackout. An explosion can be heard. The lights come on. Gent, terrified, runs onto the stage and then crouches in a corner trembling. His mother follows him onstage and tries to calm him down.]

PRANVERA. What's the matter, Gent?! What happened?! Calm down, son. Shh shh shh!

[Enver enters.]

ENVER. NATO . . . ! It's started. NATO is attacking! I knew it. They've started. Hooray! I knew they'd come to help us. I've always said they wouldn't let a whole race disappear right in the middle of Europe. Sure, there were people who said I was dreaming. And now look. Do you see, Pranvera?! Do you remember what I wrote . . . ?

[He notices that Gent is scared.]

ENVER. What's going on with you?! [His voice shaking.] You're afraid, are you? Are you a boy or a man?! Get ahold of yourself, son, because you're disgracing me! Shame on you! They're not against us. No! They're against the Serbs! Look at him! You would have been the first to run away with Fred! "No, I want to work for human rights!" Forget about it! First fight for the rights of your own people!

[Pranvera gives him a warning look.]

PRANVERA. Enver!

ENVER. I'm not saying anything . . . Just that . . . this is a time to celebrate, not to be afraid. And we all know that it's not in our tradition to be afraid. It's not our way. [*He clears his throat, as if he wants to change his tone of voice.*] I've given you examples from our history so many times. When he was just your age, Mic Sokoli held his chest to the cannon to save the lives of his men![1] And this boy . . .

PRANVERA. Enver, leave him alone, come on . . . Leave it for another time . . . !

ENVER. Ok, ok! I'm just saying that there's nothing to be afraid of. And it's just not worthy of him! A young guy! At times like these, young people should show what they're made of because they're the main . . .

[*While speaking he turns away from Pranvera and Gent and then faces them again and sees that Gent is calming down but still anxious.*]

ENVER. Aaaahhhh, no, no! I don't want to see you like this! [*Angrily, he turns towards Gent.*] Ohhh . . . You . . . !

PRANVERA. [*Holding Gent.*] Enver! For God's sake, leave him alone!

ENVER. No, no, who could believe it! Dear God, how could this be happening in my house? Why is this happening to me? What goddamn luck I have . . . [*He looks back at Gent, who is becoming more panicked.*] I can't even look at you! [*Leaves.*]

PRANVERA. Calm down, Gent! Don't be scared. They're stopping now. Calm down, son. Shh shh shh shh!

[*Gent, more relaxed now, gets up.*]

GENT. It's not what you think it is. I'm not crazy. And don't treat me like an invalid.

PRANVERA. Why are you saying that, Gent?! We aren't treating you like that, son!

GENT. I'm fine . . .

[*Enter Enver.*]

---

1. Mic Sokoli (1839–1881) was an Albanian nationalist figure and guerrilla fighter. He died at the Battle of Slivova, fighting Ottoman forces, when he pressed his body against the mouth of a Turkish cannon, an act which became legendary for its heroism.

ENVER. And when did you decide to go to America with Fred? Come on, tell me. I want to know once and for all.

PRANVERA. Enver, we'll talk about it some other time, for God's sake!

ENVER. Some other time, huh? Glad to hear that! Great! But who knows what he'll have done by then!

GENT. No . . . I won't do anything . . . ! There's nothing I can do . . . ! I just . . .

[*Enver exits without listening to him. A long pause.*]

PRANVERA. Gent, even to me, you didn't talk openly about it.

GENT. Mother, you knew that I . . . !

PRANVERA. No, Gent. You never discussed it. That day it took me completely by surprise! And it upset your father so much – that you hadn't talked it over with us.

GENT. The important thing was that you knew.

PRANVERA. You should have talked to me about it – and not at the last minute like you did, without sharing it with us. You only once mentioned that you wanted to leave with Fred. And now that I think of it, I remember Fred once mentioned it too. Is that right, Gent?

GENT. Yes, mother, but I didn't think you'd be against the idea. I don't know why you're making it such a big deal.

PRANVERA. I'm not, but . . . I don't know myself . . . It's just that sometimes you're a bit strange.

GENT. I have always been strange. Maybe I was born like that.

PRANVERA. Gent, admit you were wrong.

[*A short pause. Pranvera goes into the kitchen. Gent picks up a model from the floor. Enter Enver.
He stares at Gent, who drops the model and lowers his head. Suddenly, Enver's face takes on a soft
expression, as if he wants to make peace with Gent, and he sits down opposite him. They sit like this in
silence, in a kind of tension. Two or three times, Enver seems to want to say something. Then he gets up
and goes back to where he came from. The door opens and Merita, a neighbor, enters.*]

Scene Three

MERITA. Pranvera . . . ! [*To Gent.*] Where's Pranvera?

[*Gent doesn't manage to answer, and Pranvera walks out of the kitchenette.*]

MERITA. Oh, Pranvera! Oh God! At the Kurrizi complex[2] near where my mother-in-law lives, the police are dragging everyone out of their apartments onto the streets. Oh, good God! They say that the Kurrizi is completely empty.

PRANVERA. [*Concerned.*] Oh, no! And why?!

[*Exit Gent.*]

MERITA. I don't know. All I know is that they want to send us to Albania. And they've killed that lawyer Kelmendi, together with his sons.

PRANVERA. Oh Lord! God help us!

MERITA. All our neighbors are getting ready.

PRANVERA. For what?!

MERITA. To leave, Pranvera. They'll come here, too. And when they come, they'll force us from our homes.

PRANVERA. But where would we go, Merita? Where can we go?

MERITA. I don't know, Pranvera. Who knows where they'll take us. I just hope to God we'll survive.

[*Pranvera sits down.*]

PRANVERA. Sit down, Merita!

MERITA. Oh, my God, I just went out to the bakery. I saw all these people with suitcases, carrying their children in their arms. Oh, my God, what's happening?!

PRANVERA. I don't know, Merita.

MERITA. Here, I brought some bread for you too because there won't be any later.

---

2. A high-rise residential complex on the west side of Prishtina. It was the center of nightlife in the 1990s. Kurrizi means "the spine."

[*Enver can be seen as he stops and listens from the other side of the stage. He is holding a small radio and trying to pick up a station, holding it close to his ear. He sets the radio aside quickly and tries to look busy, putting on a pair of socks and fiddling with something. The women don't notice him. Gent can be seen behind him, holding a model in his hand but waiting because Enver is blocking the entrance. He waits a little, and when Enver notices, he lets him pass, pretending to look for something in his pockets. The women can't see any of this from where they are.*]

PRANVERA. Merita, don't go out like this again. All these policemen, all this hell around us. If something happened to you . . .

MERITA. No, no, I didn't go far. I just went to the bakery.

PRANVERA. You should be careful still!

MERITA. And you, what are you going to do?!

PRANVERA. What do you mean? What is there to do?!

MERITA. I mean, do you want to leave or . . . ?

PRANVERA. I don't know, Merita. Honestly, I don't know. I hadn't even thought about it until now. I don't know . . . I don't know!

MERITA. Well, it's easy for you. Your husband's a professor, and he thinks about everything. But my husband, he's good for nothing. Now he's not even home! He just goes out all day and does nothing. It doesn't even cross his mind that if the police were to catch him, then what would I do?

PRANVERA. Come on, Merita, he knows what he's doing. He's not a child. Maybe he went to his mother's.

MERITA. Yes, yes, he did go to his mother's. She's even sicker.

PRANVERA. You see . . . !

MERITA. And I forgot to tell you something. I saw Drita, the wife of that . . .

PRANVERA. Whose wife?

MERITA. Agron's. Agron Mala.

PRANVERA. [*She nods towards the wall as she speaks in a low voice.*] His wife . . . [*She gestures with her head.*] Our neighbor?

MERITA. Yes! She's pregnant, did you know that?! With all this hell going on, she left to go to her mother's because she was afraid she might go into labor. Agron is doing everything he can think of to get them out, seeing how things are at the border, if it's still possible to cross. He has some connections to foreign journalists, and God knows what. She said they're going to leave as soon as possible. She said the Serbs are planning to slaughter all of us.

[Gent puts the model on the floor and then continues to work on it. Enver enters.]

ENVER. It's only traitors who talk like that, and those who want to spread doubt among the people. There's no reason to panic. We have to be rational. After all, they can't kill every one of us?!

MERITA. Oh, Professor! I didn't see you! How are you, Professor? How are you doing . . . ?

ENVER. Fine, fine, thank you! What about you? How's your husband?

MERITA. To be honest, I don't know where he is! I told him, "Stay home, because you're safe here!" But him, no . . . Well, his mother is sick, so . . . What can he do!

[They fall silent for a while.]

MERITA. [To the Professor.] I brought you some bread because I have plenty. Later on, you won't find any.

[She hands the bread to Pranvera, who goes to her purse to repay her.]

MERITA. Good Lord, no, for God's sake, what . . . Come on . . . But think about buying some food because we'll be left without anything.

PRANVERA. You're right. And to be honest, we hardly have anything here.

MERITA. Pranvera, I'm off now, but come over since we're so close. 'Bye, Professor! Have a good day!

[She leaves.]

PRANVERA. 'Bye, Merita!

ENVER. [To Merita.] 'Bye! [To Pranvera.] So, he's thinking about leaving now. But how? [Ironically.] Where can we find a hole to hide our heads? Well, let him call me a political dinosaur. I don't know how a spy for the Serbs can trash anyone else.

PRANVERA. It's no use bringing these things up now, Enver. Everyone has problems to deal with. We're all living in uncertainty.

ENVER. Why are you protecting him?!

PRANVERA. I'm not protecting him, because I couldn't care less. I have my own problems. [*Calling.*] Gent! Come here!

ENVER. [*Continuing.*] Do you remember when he wrote those lies about the turmoil in my party?

PRANVERA. [*To Gent.*] Help me with these quilts. [*To Enver.*] No.

[*Pranvera and Gent start putting blankets over the window, as the stage slowly begins to darken.*]

ENVER. Then he took up writing. If you read the articles from that period, you'd think there'd never been a patriot like him. The things he said, "*No, this is our land; no, they are barbarians,*" the ideas that were in vogue then. [*He opens his bag and pulls out newspaper clippings.*] Here they are, all of them. Everything I wrote and everything he wrote.

[*As Pranvera and Gent cover the last window, Enver stops speaking.*]

Scene Four

[*In semi-darkness. Pranvera and Gent are sitting on the floor. Pranvera is holding Gent, who is trembling in fear. Enver goes to the front door and listens. There's the sound of an anti-aircraft alarm.*]

ENVER. It sounds like they're coming. Huh? Does it sound like that to you too?

PRANVERA. [*To Gent.*] Shh shh shh shh, it's nothing, nothing. Don't be afraid, Gent.

ENVER. I think they're coming up the stairs.

PRANVERA. [*To Gent.*] Shh shh shh! [*To Enver*] No, Enver. They're not coming. Don't scare me too.

[*Gent moans, very distressed.*]

ENVER. [*Angrily.*] That's enough, you idiot!

PRANVERA. Enver!

[*Enver lights a candle. Gent screams, frightened, and his silhouette can be seen going to hide in a corner of the stage. His mother goes after him to bring him back. Enver blows out the candle. A long silence. No one speaks. Enver lights the candle. He stands up, with his head bowed, as if he wants to say something. Another explosion is heard, and Enver sits down. The candle goes out.*]

Scene Five

[*The lights come up. Enver is lying on the floor, while Pranvera is on the couch. They have fallen asleep in their clothes. Enver takes his cane and gets up slowly. He picks up the small radio as well. He rubs his face to wake himself up and then goes to the corner and watches Gent sleeping. The radio makes some noise as he tries to pick up a signal. Pranvera wakes up.*]

PRANVERA. What time is it?

ENVER. The sun's coming up. [*He nods towards his son.*] Look what's become of us. Like mice.

PRANVERA. Did you get any sleep?

ENVER. None at all. What about you?

PRANVERA. [*Getting up.*] A bit.

ENVER. I think the bombing went on until a little while ago. [*Talking to himself.*] Now even this radio has stopped working . . .

[*Enver angrily tries to sort out the radio. Pranvera gets up and comes closer to him. She raises her hand to touch him, but suddenly she seems as if she can't bring herself to do so. Then slowly, as if it won't be noticed right away, she touches his back.*]

PRANVERA. Calm down. [*She hugs him from behind.*] Sit down; take a break.

ENVER. [*Setting the radio aside.*] I'm wrecked! I feel as if I've fallen from the roof!

PRANVERA. Come on.

[*She hugs him and kisses his neck slowly. Enver stops her at first, and when she tries to go on, he looks astounded.*]

PRANVERA. What's wrong? Are you not well, huh?

ENVER. I'm fine.

[*Pranvera continues kissing his neck, and he moves away slowly as if absorbed in his thoughts. Pranvera stops. Enver walks a couple of steps and then stops. He speaks without turning his head.*]

ENVER. Leave it – the boy's here. How can you think of that at a time like this?

PRANVERA. [*She pulls back guiltily.*] Gent's asleep . . .

ENVER. [*In a tired voice.*] It's not right! [*A short pause, then he turns to her.*] Are you okay?!

PRANVERA. I'm fine. But, I don't know . . . Maybe because of what's going on . . . I need you more.

ENVER. Huh?! It's nine o'clock! One way or another, we have to wake this lazy boy up. [*He walks toward the exit and calls.*] Gent! [*He returns to Pranvera.*] Now we need to fix up the basement. Get some kind of broom or whatever you need . . .

[*Exit Enver. Gent begins to stir and to get up.*]

PRANVERA. Why the basement? Enver!!!

ENVER. [*Speaking as he returns – just sticking his head through the doorway.*] Yesterday I said to that . . . neighbor . . . the husband of that . . . What's his name? I always forget it . . .

PRANVERA. Xhemajl?

ENVER. Yes! I told him to fix that broken window as soon as possible. Make him coffee or something. I'm going to the other room to listen to the news. [*He leaves.*]

PRANVERA. God help us.

GENT. He mentioned the basement yesterday, too.

PRANVERA. So, you're not asleep, then?! When did you wake up?

GENT. For three days now, I've not been able to sleep at all.

PRANVERA. You were awake this whole time, huh?

GENT. Yes, but I didn't hear anything. I was just thinking . . .

PRANVERA. But you didn't move at all. I thought you were asleep. You should have told me . . . Well, never mind . . .

[*They are silent. Pranvera sits down.*]

PRANVERA. What's going on with you, Gent? Are you unwell?

GENT. No, it's nothing.

PRANVERA. Is something keeping you from sleeping?

GENT. It's just because of the noise. The bombing went on till an hour ago.

PRANVERA. Enver didn't sleep either. Go and sleep for a bit in your room now that it's quiet.

[*Pranvera walks toward the exit.*]

GENT. Where are you going?

PRANVERA. I'm going to the basement to see if Xhemajl has started. Go and sleep a bit. There's nothing to worry about now.

[*Lights.*]

ACT TWO
Scene One

[*Pranvera is on stage having just come out of the kitchenette and opened the door. Xhemajl enters carrying tools and some boards taken from the window.*]

PRANVERA. How did the work go, Xhemajl?

[*Xhemajl leaves the tools on the ground and puts some screws in his pocket.*]

XHEMAJL. It's fixed now. But it was a bit hard to get to, and in the dark [*He shows pieces of the window frame.*] Look how this had rotted through. That's why it wouldn't close.

PRANVERA. Sit down, Xhemajl, sit down . . .

[*Xhemajl brings his tools and sits down. Enver's diary is on the table. Xhemajl glances at it with some curiosity.*]

XHEMAJL. But it's a nice place. The basement is larger than the apartment. Four rooms, huh?

PRANVERA. Yes, there are four rooms, a kitchen, and bathroom, but all the same, it's a basement — dark and damp and a mess. It's no place to live. It's better to have an apartment this size. Just a minute . . .

[*Pranvera goes into the kitchenette.*]

PRANVERA. [*From there.*] Xhemajl, did you hear the explosions?

XHEMAJL. How could I not? The whole basement was shaking. It felt like they were bombing the building. But it didn't last.

PRANVERA. I almost went mad with fear. And I guess if someone saw us now, they'd think we'd gone crazy. War outside, and we're making home improvements.

XHEMAJL. Is the Professor around?

PRANVERA. He's in the bedroom writing something.

XHEMAJL. He's writing?!

[*Xhemajl looks at his right hand which is slightly injured. Pranvera brings him coffee.*]

XHEMAJL. Thank you!

PRANVERA. What happened to your hand?

XHEMAJL. It's nothing – just a scratch.

PRANVERA. I'll get something to cover it. It could get infected.

[*Pranvera walks toward the kitchenette.*]

XHEMAJL. No honestly, there's no need. Come on, it's nothing.

[*Enver enters with some clippings and pages of newsprint. He notices Xhemajl and goes over to him.*]

ENVER. Oh, how are you, Xhemajl? Are you done in?

XHEMAJL. Not really! How are you, sir?

[*He gets up to offer Enver his chair, his mood suddenly more cheerful.*]

ENVER. No, no, stay where you are! I'll just . . . Pranvera, where are the extra chairs?

[*She comes out of the kitchenette with a bandage.*]

PRANVERA. One minute . . . !

[*Pranvera unwraps the bandage. Enver brings another chair to the table and closes the diary.*]

ENVER. [*To Pranvera.*] Look, there was one here. [*To Xhemajl.*] Was it a lot of work?

[*Pranvera withdraws into the kitchenette.*]

XHEMAJL. [*Picking up some boards to show him.*] Not that much. Look how they'd rotted through. I had to replace them with new boards and nail them in. Now you can't open the window at all. But there was no other option.

ENVER. It's better that it doesn't open. You did the right thing. It should have been repaired long ago, but you know how it is, and how could we have known things would come to this?

XHEMAJL. No one can predict these sorts of things . . .

ENVER. Are you having coffee? [*To Pranvera.*] Pranvera, have you made Xhemajl coffee?

XHEMAJL. Yes, look – here it is. How are you, Professor?

ENVER. Not bad, Xhemajl. Just hoping to God we'll stay alive!

XHEMAJL. Pranvera told me – have you started to work? I mean your writing?

ENVER. Yes, a kind of diary, some jottings, some . . . [*Instinctively he moves his hand over the pages.*] Maybe now is not the right time, but better now than never. There are some . . .

XHEMAJL. Do you know what might happen to us, Professor?

ENVER. Well, Xhemajl, as you can see yourself, God only knows. The good thing is that NATO intends to get rid of the Serbian forces and protect us. But . . . we'll see.

[*Enver stares at a spot on the floor and doesn't speak for a while. Silence.*]

XHEMAJL. I'll be off now, Professor. You have your own worries.

ENVER. No, no. Stay!

XHEMAJL. No, seriously . . . I finished the window, and I don't want to take up your time.

ENVER. Sit down, sit down for God's sake! Don't go. Come on . . . Pranvera!

PRANVERA. [*She comes out of the kitchenette.*] Yes?

ENVER. Bring us some raki![3]

XHEMAJL. No, Professor, that's not necessary!

[*Pranvera brings a bottle of raki and two glasses.*]

ENVER. Come on, one or two glasses of raki won't hurt us!

[*He starts to fill the glasses.*]

XHEMAJL. You got me now. Thank you!

ENVER. Cheers! To better days!

XHEMAJL. Cheers!

ENVER. When this is all gone, then we'll really be screwed, ha ha!

[*He laughs, and Xhemajl laughs too when he realizes he's joking.*]

---

3. Raki is a strong alcoholic drink made from grapes. It is popular in Albania, Kosovo, Turkey, and Greece.

ENVER. Difficult times. Yes, indeed. But we did this to ourselves. Because we're not as we should be. There are a lot of bastards among us.

XHEMAJL. Yes, that's true . . .

ENVER. At least we knew what Serbia was. We expected this from them, but we didn't expect it from our own people. They are even more dangerous. Because not many of us can recognize them.

[*Xhemajl glances at Enver and seems not to understand anything. Enver again seems to be lost in thought, looking at a spot on the floor. His eyes close slowly, as if he has fallen asleep. Xhemajl doesn't move. Slowly he places his glass of raki on the table so as not to make a noise. Enver suddenly opens his eyes.*]

ENVER. Oh! I didn't even read today's newspaper! Pranvera! Where's the paper?

PRANVERA. [*From the kitchenette.*] What did you say?

ENVER. Nothing. I forgot that there aren't even newspapers. Ah, in God's hands. [*For a moment he looks lost.*] Yes, yes . . . I have some weekly papers that I haven't read yet.

[*He gets up and starts to walk offstage.*]

XHEMAJL. Look, Professor, I'm leaving too.

ENVER. Why?! Where are you going? Why don't you stay a little bit longer?

XHEMAJL. [*Gets up.*] No, I'm going to my apartment because . . . I need to . . .

ENVER. Ah! Alright then . . .

XHEMAJL. [*Having gathered his tools and reaching for Enver's hand.*] Good day, Professor.

ENVER. Aaah, no, no! Look, I'll see you out.

XHEMAJL. No, no, there's no need. Go back, Professor!

ENVER. Please!

XHEMAJL. Thank you, sir!

[*They walk towards the door.*]

XHEMAJL. [*Shakes his hand.*] 'Bye, sir!

ENVER. 'Bye, Xhemajl, and thank you. Come over sometime. Come over, and we'll have a drink together.

XHEMAJL. Certainly, Professor! 'Bye! [*Exit.*]

[*Enver closes the door and looks at the papers on the table.*]

ENVER. [*As if something has occurred to him.*] God! [*Loudly.*] Pranvera, now that I think of it, do you know where I've put those weeklies?!

PRANVERA. [*From the kitchenette.*] Yes?!

ENVER. Nothing, nothing!

[*Enver exits. Blackout.*]

Scene Two

[*The lights come up. Enver is writing at a table together with Gent. Pranvera is sleeping on an improvised bed.*]

ENVER. Take a look at these pages again.

[*Gent takes a page of the newspaper and scans it as if searching for a sentence.*]

GENT. It's not here.

ENVER. Look for an earlier issue.

[*Gent pores over the pages again. Enver continues to write. Gent can't locate the article and seems intimidated by his father – in a dilemma as to whether or not to say something. Then he starts again from the beginning, going over the pages he's combed through already.*]

GENT. I can't find it. It isn't anywhere!

ENVER. [*Looks up and stares at Gent over his glasses.*] What do you mean it isn't there?! Come on, check all of them again. I know what I said. And we know it was published. That much is sure. It can't have disappeared from this world.

[*Gent once again unfolds the newspaper clippings. Enver, who has continued to write, lifts his head and watches him.*]

ENVER. I almost know them by heart, but I want to quote exactly.

[*Gent keeps going over them. Enver stops writing and joins him. He pulls more clippings from a bag and puts them on the table. He goes on for a while, unfolding them one by one at greater and greater speed. Gent suddenly stops.*]

GENT. [*Awkwardly.*] Dad, are you sure it was published?

ENVER. [*He stops and raises his head slowly, looking him in the eye.*] What do you mean, "*Am I sure?!*" [*Enver reflects a while and continues his search and stops again.*] You think I've gone crazy, huh? "*He's looking for something that doesn't exist. Just let the old man be!*"

GENT. No, no! It's just . . . it seems to me that it isn't anywhere. Maybe it's lost . . .

[*Enver doesn't speak. He edges closer to Gent, picking up some of the clippings that Gent was scanning, and continues to unfold them angrily. Suddenly, he slaps the table causing Gent to start in fear, though he goes on reading. The noise wakes Pranvera up.*]

ENVER. [*Stopping for a moment and talking to himself.*] I remember it well. I predicted everything. Everything that's happening now I said would happen: that Serbia wouldn't give up, that NATO would start bombing, that the Serbs would kick us out of Kosova. But that Agron Mala, that spy, said I was quite wrong. I just want to see again how I said it. I can't remember the wording of the sentence, and I want to quote it precisely. That's all. Even though it isn't essential when you're writing a war diary. But since I can, then why not be accurate? We should remind people that they so easily forget what they never wanted to hear. [*He keeps searching.*]

PRANVERA. What's going on?

[*Gent looks at her and shrugs as if he's afraid that if he speaks he'll make his father angrier.*]

GENT. There's a page we can't find.

[*Pranvera slips out of the covers and begins to make up the bed. After a short break, the two men feverishly continue their search. Pranvera approaches the table. Still sleepy, she looks into Gent's eyes, but he seems preoccupied and annoyed. She starts to help too. In the process, some clippings fall from the table. Enver suddenly stops and stares straight ahead for three or four seconds. Gent and Pranvera stop as well. Then Enver starts searching even more wildly, and Gent and Pranvera join him.*]

PRANVERA. [*Stops her searching.*] So . . . what are we're looking for?! Because I don't know!

[*Enver stops and looks at her. There is the sound of knocking at the door. They all stop looking through the papers. Enver straightens up and looks for his cane.*]

ENVER. [*In a low voice.*] Who is it?

[*The knocking comes again and is louder and more intense. Pranvera holds Gent. Enver looks at them and slowly makes his way to the door. When the knocking starts again, he speeds up.*]

MERITA. [*From behind the door.*] Open up, it's me.

[*Enver continues to the door, but Pranvera darts ahead and opens it.*]

Scene Three

[*Merita enters.*]

MERITA. Pranvera . . . Pranvera! They're coming.

[*Gent exits.*]

PRANVERA. What's happened, Merita?

MERITA. They're coming. Police. In masks! People have seen them coming. Everyone is leaving now. It's our turn. They're at the corner of the block. The first buildings are empty.

PRANVERA. Oh, God! This is killing me. Slow down, Merita!

ENVER. Where are they going?

MERITA. They're running away!

ENVER. Where are they running to?! Where are they going?!

MERITA. I don't know!

ENVER. They're going into every apartment, are they?

PRANVERA. Where on earth did that boy go?!

MERITA. They went into the white building and dragged people out and beat them, forced them at gunpoint to leave. Oh, they beat them – men and women. In the building lower down, they gave them fifteen minutes to leave. Everyone is leaving. They're beating people in the middle of the street. They say they're putting the women on one side and the men on the other.

ENVER. How can they separate women from their husbands?! What are you saying?!

MERITA. They're separating the women with children from the men, and no one knows where they're taking the men.

ENVER. How do they separate them?

MERITA. They pull them from one line, and they put them in a different one. They send the men to one side, and the women to the other.

ENVER. Did you see it?

MERITA. No. That's what they're saying.

ENVER. [Concerned.] I knew it.

MERITA. What?

ENVER. This is a panic situation. People are acting in panic.

MERITA. What, people shouldn't leave?!

ENVER. No, no, why should we leave? Don't you see what's happening?

MERITA. So why would he have said it's better to leave . . . ?

[Enter Xhemajl.]

Scene Four

XHEMAJL. Hello, Professor. They're coming.

MERITA. [In a low voice.] Where have you been all this time, Xhemajl?

XHEMAJL. The Qafa district[4] has been emptied. Now they're coming this way. We should all leave together. What do you think, Professor?

ENVER. No, no . . . Why should we leave?!

XHEMAJL. The paramilitaries are coming, Professor. Everyone is leaving.

MERITA. I told him.

---

4. A neighborhood of high-rise buildings on the east side of Prishtina. Qafa means "the neck."

ENVER. I . . . I can't advocate that anyone leave their country. So there.

XHEMAJL. The Serbs are coming. The paramilitaries. People are frightened! They don't know what to do . . .

MERITA. So now you're advocating?

XHEMAJL. Merita!

ENVER. [*Still distressed.*] I can only tell you that there is no need for panic. You have no need for panic. If they want to kill us all, they can do it whenever they like.

[*Xhemajl sits down in a chair shocked. From time to time, Enver looks unseeingly at the pages of his diary. A slight pause.*]

PRANVERA. Enver, shall we leave with the others?

ENVER. [*Looking at Pranvera in amazement.*] What have I been saying, Pranvera?! Why should we leave? Huh?! I say no! They still haven't come here. Why should we leave, why create panic? Who knows what they'll do with us. Just because they've kicked some people out, then we should leave too? Let them come, let them come, because when we leave our homes, we'll have nowhere else to go.

XHEMAJL. They say that there's only our block left.

ENVER. [*Distressed, in a petulant manner.*] Now our famous leaders should come out. Now [*talking to the wall.*] where are they? Apparently only they know what is right. The rest of us are wrong.

XHEMAJL. What do you think we should do, Professor? They'll come to our building too. The doctor told us so . . .

ENVER. Which doctor?

XHEMAJL. Agron Mala.

MERITA. Xhemajl, for God's sake! Didn't you hear what the Professor said?

XHEMAJL. Merita! Shut up! [*In a shaky voice, turning to Enver.*] They are . . . [*He can't go on.*] Goddamn it, damn it!

ENVER. [*Nervously.*] Now that spy should start weighing in. [*He points to the wall.*] Right! He's spreading panic among the people.

[*He sits down at the table and puts his head in his hands. His cane falls aside. He pushes the paper clippings away. Xhemajl gets up slowly.*]

XHEMAJL. Merita, let's go!

MERITA. Go where?!

XHEMAJL. We're leaving, Merita! Let's get our things.

MERITA. What do you mean, go? Don't you see the Professor is saying that this is just panic?!

XHEMAJL. Merita, we'll discuss this later; we have to go now.

MERITA. Go where?! Are you crazy?! [*She starts to cry.*] Why are you doing this to me?! [*To Pranvera.*] He always does this to me! [*Pranvera lowers her head.*] My entire life with him has been like this! He's never asked what I think, just done whatever comes into his head. Where would we go? Where the hell can we go?!

[*Xhemajl takes her hand.*]

MERITA. Let go of my hand!

XHEMAJL. Merita, I won't say it again. I'm going, and I'll leave you here.

MERITA. Go on, go wherever you want. I want to stay here. So there. What're you going to do?!

XHEMAJL. Merita, come on. Don't give me trouble.

MERITA. I'm not giving you anything. You're the one with troubles because you're incapable of anything. Go on, go . . . Go to your mother . . .

[*Xhemajl looks at each of them and walks out in rage. A heavy silence. No one moves.*]

MERITA. Where are you going, Xhemajl, stop! Where are you going?!!!

[*Merita takes a few steps and then, in a state of distraction, sits down. She wrings her hands. Enver takes his cane and gets up.*]

ENVER. We must all stay here. There's nothing for us to be afraid of. So! Now we go to the basement. Right! There we'll be . . . better off. Right!

[*Merita begins to cry. She gets up and looks at them all with tears in her eyes and then runs off.*]

Scene Five

PRANVERA. [*Carefully approaching him.*] Enver, what are we going to do?

ENVER. Pranvera, I've explained already. Where would we go?! And why?! Why don't you ever trust me?! What do I have to do to . . . [*He can't go on. His lips tremble as if in grief.*]

PRANVERA. No, Enver, it's not like that. [*Silence.*] Gent, go and take the down quilts to the basement. What's happening, Enver? Why are you behaving like this? What's up?

ENVER. What's up with me, huh?!!! What's up with you . . . ?

[*Gent sticks his head 'round the door. He seems frightened.*]

PRANVERA. Enver . . . [*She sees Gent.*] What is it, Gent?

GENT. Where are the quilts . . .

PRANVERA. They're in the bedroom. Take them down to the basement and stay there. We'll be down soon. Don't be afraid.

GENT. No, mother.

[*Gent exits.*]

PRANVERA. Enver, talk to me.

ENVER. What, Pranvera? What do you want from me?

PRANVERA. Why don't we go? What do you want for us?

ENVER. And you, what do you want? Why do you want to leave? Where do you want to go? Why don't you trust me?

PRANVERA. It's not like that. But if we are to survive, we have to leave like the others. Everything's gone to hell!

ENVER. Is it because he said so that you're thinking like that?

PRANVERA. Who?!

ENVER. Him, Agron Mala.

PRANVERA. No! Why would you say that?

ENVER. Why don't you have faith in what I'm saying? Just in him. You don't believe I'm right about anything.

PRANVERA. Why are you talking like this, Enver?! You can see what's happening. I'm just trying to think of what's best for us.

[*Enver is silent and bows his head.*]

ENVER. It's easy for him. He goes about freely because he's one of them. They'll never do anything to him. The Serbian police have given him a pass . . . The whole world knows how it works.

PRANVERA. Don't talk about him like that without having the facts.

ENVER. Why are you defending him?

PRANVERA. I'm not defending him, and I don't care about any of that, but you can't slander people in times like this.

[*Silence.*]

PRANVERA. Enver, why are you making trouble for us now . . .

ENVER. It's not me who's making trouble; it's you. Pranvera, I can't leave now. What would I do if they took you? If they took our boy? You heard that they're separating the women from the men. What would I do if they raped you in front of me and Gent?

[*Pranvera is silent.*]

ENVER. But then you don't care.

PRANVERA. What do you mean by that, Enver?

[*Enver is silent.*]

PRANVERA. Enver, why did you say that?

ENVER. I'm at the breaking point . . . Just let me be . . .

[*Silence.*]

ENVER. You understand full well what I mean.

PRANVERA. You're not quite yourself. How can you say these things to me? What on earth do you think of me . . . ?!

[*Enver sits down and covers his face with his hands.*]

ENVER. Pranvera, I'm sorry. Don't you see that I'm losing my mind? [*Shouts.*] Oh, God! Oh, God . . . !!!

[*He gets up, walks around the room a little, and sits down again. He holds his head in his hands.*]

ENVER. I'm sorry, Pranvera. It's not your fault. [*Loudly.*] I'm to blame – me. I'm responsible for everything.

PRANVERA. Calm down, Enver.

ENVER. Pranvera, be honest with me. We need to talk. I want to know now! I want to know now! Talk to me!

PRANVERA. I am talking, Enver.

ENVER. Pranvera, do you regret having married me?

PRANVERA. No, Enver, you're my husband. What's going on with you?! Why are you thinking like this? [*Enver is silent.*] Talk to me, Enver. We never talk about us. We have to talk. I'm your wife.

ENVER. Pranvera, have you ever thought of leaving me for someone else?

PRANVERA. No, Enver. No. We've never had that sort of problem. Our problem has been that we haven't spoken to each other as man and wife. We should . . .

ENVER. [*Coldly, not paying attention to Pranvera, not meeting her gaze.*] Pranvera, you felt the lack . . .

[*Silence.*]

PRANVERA. [*Sighs.*] Yes, Enver. I felt the lack of you – as someone to be close to, but also as a man. But I never considered leaving you. I've missed you. I haven't wanted others.

[*Pranvera moves closer to him. Enver embraces her, then rests his head against her stomach, like a child. He stays for a while like that.*]

PRANVERA. It's upset me that you haven't talked to me about your problem. I was interested, Enver . . .

[*Enver moves away from Pranvera.*]

ENVER. How were you interested?!

PRANVERA. I've read about this. I've looked into it. The whole problem can have a psychological basis. With certain therapies, the problem can be solved. But you never wanted to talk to me about it. And I didn't dare to be the one to bring it up. Because you were closed up in yourself. You would go off somewhere, or you changed the subject. You became a stranger – distant . . .

[*Enver gets up.*]

ENVER. No, no . . . How have you looked into it?! Did you talk to anyone, huh?! Who did you talk to?

PRANVERA. No, Enver, I read about it. I didn't talk to anyone.

[*Enver moves away slowly and takes a deep breath in relief. He stretches out and seems to expand in the space.*]

PRANVERA. But you should have talked to me about this problem, about everything, because I'm your wife. You shouldn't have ignored me. You changed so long ago. For so many years, you didn't sleep with me, and I didn't know why for a long time. You grew distant from me and from Gent. Like a stranger. You got involved with everything except us, with things that had never interested you before: politics and demonstrations, polemics, and I don't know what else . . .

ENVER. [*As if talking to himself.*] I don't understand anything.

PRANVERA. We missed you, Enver. It wasn't easy for us. But at least now don't be a stranger because we need you.

ENVER. Pranvera, what are you talking about? I don't understand you. What were you missing? You had everything. Both you and the boy. You didn't want for anything. In fact, you were living in luxury. You never complained.

PRANVERA. I'm not talking about those things . . . I had everything except you close to me.

ENVER. I did it all for you. I don't know why you're complaining now! You didn't complain before. Because you didn't have time to complain. We were taking trips to the seaside. Every time you'd hear of a nice place, we'd go there. Or you were busy shopping, buying clothes, shoes, and jewelry. But you were never satisfied . . .

PRANVERA. I didn't ask for anything. I didn't want anything except you. But you weren't satisfied with yourself. I don't know what you were looking for.

[*Pranvera starts to cry. Enver stares at the floor and shakes his head in disbelief. A short silence.*]

PRANVERA. Enver, it's not easy for me. I'm asking you today, at least for Gent's sake . . .

ENVER. And I don't have any problem. Maybe you do . . .

PRANVERA. Enver, why are you like this . . . ?

[*Enver brightens and completely changes his attitude.*]

ENVER. Wait, Pranvera! Calm down! You're upset. And I'm upset. Everybody is upset and frightened. Even me. It's war. It's completely normal. I'm sorry. My fault. Forget it.

PRANVERA. Enver . . .

ENVER. It's okay, Pranvera. I know that you're upset. We have to keep calm.

[*Gent can be seen putting his head 'round the door, seeing his parents, and not coming in.*]

PRANVERA. Why are you running away again? You have to talk to me.

ENVER. Calm down, now. We went too far. The war is enough to handle. We don't have to quarrel between ourselves. We're too old for that. Sit down! Sit down and calm down. Oh, my God, what a terrible time.

[*Pranvera dries her tears and tries to sort herself out.*]

PRANVERA. I want to talk about us . . .

Scene Six

[*Gent enters.*]

GENT. I brought the quilts down. Are you coming?

ENVER. Gent! Come here.

PRANVERA. Enver . . . !

ENVER. Come here. Listen. We're going to the basement now. Until the danger is past.

[*Merita enters.*]

MERITA. [*Crying.*] I can't find him anywhere. He's gone. He's left me. He's run away from me, Pranvera! The police are everywhere.

[*Gent starts to become agitated but tries to hold himself together.*]

MERITA. I don't even know where he could have gone. Oh, God! Oh, God!

[*She cries a while in Pranvera's arms. Pranvera looks from Enver to Gent, who is anxious.*]

ENVER. Where did he go?

MERITA. I don't know, I don't know, I don't know . . . ! [*She repeats it in a low voice.*]

[*Someone knocks on the door. Everyone steps back a little. Merita is still trembling and looking fearfully toward the door, still repeating the same words, but now almost silently. Enver steps back. The door opens slowly. Immediately we can see Agron's head and then Anita behind him.*]

ENVER. Who is it?!

AGRON. Agron, your neighbor. Agron Mala!

ENVER. You!

[*Enver, Pranvera, and Gent are dumbfounded and do not speak at all.*]

AGRON. Hello, sir! We're sorry to disturb you. Really, I'm sorry. But Drita, my wife, is pregnant . . . She's very ill. She's gone to her parents. Would it be possible for two or three days . . . until this passes . . . until I can get my wife . . . ? For now, I can't go out. Your basement is big . . . It's the safest place . . . in the neighborhood . . .

[*Blackout.*]

ACT THREE

Scene One

[*The basement. In the middle of the stage is a table with six chairs. There are three exits stage left. The first leads to a second room, the second is the bathroom door, and beyond this, a third exit leads to an alcove, and, from there, out of the basement. Gent is at the table carefully working on the model. Anita enters.*]

ANITA. What is it?

GENT. A model of a house, Anita.

ANITA. Of your house, is it?

GENT. Of the house we planned to build for our family. It's kind of a hobby of mine.

ANITA. Did the plan fall through, then?

GENT. No. I don't know . . . Maybe we'll build it someday. My father —

ANITA. And why didn't you come to my birthday party?

GENT. Me?

ANITA. Yes, you. Were you waiting for me to beg you?

GENT. No, it's not that, but I don't know. I don't know any of your friends . . .

ANITA. You know me.

GENT. I don't know! I had lots of studying to do.

ANITA. You didn't have even two or three hours, huh?

GENT. I thought that you invited me just . . . you know . . . Because we're neighbors.

ANITA. I told all my friends you were coming.

[*Gent stops what he is doing and looks at Anita.*]

ANITA. Was it that your father wouldn't let you?

GENT. Ha ha, my father . . . No, not at all, but . . .

[*Silence. Gent goes back to working on the model. Anita moves closer to him.*]

ANITA. And?

[*Gent shrugs.*]

ANITA. I really wanted to come here. I even told my dad we could come here to wait for my mom.

GENT. Well, you did the right thing.

[*Enver enters from the alcove with his diary and bag of newspaper clippings.*]

ENVER. [*To Gent.*] What are you doing here?

[*Gent shrugs*]

ENVER. Where's your mother?

GENT. I don't know.

[*Enver tries to open the door of the bathroom, but it's locked.*]

ANITA. My dad's in there.

[*Enver turns to the right. Pranvera comes from the kitchen carrying cups which she places on the table. She returns to the alcove. Agron comes out of the bathroom with his cell phone in his hand, trying to call someone, but he seems not to have been successful. He motions to Anita with his other hand and she follows him to the alcove. Gent picks up his model and begins to work again. Pranvera comes out of the alcove and goes into the bathroom. Enver returns.*]

ENVER. Where's your mother?

GENT. I don't know . . . Might she be in the kitchen?

[*Enver goes to the kitchen. Pranvera comes out of the bathroom. Enver leaves the kitchen and stops and looks at Pranvera, who is coming in.*]

ENVER. Where were you?

PRANVERA. In the bathroom!

[*Enver opens the bathroom door. Pranvera goes to the kitchen. Enver follows her. Anita enters. Pranvera carries a tureen of soup. Agron enters.*]

PRANVERA. Gent, take that model off the table and sit down. We're having soup. Sit down, Anita.

[*Anita and Gent sit down. Enver enters from the kitchen.*]

PRANVERA. Have some soup.

[*She hands a cup to Anita, then to Gent and the others.*]

ENVER. Have some soup, Agron . . . Have some!

[*Agron sits down.*]

AGRON. No . . . no, thank you! I'm not hungry . . . and there's a problem with the network.

[*Agron continues to problem-solve with his phone.*]

AGRON. Sir, I want to get my daughter out of Prishtina, to send her to Macedonia, because there's no other way out. At least for my daughter. If you leave before me, could you take Anita with you? I have to get back to my wife. She's pregnant, and now she's at her mother's. Maybe I'll leave with her, but first I'd like my daughter to get out. What are you going to do?

ENVER. What do you mean? Do what?

AGRON. When will you leave?

ENVER. Who said we were leaving?!

AGRON. If you were leaving, I'd ask you to take Anita with you. To at least save *her.* These are bad times, sir. She told me that Gent is a friend. I thought it would be better for her to leave with you because I don't really know what will happen to me. I don't know if I can get out with my wife or not. She's in the last month of her pregnancy.

PRANVERA. Is it safe to leave, Agron?

ENVER. Look at her!

AGRON. If you go with the crowd, it's safer. Here, it's not safe at all any more. They can come at any moment to throw us out.

ENVER. Maybe it's safe for you to leave, but not for us.

AGRON. What do you mean?!

ENVER. Did you know that they're separating the women from the men?

AGRON. That's happened, but here in Prishtina such things are less likely to happen.

ENVER. I'm not leaving. I'm not leaving my home, period. If they come to my house, there's nothing I can do about it. But I'm not leaving of my own accord like a lamb to the slaughter.

AGRON. I think it's much safer to go with the crowd than for them to find you hiding here. Then you won't even have witnesses. Anything could happen. There have been cases here in Prishtina where they found families in emptied neighborhoods . . .

ENVER. That's propaganda – panic . . .

AGRON. Yesterday I heard on the news . . .

ENVER. Agron, I don't want any more of this talk in my house. In my own house, I make the decisions. We aren't going anywhere. End of discussion.

[*Silence. Agron's cell phone is ringing. He gets up and moves away a bit. Anita follows him.*]

AGRON. [*On the phone.*] Hello. Yes, darling. No, I tried to call you earlier. At the moment, I don't know. Maybe we'll leave together. I can't do anything yet. I'll see if I can come. No, just me. I don't want to take Anita for now. Good. [*To Anita.*] I have to go. I have some things to do. Stay here, Anita. I'll be back soon.

ANITA. What did mom say? Is she okay?

AGRON. She's fine . . . Just fine. Wait here, I won't be gone long . . .

[*Agron gets up.*]

PRANVERA. You're going out now, huh? It's so dangerous!

ENVER. Stay here, Agron. Relax and make yourself at home. You know how things are . . .

AGRON. Yes, yes . . . I know, thank you. I'm worried about my wife, Drita. I have to see her somehow.

ENVER. Aha! No, but I wanted to say that . . . if . . .

AGRON. I'll see whether I can buy some bread as well.

PRANVERA. How are you not afraid to go out now?! Something could happen.

[*Enver gives her a warning look.*]

AGRON. No, nothing will happen to me. I'm worried about Drita. I'm careful.

ENVER. Don't pressure the man, Pranvera.

[*Agron exits.*]

Scene Two

PRANVERA. How can he go out now?!

[*Enver is staring at Pranvera with suspicion. Then, as if pulling himself together, he puts his diary into his bag of clippings.*]

ENVER. Come here. Come on, come on. Come closer. [*Anita sits down on the floor. Enver stands in front of them at the table.*] You too, Gent. Good! [*They are all sitting.*] What's your name?

ANITA. Anita!

ENVER. Right, Anita! Exactly! Now, you're adults. You're aware of the situation we're in. The enemy can't last forever. The NATO alliance and the whole world are against them. But we are still in danger. What do you think — are we still in danger?

ANITA and GENT. [*After a short break.*] Yes.

[*Anita smiles a little, but she still doesn't know if this is a joke or not.*]

ENVER. What do you think — should we be afraid? Huh? What do you think? Gent, what do you think?

GENT. No, Father!

ENVER. Yes, Gent, it's quite normal to be careful. But not to be afraid like stupid people and to create panic. No! Why? The sensation of fear can overcome caution and reason. And reason above all. Well . . . But, tell me – you've studied our folklore and history at school, I'm sure – so, how do you see our people, the Albanians, throughout history? Does an Albanian get scared? I mean in general, through historical dangers, have Albanians shown themselves to be fearful people? Well?

[*He gives them an inquiring glance. Anita lowers her eyes.*]

ENVER. Come on! Gent?

GENT. . . . No, no they were never scared!

ENVER. No, no! Look now. We don't have to take it literally. But we really have resisted the storms of time and survived them all. But like everyone, Albanians are human, aren't we? And like everyone else, we know what it is to be afraid, but, to know the difference between a reasonable fear . . .

ANITA. . . . Excuse me, where is the bathroom? Hmm, I'd...

ENVER. Yes, she'll take you . . . Pranvera, show her the bathroom, please.

[*Anita gets up with Pranvera.*]

ENVER. So, between reasonable fear and panic and loss of self-control, there is an important distinction. So, caution, vigilance, and rationality are different from panic. Is that clear to you?

GENT. Yes!

[*In the distance, the sound of an air raid siren.*]

ENVER. I don't really know. Huh, what do you think, Gent? Do you understand all this?

[*Gent lowers his head.*]

GENT. [*Humbly.*] Yes! I understand.

ENVER. No, Gent! Unfortunately, you don't understand! I don't know, my son – I don't understand you – I don't know what there is to be so afraid of. [*He speaks in a soft voice. Gent begins to get upset.*] You're a boy. In fact, you're a man now! What is wrong with you?!

[*Pranvera enters, drying her hands with a towel. She stands, listening.*]

GENT. [*Speaking haltingly and distraught.*] I don't know, Dad! But . . . I don't even know . . . I can't . . . I don't know . . . ever since that day . . . since that day when we went to that, to the demonstration . . . even though I wanted to go . . . ever since the day they beat me, I don't know, but . . . I get upset easily . . . !

ENVER. But I suffered it too, son. Look at my leg! Can you see it or not? And it's not the end of the world. [*Petulantly.*] But the way you're behaving, I don't know, I can't understand it . . . ! This . . . this . . .

PRANVERA. Enver, leave the boy alone . . .

ENVER. No! No more interfering! I want to clarify some things. [*To Gent.*] It's shameful behavior, and we've talked about this before. But now it's different. I don't want you to embarrass me in front of him. Is that clear? I don't want to be embarrassed in front of him now. Do you understand?! Be as scared as you want. Go crazy for all I care, but I don't want him to see it. Not him and not his daughter.

[*Pranvera goes to Gent. A knock at the door. Enver takes his cane and gets up, and Pranvera rushes from stage left to the door. She looks through the peephole to see who it is and opens it.*]

Scene Three

[*As before, Agron enters holding a plastic bag full of bread. An explosion is heard.*]

AGRON. I think that fell nearby!

[*Anita comes from the bathroom.*]

ANITA. What happened, Daddy?

AGRON. I don't know right now. We'll see.

ANITA. Did you talk to mom again?

AGRON. Yes, I talked to her on the phone, and she's fine! But it's not a good time to go there. [*To Enver.*] Sir, could we turn the lights off? It's dark now, and we can be seen from the street. When I was outside, I could see the windows of the basement. It's obvious there's someone here.

ENVER. Sure, of course! We completely forgot! Pranvera, are you here? All of you, come here! Turn off the lights!

[*Pranvera, who has already gotten up, has the lights off even before Enver has finished speaking. Only Agron can be seen as he walks to the edge of stage and pushes aside a blanket to gaze through the window. Otherwise the stage is almost completely dark. Agron reports what he sees.*]

AGRON. In the distance, some kilometers away from the city, you can see huge flames.

[*From time to time, aircraft can be heard.*]

AGRON. There's just one car going around the city. One moment you'll see it in one part of town, and then it will reappear in another. It's terrible! The whole town in darkness, with just one car driving around like a ghost!

ENVER. Don't be preoccupied with ghosts! There are no such things. Come away from the window! Someone might see you! If our ancestors had been obsessed with phantoms, we would have been history by now. [*A short break and then he continues in higher spirits.*] And so, some "ghost" circles 'round and immediately it's "*let's run off*" and "*let's all go mad together.*" This is no time to be an alarmist.

AGRON. I'm sorry, sir, I think you misunderstood me! I didn't mean anything by it!

ENVER. And I'm not implying anything, but there are some people who are prone to panic over the least thing. And just when they should have been analyzing and anticipating, they were in no position to act.

AGRON. I'm sorry, but I don't understand. I didn't mean to say . . . All I meant was that it's kind of murky out there. And that car seemed just like a ghost to me. Of course, figuratively.

ENVER. And I was just speaking about certain people who have strange tendencies. They're good for nothing themselves, and then they stick their noses into other people's business.

AGRON. I'm sorry, but I don't understand what you're saying. I only mentioned a ghost . . .

ENVER. And I was only referring to certain people. You shouldn't take it personally.

AGRON. Aha! Then I apologize! It's all cleared up. It was only a misunderstanding.

PRANVERA. What have you gotten into now . . .

ENVER. The ghosts come and go, but the people remain. So, there's no reason to get upset. There's no cause for it. [*An explosion is heard, then two more.*] It's nothing . . . Oh, children don't be afraid! [*He speaks as if he is explaining something very simple to some small children.*] Don't pay attention to the bombs! Don't think about them . . . Think about, for instance . . . Can you remember some poem? For instance, our Great Naim.[5] Do you know the poem "The Candle's Words?" Do you? [*He begins to recite in a voice that starts to shake from nerves.*] "I've stayed with you and I'm burning . . ." Where is the candle? . . . Here it is . . . [*He lights a candle and continues.*] ". . . and I'm burning . . ."

[*At that moment, in the candlelight, Anita can be seen throwing herself into Gent's arms, and they kiss stage right. Anita draws her hands away immediately and moves off.*]

ENVER. [*In a low voice but viciously.*] Gent!!!

[*A long pause.*]

ENVER. [*Because he is convulsed with anger, his voice doesn't project and he speaks slowly.*] In this apocalypse, you're thinking about kissing! Shame on you! [*He repeats in a low voice full of anger.*] Gent! Gent! Gent . . . ! At least you should have some . . .

AGRON. Anita!

---

5. Naim Frashëri (1846–1900), a writer and romantic poet, was a champion of the Albanian national movement for independence from the Ottoman Empire. He is widely regarded as the national poet of Albania.

ANITA. I'm sorry Uncle Enver, but we didn't do anything. We just . . . I know Gent . . . We . . .

ENVER. [*In a low voice.*] Gent, get out of my sight!

[*The dim light of the candle goes out after an explosion. More explosions are heard.*]

Scene Four

[*In semidarkness. Enver enters. He is looking for something in the gloom.*]

ENVER. Pranvera! Pranvera!

[*He walks towards the kitchen.*]

ENVER. Pranvera!

[*Enver comes back and tries to open the bathroom door, but it's locked. Just at that moment, the door opens. Pranvera comes out with a start.*]

PRANVERA. You scared me to death!

ENVER. Where have you been?

PRANVERA. In the bathroom, Enver.

ENVER. Who were you with in there?

[*He opens the bathroom door and looks inside.*]

PRANVERA. What's up with you, Enver? Why are you talking like this?

ENVER. Come on, you know full well what I'm talking about.

PRANVERA. Are you crazy or what?

ENVER. Pranvera, do you want to leave me?

PRANVERA. What's going on with you, Enver?

ENVER. Do you want to leave with Agron?

PRANVERA. How can you ask me that? Do you know what you're saying?

ENVER. He came here for you. Tell me, Pranvera. Please! Tell me now! Did you have an affair with him?

PRANVERA. How can you ask me that? Do you know what you're saying?

ENVER. You worked in the same office with him. Tell me! Maybe we'll die today. Maybe they'll kill us all. Tell me if you had an affair with that man. That's all I want to know. Say it, so I can understand. Tell me now, Pranvera! Tell me honestly!

PRANVERA. No, Enver. No. Why do you think such things?

ENVER. Tell me, have you ever cheated on me, Pranvera?

PRANVERA. No, Enver, I have never cheated on you.

ENVER. Never?

PRANVERA. Never, Enver.

[*Enver sits down. Pranvera looks at him for a while and then goes to him. Enver embraces Pranvera as they sit together, laying his head on her stomach.*]

ENVER. I know it. You want to run away with him and leave me. You want to run away with him.

PRANVERA. No, that's not true, Enver, no. Don't talk like this. I'm not going anywhere. If we go, we all go together.

[*Enver begins to cry, sobbing.*]

PRANVERA. Enver, that's enough – they can hear you! It's nighttime! What's going on with you?!

ENVER. Oh, I don't care about anyone.

[*Enver cries in silence, but sometimes a sound escapes him. Pranvera is looking at Enver and at the doors, wondering whether anyone can hear them.*]

ENVER. It's not your fault. It's my fault. Mine alone.

[*Pranvera tries to calm him down.*]

PRANVERA. Calm down, Enver. Hush now. Shush . . . come to bed.

ENVER. Is Gent really my son?

[*Pranvera stands up in shock and contempt.*]

PRANVERA. What?!!

[*Silence.*]

PRANVERA. Enver, all these years I've lived with you, it's not been easy for me. But I tell you now — tonight I would have no problem leaving you. I've had enough.

[*Enver dries his eyes and sobers. Silence.*]

PRANVERA. How could you say that about your own child? What kind of a man are you?

ENVER. I'm sorry, Pranvera. I'm sorry.

[*He stands up and reaches for her.*]

PRANVERA. Get away from me.

ENVER. I'm sorry, Pranvera. I'm upset. Don't you see what's happening . . .

PRANVERA. Leave me alone. Don't touch me, or I'll scream.

[*Pranvera leaves. Enver follows her.*]

Scene Five

[*Anita and Gent are standing onstage alone looking at one other. Gent sits down and picks up his model. Anita laughs and covers her mouth with her hand. Gent laughs too, but he keeps looking at his model.*]

ANITA. I didn't see him lighting the candle.

GENT. Neither did I.

[*They laugh.*]

GENT. Did your father say anything to you?

ANITA. No, what would he say? I've already told him I like you.

GENT. Really?!

ANITA. It was harder to tell you.

[*She laughs.*]

ANITA. But your father got really angry.

GENT. He was worried. He worries a lot about us and whether the police will come. He's worrying about us and we . . .

ANITA. Ha ha. It's not his fault. He's afraid.

GENT. No, he's not afraid, but . . .

ANITA. Honestly, he was a bit afraid . . . [*She laughs.*] The older generation is more frightened than we are.

GENT. He's afraid for us really.

ANITA. I don't know . . . But when he started with that Migjeni,[6] or whatever poet it was, I almost cracked up. Ha ha ha . . . I couldn't sit there.

[*Gent gives her a warning look.*]

GENT. It's nice that you think he's so comical.

ANITA. I'm sorry, I didn't mean to laugh at your father. It's just me. I always get the giggles.

GENT. No, it doesn't matter. I understand. Sometimes I feel like laughing too. But he was thinking of us.

ANITA. Gent, when we leave, will you come with us? Don't stay here. Did you know that I told my father I wanted to leave with you?

GENT. No, Anita. You can't leave now. It's dangerous.

ANITA. My dad is thinking of going. We might leave tomorrow. If we stay here, they might kill us.

[*Anita walks towards him.*]

ANITA. Well, anyway, I think . . . You know what . . .

[*Anita kisses Gent. Agron's voice can be heard.*]

AGRON. [*Offstage.*] There's a crowd coming from Sunny Hill.[7]

---

6. Migjeni is the nom de plume of Millosh Gjergj Nikolla (1911–1938), an Albanian writer and poet, sometimes referred to as "the poet of misery."
7. A hilly neighborhood in southeast Prishtina.

Scene Six

[*Pranvera and Enver enter. Agron is trying to put a call through.*]

PRANVERA. All those people! Where do you think they're taking them all, to Albania?

AGRON. No, they're sending those of us from Prishtina to the train station and then to Macedonia. There are lots of people at the border.

ENVER. They're sending most people to Albania.

AGRON. Yes, but those are mainly from the Dukagjini Plain.[8] Those from Prishtina are all being sent to Macedonia.

ENVER. Whatever. What matters is that they're emptying Kosovo. That matters.

[*He sits in the chair stretching.*]

ENVER. So! Now, whose turn is it of us old folks to find some bread somewhere?

PRANVERA. Where would we find it now, Enver?!

AGRON. Why? Have we finished the bread I brought, huh?!

PRANVERA. Yes, but I'll go out now. It's our turn. You've been out enough.

AGRON. No, God forbid. It's not right for women to go out . . .

ENVER. No, no! Of course not! Really . . . come on, we're not starving yet. Are you hungry, children?

GENT. I'm not.

ENVER. We had enough to eat yesterday. Maybe there's still some pasta?

[*Gent looks at Enver.*]

ENVER. It's good to prepare a bit for situations like this. Who knows what will happen later. After all, this is nothing. People have lived for days without food. They say that the human body can go nearly forty days without eating and one week without drinking water! And aren't we still yawning after yesterday's lunch?

---

8. The southwestern region of Kosovo which includes the districts of Peja, Gjakova, and Prizren.

AGRON. I can try to find some bread somewhere. And anyway, I have to go out to see if I can get Drita.

[*Gent stands up energetically and in a rush.*]

GENT. I'm going! [*He runs out.*]

PRANVERA. Gent, where are you going, Gent?!!! Gent, come back!

ENVER. Where on earth is he going?! No one told him to do that!

[*Pranvera runs out, calling "Gent." Enver follows more slowly with his cane and then ushers Pranvera back.*]

PRANVERA. [*Calling.*] Oh Gent! Gent, come back, won't you?!

AGRON. Anita, I'll be back soon.

ENVER. Don't shout like that because the police might be nearby! Why do you shout like that?! Come back inside.

AGRON. Anita, I won't be long.

[*Exit Agron.*]

ENVER. I didn't want him to go out either, but what can you do? He'll be back. I'm sure he just went to the bakery. He's not a kid.

PRANVERA. Enver, something might happen to him! God help him!

ENVER. What will be, will be! No one told him to go out! Does he have no common sense?!

[*Pranvera paces around the room, distraught, and goes to the windows to look out.*]

PRANVERA. Oh, my God! Oh, my God! He's gone. I can't see him . . . I can't see him at all.

[*Enter Agron.*]

AGRON. Anita, take this . . . [*He hands her a bag.*]

ANITA. Where are we going, Dad?

AGRON. We're leaving now.

ANITA. Aren't we going to wait for Gent?

AGRON. Sir! I'm deeply grateful to you for everything! I will never forget you! We have to leave immediately. I just received the call. Drita and her father are waiting for us nearby. They have a car, and they don't dare stay in one place for too long. Will you come with us?

ENVER. Go where? Now, eh?! No, no! You're going, are you?

AGRON. Yes. Come with us. It might be the last chance. We can't stay here any longer.

ENVER. No . . . no . . . It's dangerous . . . They might stop us . . .

AGRON. It's dangerous if you stay.

ENVER. Here I'm in my own house. No, no . . .

PRANVERA. We have to wait for Gent . . .

ENVER. Pranvera, what did I just say?!!!

AGRON. Sir, you're making a mistake. We need to go now. Come with us. There's room for you too . . .

ENVER. Mind your own business. Don't tell me what to do.

AGRON. I'm sorry sir, but . . .

ENVER. I will not run away, period. I'll stay here. Let them come. I'll be waiting . . .

[*Agron reflects. He looks at his watch.*]

AGRON. Are you sure that you don't want to leave now?!

ENVER. Quite sure!

AGRON. Well then, we're off. Anita, did you get the bags? Good. [*To Enver and Pranvera.*]

ANITA. Aren't we waiting for Gent? Maybe . . .

AGRON. Gent's not coming, Anita. Don't you see? [*To Enver.*] Thank you again. I'm so sorry that we're leaving in such a rush . . . We'll never forget what you've done for us. Goodbye!

Scene Seven

[*Agron and Anita exit. Pranvera and Enver walk a little way with them. Merita enters, upset, followed by Pranvera. Enver enters last and then goes into the bedroom.*]

MERITA. Oh, God! Is he here? Has he been here? No one has seen him. I'm going mad, Pranvera! I've looked for him everywhere!

PRANVERA. Merita, what's going on with you?! What happened?! Where have you been?

MERITA. I've been everywhere. Everywhere. I didn't find him in the flat that day. He left me a letter saying that he was going off to fight. I can't believe he could go and leave me here.

PRANVERA. Merita . . .

MERITA. No, he didn't go. I know that he didn't go. I know! He's not leaving me. But I can't find him.

PRANVERA. [*Unfocused and worried about Gent.*] Oh! Merita!

MERITA. [*In a low voice, as if explaining something very ordinary.*] I looked for him everywhere. Nobody had seen him. In every neighborhood . . . he wasn't at his parents' house either. Even his parents have fled somewhere.

PRANVERA. Merita, it's not good to wander about in times like this. Calm down. He's in God's hands. He's not alone. He's safer in the woods than we are here.

MERITA. No, no. He didn't go. I know it.

PRANVERA. Sit down, Merita, sit down and calm down. Stay here with us.

MERITA. I don't have time, Pranvera. I just wanted to see whether he'd been here. Now I think I know where he is!

PRANVERA. No, Merita, don't go out anymore!

[*Merita gets up to go. Pranvera prevents her.*]

MERITA. I know where he is, Pranvera, I know!

PRANVERA. Wait, Merita.

[*Enver enters from the bedroom, looks at them without any interest, and sits at the table. He holds his diary in his hand.*]

MERITA. [*In a low hysterical voice.*] No, no, no . . . ! [*She repeats.*] I have to find him. [*She walks out. Pranvera follows her.*]

PRANVERA. Stop, Merita. Don't go!

[*She walks out.*]

Scene Eight

[*Enver is sitting at the table which is covered with newspapers, and the diary off to the side. He has let his head fall onto the table. Pranvera is lying on a mattress and crying, looking blankly into the distance above her.*]

PRANVERA. Why, Enver?! Why . . . ? [*She repeats.*] Where's our son, Enver? Where?! Where is Gent? My son! [*She shouts.*] Where's Gent, Enver?! [*She gets up. Enver lifts his head.*] Answer me! Where is Gent?

ENVER. Calm down, Pranvera! I'm losing my mind!

PRANVERA. You know! You must know where he is! But, you! You pushed him out, you!

ENVER. I never told him to go out. You know that. You know I didn't tell him to go. Why do you say that?!

PRANVERA. But you did! All his life you kept telling him. [*She approaches the table.*] You drove us all mad. You, Enver, you! You drove us mad. [*Crying.*] But still, I took care of you as if you were the child instead of Gent. Oh, what you did to Gent, and it wasn't his fault. You were never able to talk to him like a parent. [*She is crying. She goes to the table and scatters the newspapers.*] Oh, where is Gent?!!! [*She is sobbing and covers her face with her hands.*]

[*Enver starts to collect the scattered newspapers but then leaves them.*]

ENVER. Calm down, Pranvera, please! [*He stands up and approaches her.*] Everything will be all right. Calm down! [*He starts to speak more softly and with more certainty. First, he puts his hand on her head, and then opens his arms to embrace her.*] He's probably found somewhere safe to stay and is waiting for the right moment to come back.

PRANVERA. [*Grabbing him by his collar.*] You, you, you! You . . . are responsible for everything. [*She starts pummeling him.*] Where is Gent?! Where is he?! . . .

[*Enver tries to shield himself.*]

ENVER. [*Angered and surprised.*] Hey, Pranvera!!! Calm down! Are you crazy, huh?!!! You know that I didn't tell him to go! I didn't tell him to go! [*He knocks her down. She falls down to the ground and keeps sobbing.*] You're mad.

[*Pranvera is crying loudly. Suddenly she stops as if dumbfounded. As if she's seeing something terrible offstage. She makes some inarticulate sounds as if the words she intended to speak are caught in her throat. She moves backward and points to something beyond the stage.*]

ENVER. Oh, my darling son! What happened to you, my son?! [*Pranvera gets up to look but seems unable to make anything out. Enver seems to be terrified by what he sees.*] What have they done to you!!!

[*From stage right, Gent enters – Gent's ghost. His clothes are torn, and his body is covered in blood and shows signs of torture and bullet wounds. He is lit so as to give the impression of a different dimension, and from time to time his torn clothes flutter in an invisible wind which plays only on him. Explosions can be heard along with the intermittent sound of rifles firing. Gent walks across the room, looking calm, with even a flicker of joy across his face. Only Enver can see him.*]

Three Scenes in Flashes

[*A play without words supported with music and voices. After each scene ends, the lights go down, and the next one begins.*]

Scene One

[*Enver is afraid of Gent. Pranvera is prostrate.*]

Scene Two

[*Enver follows Gent, as if pleading and looking for forgiveness as they both exit the stage. Pranvera is crouching on the floor, wailing silently.*]

Scene Three

[*Enver has grown accustomed to Gent's presence. Gent looks at the objects in the room and also glances at the pages of the diary.*]

Last Scene

[*The living room as it appeared in the first scene. Enver, Fred, Xhemajl, Merita, and Anita are drinking coffee. Enver sits at the table where his diary lies open, and he occasionally looks at a page. Fred is in his previous place.*]

ENVER. Finally, my diary is almost finished. After all these years! All that war. Now it's better. [*He flicks through his diary.*]

[*The others look at one other.*]

ENVER. It has some value, Mr. Fred.

FRED. Yes, sir.

ENVER. [*Leafing through his diary.*] For instance, "April 14th: For days no one has been seen in the streets. Neither police, nor paramilitaries. Gent came to visit us again." [*He skips to another section.*] "May 4th: Some aircraft were heard today, but in the distance. Gent came and told us that the town is completely empty. I told him not to go out because it was dangerous. But Gent doesn't know what fear is." Yes, Gent would come every day to bring us the news and tell us what was going on.

[*Pranvera enters holding a tray with a glass and some pills.*]

ENVER. [*To Pranvera, with his face lit up.*] Huh?! Already?

PRANVERA. Yes, it's time. Then you'll sleep.

[*Enver begins to swallow the pills one by one.*]

ENVER. [*As if with regret.*] Yes. After the pills, comes sleep. [*To those around him.*] She's right. After the pills, I need to rest a bit.

FRED. Ma'am, it's true that so many years have passed since then. But I'm still hoping that we can learn something about Gent.

ENVER. Eh, my Gent.

[*He points his finger offstage. None of them turn their heads in that direction.*]

ENVER. Look what they have done to my son.

PRANVERA. Come on now, let's go.

ENVER. Yes.

[*Pranvera and Enver exit. Silence.*]

MERITA. Fred, does Pranvera know you're leaving?

FRED. I've already told her that this would be my last month.

[*Pranvera enters. She sits down.*]

FRED. Ma'am, I have to go now because it's getting late.

XHEMAJL. We're going too.

PRANVERA. Thank you for coming.

FRED. This week I'll go on to another mission, but I'm sure I'll return to Kosovo often.

PRANVERA. [*Sighs.*] Mr. Fred, I'm honored that you've come back so often to see us, and I know you've tried hard to find something out about my Gent. And you too, Anita. With each of Gent's anniversaries, I have less faith that he's alive. But I can't believe that he's dead either. If I just knew what has happened to him, then maybe I could come to terms with life. But I don't expect any news from anyone anymore.

FRED. Ma'am, I wanted to tell you that my efforts will be continued by another specialist. He's an old friend of mine. I've told him about the case.

ANITA. I'll work with him in the same way I did with Fred.

FRED. Yes, and Anita will be here. I just want to let you know that recently there was another "Batajnica"[9] case, and we're expecting some new information.

ANITA. If there is any, Pranvera, I'll come and tell you myself.

---

9. The site of a mass grave just outside of Belgrade at a training ground for the Serbian Special Police.

PRANVERA. Thank you, my girl.

[*They all stand up and exit. Gent enters from stage left with his model in his hand. He is followed by Enver in pajamas. Gent stops for a moment. Enver stops as well. Then Gent exits stage right. Enver exits behind him. Gent enters again. He sets the model down in the center of the stage. He turns on a light inside it, then flips a second switch which turns on multi-colored lights. He exits.*]

[*The house lights come up.*]

THE END

By Doruntina Basha

THE FINGER

Translated by Doruntina Basha
and Janice Mathie-Heck

CHARACTERS

ZOJA — *in her late 40s, but looks much older*

SHKURTA — *early 30s, Zoja's daughter-in-law*

SHOP ASSISTANT — *may be played by Zoja or Shkurta in turn*

1. TREES KNOW EVERYTHING

[*Shkurta, in her thirties, but with the looks of a much younger woman, is in the kitchen of the house where she lives with Zoja, her mother-in-law, somewhere on the outskirts of a small town. Several pieces of luggage are spread on the kitchen floor. Shkurta, center stage, in an apron, is chopping onions with great concentration on the kitchen counter, which is also covered in other fresh vegetables that are about to be chopped. Her eyes are in tears from the onion; she wipes them with the back of her hand. Zoja enters with a batch of fresh parsley in her hands and with the looks of a tough supervisor. She notices Shkurta and what she is doing, and then scans the other items on the counter. She takes an empty jar, fills it with water and puts the parsley in it. She puts the jar with the parsley on the counter. Then she goes over to the suitcases and studies them. She opens one, smells it, then closes it again. She opens another one, smells it, and scrutinizes the rest.*]

ZOJA. [*Opens up a suitcase, smells it, frowns. Then she goes over to Shkurta, staring at her from behind her back.*] I wonder if the mold has gotten into your head, or just into your hands?

SHKURTA. [*Confused.*] What?

ZOJA. Faster with those hands!

[*Shkurta begins working faster. Zoja continues the general kitchen check.*]

ZOJA. The suitcases stink of mold. Where have they been?

SHKURTA. In the cellar.

ZOJA. Did I tell you to put them in the cellar?

SHKURTA. No.

ZOJA. So, then, who told you to do it?

[*Shkurta doesn't answer.*]

ZOJA. Who told you?

[*Shkurta doesn't answer.*]

ZOJA. [*Furious.*] Who told you?!

[*Shkurta jumps, scared, and the knife drops from her hand onto the floor.*]

SHKURTA. Nobody.

[*Shkurta bends to pick up the knife.*]

ZOJA. Pick up that knife. [Then.] When I talk to you, you answer!

SHKURTA. You don't like it when I talk.

ZOJA. Answer, not talk.

SHKURTA. What's the difference?

ZOJA. What is this? Speak only when I ask you to. Put the pan on the stove burner.

[*Shkurta does so.*]

ZOJA. Why is there an extra bag?

SHKURTA. I've packed some of my personal things.

ZOJA. [*Looks at her wristwatch.*] And again, we're gonna be late.

[*Shkurta pours oil into the pan.*]

ZOJA. Don't fill it up with oil like you usually do. We don't have money to burn.

[*Shkurta opens a kitchen drawer.*]

ZOJA. The wooden spoon. Not the steel one.

[*Shkurta takes out the steel spoon.*]

ZOJA. Is the oil hot yet?

[*Shkurta puts her hand over the pan. Doesn't answer. She takes the onions and puts them in the pan. Shkurta notices the steel spoon. She replaces it immediately with the wooden one. Zoja has noticed all this.*]

ZOJA. I looked for you all morning all over the house. You disappeared into thin air.

SHKURTA. I was in the cellar.

ZOJA. Turn the temperature down.

[*Shkurta does so. Zoja takes a little crossword puzzle magazine out of her pocket and sits on the chair by the counter beside Shkurta, who is now chopping other vegetables.*]

ZOJA. [*Reads with difficulty.*] "Branch of mechanics which studies the relation between air and object." "A-E-R-O . . ." [*To herself.*] One, two, three, four . . . [*counts in a low voice*] twelve?! [*Closes the magazine, looks at its front page.*] How much did you pay for this piece of shit?

SHKURTA. Seventy cents.

ZOJA. When I was young, with that money you could fill the house with food for one week, or even more, depending on how you prepared it. [*Glances at how Shkurta, when cleaning the peppers, lets the seeds fall on the floor.*] For sure not like you do. It's obvious you come from a rich family. [*Folds the crossword puzzle and returns it to her pocket.*] Do you ever think of the poor and destitute?

SHKURTA. My family has always . . .

ZOJA. You think that the carrot will peel itself, chop itself into pieces, and then jump into the frying pan?

[*Shkurta leaves the peppers, takes a carrot, and starts peeling it.*]

ZOJA. Who's gonna finish the peppers?

[*Shkurta stops; she's confused.*]

ZOJA. When I was your age, I didn't need anyone to tell me what to do. When I was your age, I was already the mother of two.

[*Shkurta continues with the carrots. From time to time she goes over to the stove to stir the onions. She is doing everything very quickly. Zoja goes over to the suitcases, opens one, takes something out, and smells it. Then she smells something else. Then she smells her own hands.*]

ZOJA. All the junk of a house accumulates in the cellar. What were you thinking?

SHKURTA. When we get back, I'll put the luggage in the attic. There's more air there.

ZOJA. Were you born in a cellar?

SHKURTA. I was born in a hospital.

ZOJA. What makes you so sure?

SHKURTA. My mother told me so.

ZOJA. What makes you so sure that the carrot should be cut that way?

SHKURTA. I've always cut it that way.

ZOJA. It doesn't matter how you've always cut it.

SHKURTA. But he likes it like that.

[*Tension.*]

ZOJA. You know better than I do how he likes his carrots?

SHKURTA. I didn't say . . .

ZOJA. [*Waits for her to finish, then.*] You didn't say what?

[*Shkurta doesn't speak.*]

ZOJA. [*Takes the knife from her hands, starts to chop carrots herself.*] You don't know anything.

SHKURTA. He likes how I cook.

ZOJA. He only says that to please you.

SHKURTA. He's not like that.

ZOJA. I made him like that.

SHKURTA. He always eats with a big appetite.

ZOJA. Exactly. Well brought up.

SHKURTA. He gives me compliments.

ZOJA. I knew that before you. He gave his first compliments to me.

SHKURTA. He did it to please you.

[*Zoja stops. Shkurta uses the opportunity to take the knife from her hand. She takes over the carrots.*]

ZOJA. What did you say?

SHKURTA. [*Alarmed.*] The onions are burning! [*Runs for the pan.*]

ZOJA. When a man says things to please his mother, it means that he loves her. When he says things to please his wife, it means that he's not being honest with her. It's as simple as that.

[*Shkurta removes the blackened onions. She throws them into the garbage bin.*]

ZOJA. [*Doesn't look at Shkurta.*] You've blackened my life as well.

SHKURTA. I'm not doing anything wrong.

ZOJA. True. But you're not doing anything right either.

[*Suddenly, a strong wind is heard outside. Shkurta and Zoja look towards the window.*]

SHKURTA. Everything will be ready on time.

[*Shkurta quickly begins to peel and chop onions. Her eyes well with tears again.*]

ZOJA. You know, when I saw you for the first time, I didn't like you at all. I even said that to my husband. But he told me that it was only important that our son liked you. How can that be important?

SHKURTA. Maybe because it's important for people who are going to live together to like each other.

ZOJA. But now you're living with me and not him.

SHKURTA. It isn't necessary to remind me.

ZOJA. It isn't natural for a girl to try so hard to go against the *flow* of things!

[*Shkurta doesn't react.*]

ZOJA. When I was young, marriages were made upon agreement of the families, and not the couple to be married. And for that reason, all of them were a success. At that time, families which had clumsy girls would usually keep them out of the public eye; they would never offer them in marriage. I pity the poor mothers who had to deal with them! The poor mother who raised you . . .

SHKURTA. And poor you!

ZOJA. Yes, poor me.

SHKURTA. My mother always told me that . . .

ZOJA. [*Taking out the crossword puzzle again.*] I don't want to hear about the woman who raised you.

[*With this sentence, Shkurta raps her own finger very hard with a knife. Blood begins to flow. Her face suddenly shows immense pain, but she doesn't make a sound. Zoja, who is now completely absorbed in the crossword puzzle, doesn't have a clue as to what just happened. She only notices that Shkurta has stopped. Eventually she turns her head to question her.*]

ZOJA. Why have you stopped?

[*Shkurta doesn't respond.*]

ZOJA. [*Stands up and gets closer to her.*] What's happened now? [*Sees the blood.*] What is this?

[*Zoja grabs the hand that Shkurta has been holding with her other hand. She sees that Shkurta has cut her finger. Blood is flowing.*]

SHKURTA. [*Out of context, instead of a scream.*] Aerodynamics.

[*Suddenly, Shkurta is in a shop.*]

FIRST INTERMEZZO:
SHKURTA IN THE SHOP OF HAPPINESS

[*Shkurta has wrapped her finger with her apron, which is now bloody. She glances around and goes over to the counter where the shop assistant is smiling at her. Shkurta feels a bit embarrassed about how she looks. The shop assistant gets to the point.*]

SHOP ASSISTANT. Good afternoon, ma'am.

SHKURTA. Good afternoon.

SHOP ASSISTANT. How can I help you today?

SHKURTA. I want to buy a house.

[*The shop assistant disappears under the counter and reappears with two cartons containing models of houses.*]

SHOP ASSISTANT. These are our latest models. They're selling extremely well.

SHKURTA. I'm not here to buy what everyone else is buying.

SHOP ASSISTANT. That's fine. [*She again disappears under the counter and reappears empty-handed.*] Have you already decided what you would like?

SHKURTA. No. Yes. A house in the middle of the city.

SHOP ASSISTANT. Ma'am, houses in the city are not in fashion anymore.

SHKURTA. Great. Neither am I.

SHOP ASSISTANT. Cities are polluted. They don't have enough green spaces. Wait, I'll show you another model of a country house. [*Takes out a new model from under the counter.*]

SHKURTA. I don't want a country house!

SHOP ASSISTANT. [*Returns the model.*] As you wish, ma'am.

SHKURTA. I want a house with windows that open, views down never-ending streets. Other houses, cars going up and down the street, heavy traffic, bus stops everywhere, mailboxes on every corner, billboards all over the place. I want a house right in the middle of car horns and police and emergency sirens. And on the horizon, I want skyscrapers.

SHOP ASSISTANT. Let's see what we've got. [*Opens a catalogue and starts going through it.*]

SHKURTA. I've lived all my life in the country. Surrounded by trees and hills, ploughed fields and furrows. I want asphalt. I want smog.

SHOP ASSISTANT. All right. [*She brings a new house out from under the counter.*] What do you think about this one?

[*Shkurta looks at it for some time. She turns the house around. She peers at the doors, windows and balconies.*]

SHKURTA. It's fine. But not perfect.

SHOP ASSISTANT. No. It isn't perfect at all. [*Removes the model and displays a new one.*] And this one?

SHKURTA. Too big.

SHOP ASSISTANT. And yet deficient. [*Removes this one as well.*]

SHKURTA. I want a perfect house!

SHOP ASSISTANT. So, describe it a bit to me.

SHKURTA. In fact, I don't want a house. I want an apartment.

SHOP ASSISTANT. That can be done. [*Goes under the counter to bring models of several apartments, which she exhibits for Shkurta.*] Apartments for sale!

SHKURTA. [*Bends to have a close look at them. She's fascinated.*] They're all wonderful.

SHOP ASSISTANT. Like our clients.

SHKURTA. I can't decide which one is best.

SHOP ASSISTANT. That's only from the outside.

SHKURTA. What's inside?

SHOP ASSISTANT. [*Opens a little window.*] Have a peek and tell me what you want.

SHKURTA. [*Peeking through a little window.*] I want all sorts of machines and devices that peel, chop, slice and dice. I want a device that cleans absolutely everything. A dishwasher is a must.

[*The shop assistant has selected all the items in miniature and has put them inside the apartment through the open window.*]

SHKURTA. I want a big sofa in the living room, with a lot of little cushions that smell of my mother's perfume. In fact, please put those kinds of cushions everywhere in the apartment. In the kitchen, too.

[*The shop assistant takes some miniature cushions and sprays them with a miniature perfume bottle. She places them in the apartment through the same opening.*]

SHKURTA. I want street lamps right outside my bedroom window. But I don't want the light of passing cars to reflect on my ceiling at night. It would look like ghosts approaching the window.

SHOP ASSISTANT. [*Fulfilling her wish.*] Everything for the apartment of your dreams.

SHKURTA. More lamps. Put them everywhere in the apartment.

[*The shop assistant throws a handful of miniature lamps inside.*]

SHKURTA. I'll take it.

SHOP ASSISTANT. Excellent choice.

SHKURTA. How much?

SHOP ASSISTANT. Oh, I'm sorry, it's not that easy.

SHKURTA. Excuse me?

SHOP ASSISTANT. You want to buy an empty apartment?

SHKURTA. But this one is full.

[*The shop assistant goes under the counter and comes back up immediately with a collection of miniatures which she displays on the counter top for Shkurta. It's all miniatures of people, and some cats and dogs.*]

SHOP ASSISTANT. For the price of the apartment you can get a full family, including a cat and a dog that get along perfectly well with each other.

SHKURTA. Really?

SHOP ASSISTANT. This offer is only for you.

SHKURTA. But . . . can I choose the family?

SHOP ASSISTANT. [*Gives her a catalogue.*] Go ahead.

SHKURTA. [*Goes through the miniatures.*] There's everything in here . . . Can I choose their characters, too? Their hobbies? How good they are at housework?

SHOP ASSISTANT. [*Discreetly.*] You could also get some that do all the housework for you. You'd only have to sit and watch.

SHKURTA. No. I could never just sit, not alone with my thoughts. That would drive me crazy.

SHOP ASSISTANT. Believe me, this opens the door to a whole new world.

SHKURTA. In fact, I don't want any family. At least, not now. If I wanted them, then I'd prefer them to do the housework only when I ask. The rest of the time I'd rather be left alone.

SHOP ASSISTANT. Would this be a big or a small family?

SHKURTA. How small is small?

SHOP ASSISTANT. [*Introduces her to miniature family members.*] One husband. One daughter. One son. One pet.

SHKURTA. Small! [*Then.*] But is it really necessary?

SHOP ASSISTANT. Of course! How else will you live?

SHKURTA. Alone. On my own.

SHOP ASSISTANT. But whom would you talk to?

SHKURTA. To myself.

SHOP ASSISTANT. People would think that you've gone out of your mind.

SHKURTA. I wouldn't worry about what other people think. Besides, there wouldn't be anyone around to listen.

SHOP ASSISTANT. The house of your dreams is so sad.

SHKURTA. No, just the opposite. It's full of life.

SHOP ASSISTANT. One pet at least?

SHKURTA. I don't know. What do you recommend?

SHOP ASSISTANT. From what I've understood so far, a cat would suit you perfectly.

SHKURTA. Is it compulsory?

SHOP ASSISTANT. Nothing is. But it's included in the special offer.

SHKURTA. All right, a cat. A little one that minds its own business.

SHOP ASSISTANT. A kitten then. You like to start things from scratch, don't you?

SHKURTA. For the first time in my life.

[*The shop assistant wraps everything up. Shkurta takes some bills out of her pocket and gives them to the shop assistant.*]

SHKURTA. I'm sorry. I've only got the paper money I made when I was little.

SHOP ASSISTANT. That's the only currency we accept here. [*Takes the money, gives Shkurta the package.*] Good luck.

SHKURTA. I . . . where should I put all this?

SHOP ASSISTANT. Wherever you like.

SHKURTA. Wherever I like?

SHOP ASSISTANT. Wherever you like, dear. It's all yours now.

SHKURTA. But it's so . . . heavy.

SHOP ASSISTANT. That's how every new beginning feels.

SHKURTA. What if it rains? I'm afraid it will all be damaged by the dampness.

[*End of Shkurta's intermezzo.*]

2. TREES KNOW EVERYTHING

[*Shkurta is back in the kitchen. She doesn't have her package anymore. Her finger is still wrapped in the bloodstained apron. Zoja is there also.*]

ZOJA. Did you say something?

[*Long pause.*]

SHKURTA. I answered your question from the crossword puzzle.

[*Another long pause. Suddenly Shkurta assumes a different mood. She goes back to the stove to continue what she had been doing. Zoja follows her everywhere, not knowing how to behave or what to say.*]

ZOJA. Sit down.

SHKURTA. Hmh?

ZOJA. I said sit down!

[*Shkurta sits by the table. Zoja removes the frying pan from the stove. Then she clears all the other items from the table to create some space. She sits down, takes Shkurta's finger, and begins studying it.*]

ZOJA. This is nothing.

[*Then she takes a bandage from a kitchen drawer and some iodine. She carefully takes Shkurta's finger again and starts to slowly blow on it.*]

SHKURTA. You don't have to take care of me.

ZOJA. [*Bandaging her finger.*] I won't have any use of you if you're injured.

SHKURTA. An injured daughter-in-law is worse than a wounded horse.

ZOJA. We still have a lot of work to do.

SHKURTA. Everything will be ready on time. The ceremony doesn't begin until evening.

ZOJA. The ceremony? [*Laughs.*] Sometimes you have a funny way of talking.

SHKURTA. Maybe you have a funny way of understanding.

ZOJA. You can't call a thing like that a ceremony.

SHKURTA. [*Draws back her finger.*] Really, don't bother.

ZOJA. Almost done. You'll have bloodstains on everything you touch.

SHKURTA. That's already happened.

ZOJA. No. Only the apron is stained.

SHKURTA. It happened even before. But with invisible blood.

ZOJA. You're raving mad.

SHKURTA. I don't believe anyone has ever gone mad from a cut finger. From invisible bleeding, yes.

ZOJA. Whatever!

SHKURTA. Everything in this house is stained with my invisible blood. Even you are, although we've rarely touched. Maybe it got on you when you were sitting on the sofa. When you're not home, I lie on the sofa, shed my invisible blood, and enjoy it a lot!

ZOJA. I don't understand you.

SHKURTA. It's been a while since you said "whatever." Once it was one of your favorite words. What happened?

ZOJA. Oh, I don't know. An expression I abandoned a long time ago.

SHKURTA. Like virtue.

ZOJA. Always, even when I was young . . .

SHKURTA. I don't want to hear about your youth! Must have been very boring.

ZOJA. [*Finished with the bandage.*] Now you can use your finger again.

SHKURTA. What if I don't want to?

ZOJA. I need your help.

SHKURTA. You need me only to treat me badly. That's why it doesn't matter if I'm wounded. It even gives you an advantage. The weaker I am, the stronger you are. This is the basic principle of your kind of people.

ZOJA. Rubbish. You're like a daughter to me.

SHKURTA. And you're like a stepmother.

ZOJA. God forbid!

SHKURTA. You have a daughter. Why should I take her place?

ZOJA. Because you are the wife of my son.

SHKURTA. [*Angry.*] Ex-wife of your son!

ZOJA. Hush!

SHKURTA. I'm sorry. Mistake. Ex-son!

ZOJA. How dare you!

SHKURTA. The neighbors can hear us?

ZOJA. You think I'm ridiculous, don't you?

SHKURTA. The neighbors have better things to do than eavesdrop on our chitchat.

ZOJA. No. Believe me. They don't.

SHKURTA. I don't even think they come close to our garden fence, and that's probably because of our weird way of living. Or maybe it's because of your "interesting" views on life and death and *the nature* that surrounds them.

ZOJA. I'm a woman of principles. If people don't like it, I don't care if they ever knock on my door.

SHKURTA. Or maybe . . . [*whispers*] the trees can hear us.

ZOJA. You should be ashamed of yourself for joking about things like that.

SHKURTA. I could never be your daughter. I am my mother's daughter. But you have forbidden this.

ZOJA. I've never forbidden you from doing anything. You can do whatever you want.

SHKURTA. Only in my free time.

ZOJA. Why are you being so difficult?

SHKURTA. Because right now, unlike the rest of the day, I'm sitting in my chair, and that means it's my free time.

ZOJA. You sound as if I've imprisoned you.

SHKURTA. Yes. I'm your slave. Slaves have a difficult life. That's why in my free time I get to be difficult.

ZOJA. Shkurta!

SHKURTA. That's not my name. You gave me that name so that my days would be short. But, as it turned out, somebody else's days were short.

[Zoja slaps her face immediately, but this doesn't have an effect on Shkurta.]

ZOJA. You are mean.

SHKURTA. [Stands up.] I'm tired of this life. I'm tired of this luggage. Every year is the same. [She kicks the suitcases. Zoja makes sure to return them to their original position.] I'm tired of following you on every anniversary, on your escape from [ironically] ghosts that descend from the trees to tell the untold truth, because only the trees know everything. [Bland.] I'm tired of living in your fantasy world.

ZOJA. You'd better sit down.

SHKURTA. I want to throw up just thinking how this meal is going to smell. Not to mention that I have to spend all day over the stove.

ZOJA. I'm going to give you a sedative now.

SHKURTA. Give me some air.

ZOJA. Do you want a cigarette?

SHKURTA. My mother, that evil woman who raised an evil person like me, turned everything upside down, only to get it into my head that I didn't enter this world in vain. And you step on me as if I were a rag, just because I was once your son's wife.

ZOJA. You still *are* my son's wife.

SHKURTA. In your head!

ZOJA. Not true. You have a husband!

SHKURTA. No, I don't!

ZOJA. Yes, you do!

SHKURTA. Don't!

ZOJA. Do! If you didn't have a husband, it would mean that I don't have a son. And I do have a son! And I don't want to hear another word!

[*Shkurta gives up.*]

ZOJA. I'll go and get the sedative.

SHKURTA. I don't want a sedative. I don't want a cigarette. I don't smoke. I'm not like you. I don't feel better by using the things that make you feel good. The only thing that you and I have in common is that both of us don't have husbands anymore. But this shouldn't make you think that I'm like you. We're not the same.

[*Tension.*]

ZOJA. May this be the last time you mention him.

SHKURTA. Amen.

ZOJA. [*Change of subject.*] If you want, we can have coffee before we leave.

SHKURTA. What makes you so sure that the loyal fetching-dog is going to follow you this time?

ZOJA. All right. Let's have coffee first, and then we'll see.

SHKURTA. I just want some water. My throat is dry.

[*Zoja gives her a glass of water.*]

SHKURTA. Why does it have to be so hard each year?! [*She empties the whole glass.*]

ZOJA. It's from the pain. You cut your finger really badly. Maybe I should take you to see a doctor.

SHKURTA. It doesn't hurt.

ZOJA. Maybe it needs stitches.

SHKURTA. I've suffered greater pain in my life.

ZOJA. Yes. I'm sorry.

SHKURTA. You don't have to be.

ZOJA. I'm really sorry.

SHKURTA. OK, please!

ZOJA. Good.

SHKURTA. [*Stands up.*] Let's continue. We're gonna be late.

ZOJA. [*Satisfied. Looks at her wristwatch.*] Yes. We're late.

[*Zoja goes back to the counter. Shkurta fills her glass with water and drinks it all. Then she drinks another glass and joins Zoja at the counter. They continue working together. They pass things to one another. A moment of quiet, if fragile, peace.*]

ZOJA. I call you Shkurta because you're short.

[*Shkurta bursts into fits of violent laughter. At first Zoja laughs with her, but soon Shkurta's laughter gets on Zoja's nerves.*]

ZOJA. What's so funny?

SHKURTA. When I was little, we had a cow. It had a spot on its neck, and for this reason, I called it Spotty Neck. Because it had this spot. On its neck. Spotty Neck.

ZOJA. When I was little, we had sheep. One day, during bayram,[1] my father and my uncle took a little lamb to the butcher, and they took my little brother with them. He was only ten at the time. When the lamb was slaughtered, my little brother fainted. Since that moment we've called him Fainty.

SHKURTA. Uncle Fainty . . . is called Fainty because he fainted once as a kid?

ZOJA. Yes.

[*Shkurta goes into another fit of laughter. Zoja is pleased that Shkurta is laughing at her story.*]

ZOJA. You see, we can also have fun together.

SHKURTA. [*Back to business.*] Give me the knife.

ZOJA. Careful this time.

---

1. A Muslim religious holiday, Eid-Adha, the Feast of the Sacrifice.

SHKURTA. It won't happen again.

ZOJA. Well, just be careful.

SHKURTA. It's not the first time I've handled a knife.

ZOJA. When I was about five years old, my mother cut her index finger off. We were in the kitchen. She was cooking, and I was playing under her counter. Suddenly, she screamed, and her whole finger fell on the floor right in front of me. Next thing she fainted, and I started screaming until my grandmother came running into the kitchen. She gave my mother a couple of slaps until she came to, and then shoved the pacifier back into my mouth. She threw the finger in the garbage bin.

SHKURTA. I always thought only butchers cut their fingers off.

ZOJA. My mother was a quiet woman, but hardworking. Poor thing, when she was 50, she started getting these back pains, and she couldn't do any of the housework anymore. I was 25 then, and I had to bathe her. It was the first time I saw my mother's naked body. Her arms and her hands were covered with scars. When I asked her where she got them all, she told me about a little kitchen accident for each and every scar. Her hands were mainly burned. Either from the fire or from the iron.

[*Shkurta is focused on cooking.*]

SHKURTA. I'm putting the frying pan back on the stove.

ZOJA. [*Content.*] All right.

SHKURTA. The vegetables are ready.

ZOJA. The meat is defrosted?

SHKURTA. Defrosted and cut into pieces, fatty bits carefully removed.

ZOJA. What about the garlic and the parsley?

SHKURTA. Maybe we shouldn't put any parsley in it.

ZOJA. Parsley adds to the aroma.

SHKURTA. But I don't like it.

ZOJA. Well, you're not the one who's gonna eat it.

SHKURTA. He doesn't like it either.

ZOJA. What? He's crazy about parsley!

SHKURTA. No, he isn't. He doesn't like it at all.

ZOJA. That's not true.

SHKURTA. He always scrapes it off the plate with his spoon.

ZOJA. I've never seen him doing that.

SHKURTA. When you're not looking.

ZOJA. Maybe he was removing the bay leaves. It happened a few times when I added bay leaves by accident.

SHKURTA. Then he puts them on my plate. I eat them, although I don't like the taste. I do this to cover up for him. This is our little pact.

[*Tension.*]

ZOJA. Pact?

SHKURTA. I eat the chopped parsley leaves off his plate, and he eats the gristle off the meat on my plate.

ZOJA. He can't put any gristle in his mouth!

SHKURTA. Exactly. It's a secret pact. We take turns eating things we don't like from each other's plate. This is our way of saying "I love you" to one another.

ZOJA. What are you talking about? What is this blabber?

SHKURTA. It's a token of appreciation.

ZOJA. My son keeps secrets from me?

SHKURTA. He does it so you don't feel bad.

ZOJA. Why should I feel bad?

SHKURTA. Because you were always such a devoted cook for him.

ZOJA. Are you implying that I'm unable to detect my son's dislike of an herb?

SHKURTA. Why are you taking it out on me? He started this thing, not me!

ZOJA. A secret! It's not a thing! It's a secret!

SHKURTA. It's not a big deal. It's just our little game.

ZOJA. [*Crestfallen.*] You two play games behind my back.

SHKURTA. No, Zoja. It's our thing only. It doesn't have anything to do with you.

ZOJA. You are playing games behind my back.

SHKURTA. What? I just suggested that we not add parsley. It really doesn't change anything. Go ahead, add some if you want.

ZOJA. How is it possible that my son turns out to dislike parsley, and I only discover it after decades of feeding him?

SHKURTA. He didn't want to bother you.

ZOJA. While, oddly, behind my back, he turns out not to mind eating the gristle of the meat, although I spend hours cutting it out just to suit him.

SHKURTA. Please. If you want to finish the dinner on time, just drop it.

ZOJA. You're trying to turn him against me.

SHKURTA. Never!

ZOJA. You, young woman, your head is filled with filthy ideas.

[*Silence. Shkurta is at a loss for words.*]

SHKURTA. He's not here . . .

ZOJA. Exactly! But he will soon be back. My faith in him is already ruined, and now that you've told him God knows what about me, his faith in me will be ruined as well. This is so that you can have him all to yourself. That is what you've been up to all the time. You're using his absence to take power in the house. Yes, you're trying to take power!

SHKURTA. That's not true!

ZOJA. And then, when you have full authority over him, you'll make him hate me . . .

SHKURTA. No, Zoja . . .

ZOJA. . . . and then you'll get him to kick me out of the house. That's how these things usually go.

SHKURTA. Zoja, he's not coming back!

[*Tension.*]

ZOJA. How dare you say something like that?

SHKURTA. It's not a *dare*. It's a fact.

ZOJA. You should be ashamed of yourself.

SHKURTA. All right!

ZOJA. Who have we been cooking for then since morning?

SHKURTA. Forget what I said.

ZOJA. For a *ghost?* For an imaginary person?

SHKURTA. For someone who is *not*.

ZOJA. If he only knew how you're talking to me. He would pull your hair out by the roots!

SHKURTA. Does it ever occur to you that he might be dead?

ZOJA'S INTERMEZZO ALL THE QUESTIONS YOU EVER WANTED SOMEONE TO ASK YOU, BUT NO ONE EVER BOTHERED TO ASK

[*The counter from the first intermezzo with Shkurta is now visible again. The shop assistant is behind the counter. Zoja approaches her with some discomfort. The shop assistant welcomes her with a big and patient smile.*]

SHOP ASSISTANT. Good afternoon, ma'am.

ZOJA. Hello.

SHOP ASSISTANT. How can I help you today?

ZOJA. I'd like you to interview me.

SHOP ASSISTANT. About?

ZOJA. [*Taking out a piece of paper, she unfolds it carefully and hands it to the shop assistant.*] It's all in here. I wrote everything down in case you forget what to ask. It wouldn't be the first time.

SHOP ASSISTANT. [*Leading Zoja towards a table with two chairs.*] Please have a seat.

ZOJA. I don't have much time. I've left the dinner cooking on the stove.

SHOP ASSISTANT. All right. [*Reading from the letter.*] What have you been thinking about recently?

ZOJA. About my son. I think of him every moment I'm awake, and when I'm sleeping, I dream about him.

SHOP ASSISTANT. Where is he?

ZOJA. He left home on the 10th of June, ten years ago, and he never came back.

SHOP ASSISTANT. Do you know where he went?

ZOJA. No. No one has seen anything of him since that time. They were taken as a group. Ten or fifteen of them. Most of them were either his friends or relatives. There's some talk that they were loaded onto a truck. Like hay.

SHOP ASSISTANT. Did anyone from that group come back?

ZOJA. Yes.

SHOP ASSISTANT. And they didn't tell you where they had been or where your son is?

ZOJA. They returned in black plastic bags. Skeletons.

SHOP ASSISTANT. Do you think your son is dead, too?

ZOJA. No. If he's dead, he would have returned in one of those plastic bags, like the others. But since his body was never found, it must mean that he is alive. He's quite a clever fellow. I'm sure he has survived.

SHOP ASSISTANT. Why did you let him go?

ZOJA. That's a good question. No one has asked me this until now. You know, no one has ever asked if he should have left the house that day or not. In fact, no one has ever asked me anything about my son, not even when he was a baby. My husband was always in charge; he made all the decisions about him. One day, when my son was five years old, my husband put him on his shoulders and started climbing up the cherry tree in our yard. I begged him not to take the boy with him. I was scared he'd fall and get hurt, but my husband just showed me the back of his hand and told me to be quiet and go back into the house. I had to watch from the kitchen window as they climbed up the tree. I could tell by the expression in my little boy's eyes that he was terrified. When they were almost at the top, while my husband was stretching to reach for the cherries, my son slipped off his shoulders and plummeted to the ground. For the first few seconds he didn't let out a sound. I ran outside and found him all blue in the face. My husband quickly came down but hid behind the tree in shame, clenching a fistful of cherries. Red juice dripped from his fingers. Suddenly, my son let out a scream as I held him in my arms. He looked better. We took him to the doctor who said that he had multiple fractures in one leg. It was this accident that gave him the permanent limp. [*Pause.*] Then there was that day, that awful day, exactly ten years ago. My husband told the boy to go outside and see what was happening in the yard. He made him leave the table without finishing his meal. Then we heard a rattling sound. At first we thought it was a sudden rainstorm that was causing havoc in the yard. My husband was such a coward.

SHOP ASSISTANT. How would you have acted if you had been your husband?

ZOJA. The moment I heard the noise, I would have told my son to go down to the cellar to get us some pickles, and then I would've begged my husband to go after him and talk so as to distract him. I didn't want him to feel scared or upset. Then I would've locked the cellar door and hid the key. I would've sat in the living room, turned on the TV, taken my knitting, and waited calmly for evil to burst through that door. They wouldn't harm me. They weren't coming to get me.

SHOP ASSISTANT. You have a daughter, too, isn't that right?

ZOJA. [*Reluctant.*] I used to.

SHOP ASSISTANT. What happened to her?

ZOJA. We married her to a man from a distant town. Why are you asking me about her? That's not one of the questions I wrote down!

SHOP ASSISTANT. Why so far away?

ZOJA. [*Despite her reluctance, she cannot resist speaking.*] The daughter was my first child. [*Then.*] I had just started menstruating and was only 14 years old. My mother was hiding the fact from my father that I'd become a woman, but he knew, because for some time he had been checking my underwear drying in the yard for stains. So, he engaged me to a man without my approval and without my mother's consent. Young girls and women are never asked about anything, not even about basic matters concerning their lives. The day they married me off, I was quiet and did what I was told to do. I had no idea what awaited me. Everything happened so fast. My mother wept all the time while they were taking me to my future husband. [*Pause.*] On my wedding night, the moment he got on top of me, I was in such pain that I lost consciousness. Nine months later, I gave birth to a little girl. That very day, he came up to the room in the attic where I was recuperating, and, as I was breastfeeding our newborn, he slapped me so hard that the nursing baby fell from my breast. He had wanted a boy. Neither he nor his family spoke to me for one year. Then I got pregnant again after he came into my room one night, to my great surprise. Again, that night I fainted and nine months later I gave birth to a little boy. They fired guns in the air, danced traditional dances, and made *baklava, tatli,* and *flia.*[2] People came around all day while I was lying in my room, weak and alone with my baby girl and my newborn baby boy. While I was still weaning the boy, his father would take him away whenever he went somewhere. I would only see him in the evenings. Still nobody ever talked to me, unless someone gave me an order. All the other members of the household would compete to see who could get to hold the little boy in their arms. When my daughter was a bit older, my husband married her off somewhere faraway, without even asking me. When our son turned 20, he brought a bride home himself. So, I never really had the opportunity to raise my daughter or my son. Years later, when my husband had started drinking, whenever my daughter-in-law would go to visit her parents, my son would talk to me, ask me questions, stay close to me, sometimes even kiss me on the cheek. But then, on that spring day, he left home and never returned.

SHOP ASSISTANT. What happened to your husband?

ZOJA. Nothing. He's still somewhere in the house. We don't talk at all. Whenever we catch a glimpse of one another, we swear. Half of the time he's drunk anyway. The rest of the time I silently curse him. Sometimes we bump into each other in the hallway. Our moaning and groaning fills the

---

2. Baklava and tatli are pastries of Turkish origin. Flia is a savory layered pie unique to Kosovo.

hallway with a bad smell — his of foolishness, and mine of regret. Never in his life, not even for a second, did he put his arm around my shoulder.

SHOP ASSISTANT. Maybe he drinks now because of your son.

ZOJA. He never loved my son. He doesn't know how to love. To love someone means to care about him. Not to let him down. In that house, I was the only one who knew how to love. No one else.

SHOP ASSISTANT. What about your daughter-in-law?

ZOJA. Oh, she's funny. She's so tiny, like a child. When I saw her for the first time, she worried me so much that I couldn't sleep for a week. I couldn't imagine her pregnant. And that's how it turned out. After three years of marriage, my husband started telling my son that he should get rid of his wife, but he wouldn't agree. He kept saying it was too early for children.

SHOP ASSISTANT. Is she still with you?

ZOJA. It's been ten years since my son disappeared, and she's still living with me.

SHOP ASSISTANT. She's very loyal.

ZOJA. I have the impression that if she had the chance, she'd run away.

SHOP ASSISTANT. Why is that?

ZOJA. She often looks absent-minded when she's doing the housework. If I don't tell her what to do, she can spend the whole day staring out the window at the trees. She's very slow. It's so strange. She thinks people around her care about what she has to say. She says she loved my son.

SHOP ASSISTANT. Why do you still keep her at home?

ZOJA. But she's the wife of my son.

SHOP ASSISTANT. But your son isn't there anymore.

ZOJA. What do you mean? That I should let her go? And what would I say to my son when he returns? How would I face him?

SHOP ASSISTANT. So, he is coming back, is he? When?

ZOJA. Today is the 10th of June. A rainstorm has been forecast for the evening.

[*End of Zoja's intermezzo.*]

3. TREES KNOW EVERYTHING

[*Everything is back to normal. Shkurta, guilt-ridden, is staring at Zoja. A pause.*]

SHKURTA. Zoja?

[*Zoja doesn't respond.*]

SHKURTA. Zoja, the meal is ready. Should I take it off of the heat?

[*Zoja doesn't respond. Shkurta removes the pan from the heat. Empties its contents onto a plate. Puts the plate on the table. Everything is done swiftly and quietly.*]

SHKURTA. The table is set, Zoja.

[*No response.*]

SHKURTA. Zoja, I only wanted . . .

ZOJA. I feed you, I give you shelter, a soft bed to sleep in, hot water, fire in the winter, shade in the summer . . . everything! I give you everything that you don't have! And what do you give me?

[*Silence.*]

ZOJA. What do you give me that I don't have?

[*Shkurta doesn't respond.*]

ZOJA. You mend my clothes when needed, but the stitches always come out.

[*Shkurta stays still.*]

ZOJA. Your hands . . . they're simply . . . they're no good.

[*Shkurta stays still.*]

ZOJA. But still, you have the nerve to give me advice about my own flesh and blood!

[*Shkurta stays still.*]

ZOJA. If your stitches didn't come out of whatever you sewed, maybe I'd consider your advice.

[*Shkurta stays still.*]

ZOJA. But you're . . . insufficient.

[*Shkurta stays still.*]

ZOJA. I can't take your advice because you're incomplete as a woman, and there's no connection between your head, your heart, and your hands. I don't understand you.

SHKURTA. I just wanted to . . .

ZOJA. Empty the luggage of your personal belongings. You're not coming with me.

SHKURTA. I didn't want to . . .

ZOJA. "*I wanted to, I didn't want to* . . ." Can you hear yourself speaking? You're not even able to put a sentence together. How am I supposed to believe that you're able to put thoughts together? It's a fact? You talk to me about facts? [*Stretches her hands towards her.*] Do you see these hands? Do you see a single scar on them? Forty-five years and not even one burn or cut. You know why? Because I've seen my mother's body, and the facts told me that there are far more serious pains in life, and I shouldn't try to hide them with some frivolous, trifling pain.

SHKURTA. If you could please allow me to finish.

ZOJA. [*Takes the knife in her hand.*] It doesn't matter how many times you've had a knife in your hands. What matters is where your head is when you use it. [*Throws the knife on the table; it falls on the floor.*] Your mind is always all over the place. It's why everything you say is deficient.

[*Pause.*]

ZOJA. Pick up the knife.

[*Shkurta obeys.*]

ZOJA. Actually, don't empty the luggage.

SHKURTA. Just listen to me once . . .

ZOJA. Take it and leave.

SHKURTA. Excuse me?

ZOJA. Go back to your mother and never return.

SHKURTA. Please listen to me . . .

ZOJA. What?

[*Pause.*]

SHKURTA. Never mind.

ZOJA. Go on.

SHKURTA. I want to come with you.

ZOJA. I'm setting you free.

SHKURTA. Why now?

ZOJA. Your mission in life has come to an end.

SHKURTA. I was not on a mission here.

ZOJA. Whatever. It doesn't matter what it's called.

SHKURTA. It does. I was here out of *love* for your son.

ZOJA. The luggage!

SHKURTA. Take me with you.

ZOJA. Leave this house immediately!

SHKURTA. No, I won't.

ZOJA. Why are you talking? Who asked you to talk?

SHKURTA. Zoja, let me come with you.

ZOJA. You don't have to do things you don't believe in.

SHKURTA. You won't make it on your own. The luggage is too heavy.

ZOJA. Girl! Do you have ears? Get out of my way! I don't ever want to see you in this house again!

[*Pause.*]

SHKURTA. All right. I'll leave.

ZOJA. Very well.

SHKURTA. I just want to say one thing.

ZOJA. You don't seem to grasp that your opinion is of very little interest to me. Especially now after showing how little you respect me and my son.

SHKURTA. In the ten years that have passed, you've only buried yourself deeper and deeper in a fantasy world, instead of going in the opposite direction, towards the surface which is closer to reality. You know, the deeper you go, the more difficult it will be to rise to the surface again.

ZOJA. [*Suddenly she is looking at her with a smile on her face.*] Is this all you had to say?

SHKURTA. I just wanted to say that it's all making you suffer even more.

ZOJA. Really? Now you've made me curious. How, then?

SHKURTA. No rainstorm will bring him home. But you can't accept this. You have it in your head that the morning after the storm, when it's all calm again and you return, you'll find him just as in the old days, as if nothing had ever happened. The truth is that every year the storm brings only water, mud, some broken seedlings from who knows which village, and trash. And while you are watching me clean up the yard, I hear you say: "*Next year.*"

ZOJA. You know, if you're not good at anything else, at least you're good at talking rubbish.

SHKURTA. I feel sorry for you.

ZOJA. [*Roughly.*] I've lived more than you. Look at yourself. You're pathetic.

SHKURTA. [*Zoja's words sink in. A discreet smile.*] That is true.

ZOJA. You said what you had to say. Now go.

[*Shkurta goes over to her luggage.*]

SHKURTA. Life with you has been hard.

ZOJA. I'm glad it's come to an end.

SHKURTA. I'm sorry it had to end this way.

ZOJA. At least from now on, I don't have to see your face anymore.

SHKURTA. You know, there were moments when I could've accepted you like a mother.

ZOJA. Poor thing. And betray your real mom?

SHKURTA. My mom is happy. She has everything. You have neither a son, nor a daughter, nor a husband. And now, not even a daughter-in-law.

[*Zoja is shaken by this, but she won't show it. She takes her crossword puzzle and starts fiddling with it, while Shkurta is standing beside her luggage and staring at it.*]

SHKURTA. Considering the 12 years that I've lived here, I don't have a lot of personal things. They all fit in one suitcase.

ZOJA. Easier to carry.

SHKURTA. In fact, since I never had a life of my own, the things in it aren't even mine.

ZOJA. Whatever you say, girl, just get out fast!

SHKURTA. I packed this suitcase this morning, in the basement, for a special reason. I wanted to leave with you today, on our annual trip. I planned to go with you to your stop, and then continue down the road . . . to my mother's. For good.

ZOJA. I guess our thoughts were on the same wavelength!

SHKURTA. Do you want to know what's in this suitcase? [*She opens it and starts taking out some clothes.*] Take it as a chance for us to finally get to know each other. One day we might regret not having given each other a second chance.

ZOJA. One day I won't even think of you.

SHKURTA. [*She spreads some of the clothes on the floor; they are all men's clothes.*] Maybe you'll think of my personal belongings.

ZOJA. Your belongings smell moldy.

SHKURTA. I've saved them from being ruined.

[*Silence. Eventually Zoja turns to have a look at what's on the floor. It's her son's clothes. She slowly rises from her chair.*]

ZOJA. Where'd you find these?

SHKURTA. In the cellar. Where you hid them, where they were covered in water and mud during the flood.

ZOJA. How dare you touch my things?

SHKURTA. They're not yours! You've abandoned them!

ZOJA. You've no right to take them.

SHKURTA. Of course, I do! They belong to me because I looked for them, and I found them.

ZOJA. They're his things!

SHKURTA. I'm so tired of you using the present tense! Those were his things! Now, since they don't belong to him anymore, and since you don't want them, I'm taking them! [*She gathers some clothes together on the floor.*] Your son on his wedding day. Do you remember?

ZOJA. Get them out of my sight!

SHKURTA. I remember. It was the happiest day of my life. Why did you try and make me forget the happiest day of my life?

ZOJA. It's not about you forgetting. It's about me not remembering.

SHKURTA. Naturally! It's the day I came into your life.

ZOJA. Why do you always have to get in between?

SHKURTA. In between what? You and what you want to forget?

ZOJA. I don't want to forget forever! I just want to forget for now!

SHKURTA. What is *now*? When is *now*?

ZOJA. Now is this day!

SHKURTA. [*She throws a hat onto the floor with the other clothes.*] Do you remember this one?

ZOJA. Please! Get them out of my sight!

SHKURTA. Here! That was the day when he went into town to sell the first cherries of the season from our cherry tree. Remember now? It was a mere six months after we got married. When he came back, he told us that he'd sold all the cherries. His father said that naturally the town ladies couldn't resist the hat he was wearing that day, which was, in fact, his father's. Remember now? You refused to speak to me for a whole week because, when he came through the door, I gave him a hug. You dropped a glass, and it shattered.

[*Zoja is staring at the clothes. Shkurta takes some shirts out of the suitcase and spreads them on the floor by Zoja's feet.*]

SHKURTA. These shirts were a gift to him from my family on our wedding day. This one was from my aunt, this one from my grandmother, and this one from my mother. They're still in their packages. You didn't allow him to wear any of them, ever.

[*Shkurta continues taking out clothes, displaying them on the floor.*]

SHKURTA. These trousers his aunt mended several times. This t-shirt he wore when he played soccer. [*Smells it.*] Now, even the smell of his sweat is gone.

[*More.*]

SHKURTA. These sandals we bought at the market. These slippers my brother passed down to him, as they were too small for him.

[*More.*]

SHKURTA. This watch he bought with the first money he earned.

[*More.*]

SHKURTA. His overalls.

[*More.*]

SHKURTA. These jeans he wore on our first date. [*Rhetorical question.*] Would you like me to tell you how we met?

[*Zoja covers her ears with her hands. Shkurta displays more clothes.*]

SHKURTA. These shoes I bought him for his first birthday as my husband. Until recently they were always at the front door of the house. However, I noticed that they were missing and started to look for them.

[*More.*]

SHKURTA. These clothes are the ones he probably wore before we got married, before I even knew him. I don't want to forget them either.

[*Shkurta has now covered the whole kitchen floor with her husband's clothes. They look like an exhibition. Zoja goes through each and every item.*]

SHKURTA. You understand now? This is the reason why I put up with you for all these years: for the man who went missing and who wore these clothes. [*Then.*] It has been horror living with you, Zoja. In all those years, you didn't allow me either to remember him or to forget him. But the one thing I really can't understand is how you continue to expect him to return while, at the same time, you try to erase all signs of him from the house.

ZOJA. I'm not trying to erase anything. I just want some things out of my sight, temporarily. Until he comes back.

SHKURTA. [*Harsh.*] You have no right to think that this happened only to you!

ZOJA. [*Staring at some clothes from the last pile that Shkurta took out of the luggage. Takes them in her hands. Then she bends over some other items, the ones he had worn before he got married to Shkurta.*] He wore these on his first day at high school. He was always very proper. But that day, his grandpa gave him a pen, and he kept it in his shirt pocket. The pen leaked, and the ink stained the shirt. You can still see the stain here. The only stain he ever had on his clothes. He would never allow his clothes to get dirty; he always went out with them ironed, even for chopping wood. I've washed and ironed these clothes so many times; I know all of them by heart. [*Then.*] It isn't possible for someone simply to disappear from the face of the earth!

SHKURTA. He hasn't disappeared from the face of the earth. He *must* be somewhere.

ZOJA. Somebody should know something. There should be witnesses!

SHKURTA. It's just a matter of time until his body is found.

ZOJA. He did no harm to anyone.

SHKURTA. He had a big heart.

ZOJA. He still has. Wherever he is.

SHKURTA. [*Stretches her arm out and touches Zoja's arm.*] Zoja . . .

[*Zoja doesn't respond. Shkurta withdraws from her.*]

SHKURTA. I didn't have a lot of time with him.

ZOJA. Neither did I.

SHKURTA. I wasn't even here on that last day.

ZOJA. These clothes . . . how could you take these clothes out? How could you touch something so sad?

SHKURTA. These are all that's left from the short time we were together.

[*A longer pause. The sound of the leaves on the trees from the yard is audible. Zoja starts folding the clothes and putting them back in the suitcase. Shkurta is still standing in the same place.*]

ZOJA. You can take all of them with you. Just leave me the shirt with the stained pocket.

SHKURTA. Zoja, can you tell me what he was wearing that day?

ZOJA. [*Thinking about it.*] I can't remember.

SHKURTA. Try to remember it, Zoja. Try harder.

[*Zoja tries harder, but cannot remember. This upsets her, and she takes all the clothes out of the suitcase again and starts inspecting each and every item, trying to think about which ones are missing. Finally, Zoja remembers.*]

ZOJA. The sky-blue summer jacket with the zipper. Left hand in the pocket, where he was probably playing with the handkerchief that had his initials. Under the jacket, a white t-shirt, one size smaller. His favorite jeans with a printed brand on the back, right pocket, and frayed at the cuffs. When he reached the door, he put on a pair of his father's shoes, which were bigger. He left wearing those shoes.

[*Pause. Shkurta has put two spoons by the plate on the table.*]

SHKURTA. Let's eat.

[*Zoja goes over to the window, opens it. The rustle of the leaves is even stronger now. It starts to rain. Zoja is looking outside.*]

ZOJA. They're so tall. As if they want to crack open the sky. I'm sure they know everything.

[*Zoja goes over to her luggage. Takes it and heads for the door. Shkurta is following her every move. Then.*]

SHKURTA. You're leaving?

ZOJA. A rainstorm is going to break. The house could collapse.

[*Exit Zoja.*]

EPILOGUE THE SECOND CHANCE CLUB

[*Zoja is sitting at a table, alone. Her luggage is by her side.*]

ZOJA. It's not really true that you're living in the next room, right? Are you doing it to make me angry? Or to make me feel better? Which one?

My dear husband, you're so considerate.

Which is the reason why I forgive you for everything.

All the swearing.

All the beatings.

All the plates of food you threw at the wall when you didn't like the taste.

All the forks you threatened to scar my throat with when your favorite team didn't win the game.

All the nights you didn't come home. All the weeks when you'd disappear without a trace.

All the things I would accuse you of in my head when you weren't with me.

And if you really were doing all the things that I imagined, I forgive you, too.

But there are three things that I can never forgive.

The day you sent our daughter so far away from home and never bothered to find out how she was.

The day you interrupted our son's meal and told him to go out into the yard and see what was going on — the day he left the house limping in your shoes and never came back.

And the moment you went out after him, swearing through your teeth that he took your shoes, and you didn't come back yourself. Behind you, you left half a cup of coffee. I wondered whether the coffee contained a secret message for me. Right away, I regretted washing the cup, erasing what could have been a very important message hidden in those black coffee grounds.

I think you love me, too, but in your own way. Or at least I like to think that. But, if I'm wrong, please forgive me.

And if you never really loved me, I forgive you that, too.

If you meant it when you said that you'd prefer me dead, I also forgive you that.

But those other three things I can never forgive. I'm sorry, but I can't.

I also can't forgive the trees outside the house for not having a mouth. I know they have eyes because they keep their heads high and often lean in the direction where those foreign languages come from, but I know that they have no mouth. If they had one, they would speak. If they could speak, they could tell me where all of you went that day. Every time the wind blows, I think that you're trying to tell me where you are, through the murmur of the leaves. When it's windy at night, the rustling wakes me up, and I can't get back to sleep because I'm trying to understand what it means. I've become a slave to signs and symbols ever since the day that you and my son vanished. I haven't managed to interpret any of them yet, and this is driving me crazy. Especially the rustling of the leaves.

Please forgive me for not being the wife that you wanted, or for being a wife unsuited to your needs. I did my best not to upset you. Please forgive me for that, too. Forgive me for not always knowing which socks you wanted to wear. Maybe if you give me a second chance, I might be able to understand your whims and learn your tastes.

Please forgive me for not being able to hide all the love I had for my son, for worrying myself sick about him all the time, for exclaiming, *"Be careful son!"* the day he left the house in a limp, all of which caused you to blow your top.

Forgive me, forgive me, forgive me. I forgive you everything. Apart from those three things . . .

Apart from those three things. And, please, forgive me for not forgiving you those three things.

END

SLAYING THE MOSQUITO

By Xhevdet Bajraj Translated by Ani Gjika

PROTAGONIST: A MAN

[A room with a table and two chairs beside it. On the table, a bottle of alcohol and a shot glass. A dog (in the absence of a real dog, a toy one) near the table. A window and a shelf filled with books.]

[The man reads out loud from an open book.]

The angels I once carried on my shoulders
committed suicide
when snow fell on my hair
on what now is nothing more than snow
I was a groom who rode the horse of death
searching on the footprints of a day long gone
for a familiar face
to give me the nerve of a flower
that dares to bloom by the window
this very same one
from where you see
what's left of the world

Until someone dies of gunshots
                        of knife cuts
                                    of hunger
because of an absence of love or a surplus of it
while listening to grass grow

he thinks in two months
certainly
it will reach heaven
but the sun is no fool
it burns everything reaching for the blue

Eagles swallows nightingales
fly
inside cages hanging inside rooms
Snake bear lion survive in zoos
Shark fish snail
swim the waves inside cans
The bull and all the cows of his harem
all ground up and salted
dream
shoved forcefully
inside their own intestines

I don't know if I'm standing on my head
or if the world has toppled over
From here it seems reality will never stoop so low
as to deny our own imagination
meanwhile each day we wait among loved ones
for a cold kiss from the blade of a thief's knife
a bullet's flight from its black nest
       straight into a kidnapper's chest

or the liquid wail of drug traffickers' axes
who deliver illusory collages
made of flesh from our bodies

So
we wait
with a smile on our faces
We prove Aristotle's words
that man is the only animal
capable of such a thing
smiling

[*He stops reading in order to continue his monologue.*]

Wind blows from all directions
the sky committed to making a mess
Goddammit
life must be lived
But
I don't give a fuck about anything
I'm nearly dead but I'm rich
I got seven Bozhur[1] cigarette packs
and a load of bottles
filled with fresh Rahovec[2] air

1. Bozhur cigarettes are produced in Kosovo.
2. Rahovec is a town in Southeastern Kosovo.

while the world exists solely for poetry

for a glass of raki[3]

and love making

I say this from the land of the feathered serpent[4]

it grew wings

because it swallowed a dead

                                                        seagull

I know this

because I am

the son of the Knight of the Black Eagle[5]

                                                        black as the final night

emperor of the red sky

and for my swift return to the empire of silence

I need nothing

because I'm the king of nothing

I'm the holy nothing

God of nothing and more than that

I am nothing itself

I

who have just found another house

and now live here

---

3. Raki is a strong alcoholic drink made from grapes, popular in Albania, Kosovo, Turkey, and Greece.

4. The Feathered Serpent was a prominent supernatural deity, found in many Mesoamerican religions.

5. The black eagle is one of Albania's national symbols, meaning the speaker is the son of an Albanian nationalist.

my belly full my soul empty

and while time flies stealing days from the future

no one complains about this

[*He listens attentively, seems concerned about the mosquito's buzz, starts to go after it.*]

Last night I went to bed at 2:00 am

From 2:00 to 3:00

a mosquito tried to deafen me

I turned the light on four times

four times I turned it off

four times my wife yelled at me

four times I had no time to listen to her

Her timing to tell me things is always off

Be quiet

I told her

but no

on these occasions

or when she showers

or puts on make up

or sings

or thinks of family work God

life stuff

As if surviving were the right way to live

Anyway

she excels in one thing

she sleeps well

when this happens

if the room is cold

I tuck her in with a line by Neruda

But I should admit

she didn't steal my love

I willingly gave it to her

at first sight

she

a young thing back then

by the name of a flower blooming out of a beer can

I rejoiced the way a lamb rejoices

       when it survives Bayram[6] celebrations

my shoes trembled

       not my legs my shoes

and I understood then

what an idiot whoever named such a thing with one word

love

You can imagine

in my bed

---

6. An Islamic religious holiday, Eid-Adha, the Feast of the Sacrifice.

like a spring flower
until I water it with rain
under bright lightning and thunder
and then at day's end
as I transform into a rose
at the expression of her face
when she smiles as she rarely does
so when you first look at her
she seems nearly blissful

[*He takes a sip from the shot glass on the table.*]

Uselessly I've been looking for the mosquito
on the ceiling on walls on the window on my bed
on the closet on the moon
on the head of Ursa Major standing on the Big Dipper
setting off for the Milky Way
From 3 o'clock to 4 o'clock
five times that mosquito bit me
It really hurt the last time
that's when I discovered mosquitoes have teeth

This happened
when I was dreaming of Stalin on Skanderbeg Square in Prishtina

Have you heard of the former leader of the former Soviet Union

the one who used to stroke children's hair

even though he could kill them all

like he killed Daniil Kharms[7]

Doesn't matter

he's known about you

but someone needs to inform people that he's dead already

like his peace period over the Soviet land

until under it

the Soviet Union's most precious ones began to hum

miners and naturally

as they turned in their graves

Mayakovsky Esenin Tsvetaeva Akhmatova Mandelstam

when trying to escape the political system

people found refuge in the monasteries of poetry

and knelt before a vodka-made god

But who cares about dead poets

when people

without enough water

even a few drops

face a crucial dilemma

should they wash their eyes their asses or save it for coffee

---

7. Daniil Kharms was a Soviet-era surrealist and absurdist poet who died in a psychiatric ward. The cause of his death was starvation.

or tea
If only it were the Apocalypse already
or even one or two days after it

What does it matter if the sun keeps moaning
barking screaming yelping
like a tortured dog
The day passes without returning never lays down its head
never stops a single moment
in a man's heart
where the scream of a flower blooming
coexists with the cries of a pigeon
seeing how her squab
caught mid-flight
the shadow of a falcon crossing its motionless wings
falls without a crumb of life left
like the light of death itself

Anyway
I was talking about the mosquito
When it bit me
I launched at it like the king of animals
and
fell down the stairs
Nothing serious
I broke a rib and my nose started bleeding

I hurried slowly and got up

and went to the kitchen

then like the black wind of the desert

returned to the bedroom

knife in hand

Come show yourself now

get closer if you dare

yelled I who else

not The Brave One with Many Friends[8]

which is my dog's full name

he came out of the bedroom looking at me all puzzled

I placed my knife near the bed

and at 4:20 am

I tried to sleep thinking

what are the state police or the local ones doing

what is SHIK[9] doing

what are Our Armed Forces doing

what is the United Nations doing

Eulex

Nato

all those secret services afoot

who can't protect a single citizen

from a mosquito

---

8. The dog is named after an Albanian children's book by the same title which
   tells the story of George Castriot Skanderbeg, Albania's national hero.

9. An Albanian acronym for the Kosovo Intelligence Service.

If there were two
or if there were a spider or a bee
If there'd been a wolf two wolves three wolves or a volcanic eruption
of them
if there'd been The Animals The Birds Pantera The Pussycat Dolls
Los Tigres del Norte Scorpions Sex Pistols
If there'd been a priest
   my neighbor to the right
If there'd been the old lady who lives to the left of my house
If there'd been Muji's[10] horse
or Skanderbeg's black horse
or the White Horse of which Ermira Babaliu Xhoi[11] and others sing

Life is too short to send everyone to hell one by one
all those who deserve it
and so sometimes
instead of organizing an election
   where people could decide
   if water is wet or not
   I wait for an increase in numbers of those who've written
   or at least try to write down the history of mankind
     leaving not even the smallest trace of peace
     not even in the heart of a stone
and in between every dumbass I stick carbon paper

10. In the Albanian Epos of Heroes, Muji is a protagnoist and heroic figure.
11. Names of Albanian pop singers.

so that

by sending the first one to hell

the rest are taken care of

People who walk the way of god

with bells on their necks

whether they're the opposition or otherwise

are the same shit

stink the same

they only look different

At least

that's what I think when I lie on top

of my country's daily collection of garbage

and ask myself

which evening's sun must I become

whose inebriated shadow

song of what bird

grunt of what barbarian

moustache of which Tatar[12]

In the end

the one who for a moment happens to be on top of the garbage

sees way farther than the one who's under it

---

12. Turkic-speaking people living in Asia and Europe.

If I am sitting

I don't think

my lips are sealed

like a portrait hanging in the gallery of psychopaths

Thinking can be bad for your health

it can convince you to go naked in the forest to the animals

and stay there

[*Again the mosquito buzz is heard, and again he goes after it.*]

Little brother

the worst thing in the world was

when in the middle of life's last flower field

there where the grass meets the sky

as the girl dreams of a first kiss

they managed to separate the meaning of the word love

from the thing it names

This had to have hurt them deeply

much more than a tooth hurts

[*He drinks his shot of raki and fills it right up again.*]

At 4:35

the cursed mosquito flew right next to my ear

Enough

the end fin konets fund[13]

I switched the light on and put on my camouflage uniform

my bullet-proof vest too

I stood there watching with binoculars for fifteen minutes

until I found it on my wife's cheek

on the very spot I'd kissed her earlier that day

mmm how I rejoiced

because if it had been on the tip of her tit

it would have sucked my life's milk

and I couldn't have intervened

because I would have likely awakened the bird

I'd bought her in the town's bazaar

gifting it to her when she gave me her heart

I said

so her rib cage would no longer be empty

And if I'd found the mosquito on the hill where I've raised my flag

as a sign of occupation

a forested hill under which

a moist and warm cave exists

where human beings typically come out

And if the mosquito had sat on one of her arms

and I would have hurt her there accidentally

who would have cooked for me

who would have scratched my back

13. The phrase "the end" repeated in French, Russian, and Albanian respectively.

who would have tied my shoes
who would have worked
Some of you need all your life
to do nothing
whereas I have carpeted my life's path with flowers
annoyed ones

I approached her slowly
and with all the strength I had left from a sleepless night
I punched her
BAM

How strange
it was the only time my wife made no comment
for this reason
after all those hours I kissed her again
a kiss warm as tears
it always kills me the kiss of a woman
even when I do the kissing I die too
I forgave her all her week's chatter
when she won't shut up
and resembles an open window
which for as long as the wind blows
lets all good memories fly out
and all sorrow seep in
When this happens

the season of dead flowers begins
all the world's roads cross through my heart
and I carry her love with me
on my shirt pocket
like an ink stain

In any case
when I drink hash tea
I feel like Paul Gauguin long ago
I always see naked women on white horses
galloping through wide fields of flowers
among tall oaks

[*He takes a sip of raki.*]

I called to her noblewoman oh noblewoman
two times
but uselessly
she didn't even move
Doesn't matter I said
I'll celebrate by myself
and I turned on the music
Don't bother me mosquito by Ludwig Von The Doors
turned the volume all the way up
from the portraits on the walls
historical figures watching me

I took the bottle of grape raki
didn't want to die of thirst
like a shipwrecked sailor in the sea
In the end
I'm sure you remember that famous Archimedes line
let me have a sip of Rahovec raki
and I will move the world
Or else this town's raki springs from the earth
meaning it's not men and women who make it
on the contrary raki makes them better humans

I rolled a cigarette and lit it obviously
I'm not a sheep who eats grass
I spilled some raki on the plate and started drinking it with a spoon
went to heaven
Amen
may god bless my country
or simply as the holy scriptures say
domine memento mei[14]

Drink locally and think globally
it's better to get drunk sometimes
than be idiots all your lives
The goal is to avoid water
you know how disgusting it feels

14. Domine memento mei from Latin meaning, remember me, Lord.

when it seeps into your shoe
never mind to wet your mouth with it

After a while I went up to the bedroom
it was time to wake my wife up
so she'd shower dress up put on make up
and then go waste all her time at work
Because she wasn't getting up
I threw a glass of water at her, lukewarm as piss

She awoke with some unusual questions
why is my jaw hurting
why is there blood on my lips
why is my tooth broken

Hey hey hey
don't ask me
it's true I know a lot of things in life
        but not everything
you should know better than me
where you've wandered off in your dreams
Now go to work and come back whenever you want
but watch out for your necklace
don't lose the beads
because before you can collect them all
under this beautiful sky

the doves will have taken them

these ones dying of hunger

and please

tell the crowd today I don't take visitors

and I don't feel like leaving the house

I hope they can still find the sun's shadow without me

if not

let them come up with a game for the bread and circuses

they can take their time for example to figure out

what's going on with us

why politicians of the strongest parties

right before the election have come to an agreement

to increase the production of leather

and donate to the populace

long-sleeved shirts that crisscross and tie in the back

Well this is how things go

life is a coin tossed in the air

heads or tails doesn't matter

your face wears a sneer

caused by the weight of the cross

But if it's neither heads nor tails

you'll never have offspring

For masks to fall off in life's dramatic play

sometimes a banana peel suffices

the major parties have an agreement
turn a deaf ear to the people's will
consciously
to do as they please with the people's vote
They want to ignite the country
so they can put out fires with blood
people's blood obviously
while they give us just two options to choose from
rise or I'll kill you
fall or I'll kill you

So you see
the wise one knows of what he speaks
but the ignorant only says what he knows
I didn't mention politicians
because it doesn't matter what anyone says
Americans are right
an opinion is like an asshole
everybody has one

Looks like
a good politician here
is the one who's had plastic surgery
his face covered with skin from his ass
he speaks briefly

but when he speaks

he says nothing

he takes no steps forward

or backward not even to the left or to the right

so those born to follow him will not weary

and he always keeps his head up and his gaze resolute

toward the future of the country obviously

he spits out jewels from his political thesaurus

      I represent the government

      I am here to help you

and continues

      honored citizens

      our promises have reached all corners of the land

      every house every field

      like Coca Cola ads

      but we're working day and night to get a place in
      the UN

      before this company does

      long live So and So

      long live our fallen friends

ending his reading of the text

as if he were a classical essayist

with a citation

      eat shit

      how could millions of flies have got it wrong

After his speech is over

he turns to look at his wife by his side
who is also wrapped up in political life
a truth evidenced by her huge ass
grown bigger while she sits on it
through long meetings
she smiles
until in the nearby mosque
a few saints weep
because they know that every minute on this planet
a dumbass is born
someone once said man is the most complicated machine
in the world
but even the biggest dumbass even the major dumbass
can be produced
naturally
with the help of a dumbass woman

This is the reason why I always vote for the bad guys
so those who are much worse won't win
I've no idea who the dead vote for
it's enough that they vote too

[*He takes another sip of raki.*]

I don't remember what time I went to bed
maybe a little later

with a bad feeling that I hadn't spent the night the usual way

when I set the alarm

to wake up exactly at 3:29 in the morning

to smoke a cigarette

listening to Funeral Blues

then go back to sleep

with the rhythm of a dead man

But nothing's perfect in this world

except for the grape raki from Rahovec

and Oaxaca's mezcal

with a worm at the bottom

that calls me by my name

Whoever hasn't seen a bottle of mezcal

with a worm inside

has no idea what it means to see the universe and his own soul as one

[*The mosquito is heard buzzing; the man goes after it.*]

The sun had risen a while ago

just when I started to dream

because finally I fell asleep

someone rang the doorbell

I opened one eye but quickly shut it

it's the alarm clock it's not the alarm clock it's the alarm clock it's not the

alarm clock

the moment I wanted to light a cigarette

drink drunk drink drunk

for a long time the bell rang

this would have hurt

even Van Gogh's ear

The Brave One with Many Friends started foaming at the mouth

what should I do if he bites me

when a dog bites a man

nothing happens

but when a man bites a dog

even in self-defense

it becomes breaking news

the CNN Bin Laden kind

no no no

I don't need fame

now I'm reminded of that nongovernmental organization

that opposed Pavlov the scientist

who used to torture stray dogs with a bell

ah

they're good people these Jehovah's . . .

but they're a little stubborn

if they were saints

they would bore God to death

who knows what they'll become when they grow up

just think about it

if I were to wake someone up at this hour

they would throw me past the gates locked with seven keys

I went down with The Brave One with Many Friends

we slowly reached the door

his eyes were open mine were half-closed

I open the door

stick my head out and look to the left

      I can't see anyone

I look to the right

    nobody

I get back

again the doorbell rings

I open the door quickly

look to the right

    no one

look to the left

    no one

look behind me

    no one

look in front of me

    goddammit

      there they were

and before they could start with good morning we are Witnesses

I stopped them saying

good morning my ass

again my eyes half-closed

since American coins don't say

In Gold We Trust

I have no reason to doubt your relative

but whenever your creator wishes to

let him address me directly

and if I wanted to

      you know chat with him

we would go to Paradise restaurant

      because a sober god doesn't deserve to be in Olympus

or we would stay here at home

it's the same to me

in between glasses full of Rahovec raki and wine

and food which could be a few doves

I'd have taken out of my rib cage

out of their rib cages

or from your rib cages

I would have stroked them for one two three or four seconds

then wrung their necks with my teeth

and I would have enjoyed eating them accompanied with
red wine

clearly

because red and white wine

produce the same urine

In any case I learned then that red wine

leaves something in the soul

and I love the only song ever sung to white wine

oh white wine

why aren't you red

In the end

we'll wind up at the Corpse Bar

found 2007 km ahead

and then at the first intersection to the left

on an island in the middle of the abyss

because there they offer good space cake

and we would talk as usual

about ribs

the serpent that speaks

sings dances and instead of selling apples

sells deceit

We'll speak of the world

of the good bad stuff and the bad good stuff

of his child my child your child

of the child of those over there and of those others a little farther away

of pain joy sorrow

of the envy I have for the albatross

because by batting his wings just twice

he can hover in the air for hours on end

he can peacefully sleep in the sky

nothing can wake him no bells

much less the buzz of a mosquito

which would die

before it would approach him

I know that a man without faith is like a fish without

a bicycle

maybe it's not god's fault

maybe it's the fault of his representative on earth

[*Takes another sip of raki.*]

Sir

they kept insisting

What Sir

my role here is different

similar to that of a poet who used to state in the newspaper

that since we're all covered in darkness

I eat and excrete light

obviously

the light of reason

A cow would need to live a hundred years

whereas people at least a few hundred

but no

they've made life short as a pepper

a small spicy one

and here

even dessert is spicy

To crush this feeling

I say to the unemployed who can't find a good reason

       to leave the house

even less to stay indoors

       doing nothing

I say to them

look people in the eye

from this gesture poetry rises

If in doing so you can't save the world

don't worry

at least you'll save your souls

Waiting for a miracle

the starless night plucks our dreams at the roots

arranges space to plant anxieties

flips the pages of our fear off the record

like a manual for the miserable

And you have put me here to honor me supposedly

I know how you love and wish me well

       dead

and I love you
like Sisyphus his rock

Sir
leave the dog at home and come with us they told me
I hardly hear you anymore
are you talking to me or to that other guy
The finger where the mosquito bit me
raised at The Brave One with Many Friends
and of course I opened my eyes and ears
so I heard them singing the blues all the birds
from Prizren Gjakove Peje[15] and Rahovec

Look
through much struggle life gives birth to laws
without intending to exploit
my absolute democratic and demoswastik right
I tell them
go in peace to heavenly paradise
surfing the waves of the Dead Sea
butdothisquicklywithatailbetweenyourlegslikeadog
or do it while triple stepping
andale andale arriba arriba epa epa
never turn to look back at my children
my only ones my dears my I don't know what

---

15. Names of towns in Kosovo.

because the ticket to paradise is still free
allow me to inherit this cursed planet
and remember
if you keep on hating the world
then please
                    hate her without me

[*He takes another sip of raki and fills his shot glass again.*]

I completely agree with what all religions say
that our Creator and my gods are perfect
like men's breasts
which exist
to serve only for personal pleasure

But
oh
someone please wake me from my daydream
this state has gone on too long
go away now
in a little while I need to welcome the President of New Guinea
New Zealand New Jersey New York Nuevo Laredo and New Mexico
and those who have an IQ higher
than the size of a snake's shoes
know how important this is to me

to my dog
and finally to my people
even though I hate what's mine
and to tell you the truth
what's yours I hate even more

Sir we insist you come with us
they boomed
What movie did you come out of I responded
What horror story did you flee from
you've even outmatched yourselves
with these maddening onomatopoeias

Even though they spoke clear Albanian
I didn't like it
fuck these motherfuckers
what should I do now
so I kept going

Hey

the weather in our land will be cloudy tomorrow

the sun will rest a little in fact for quite a while

it's possible it won't come out all night

vegetation is greener than ever before

I need to return to my neighbor the day before yesterday's newspaper

I got gastritis for free

A good explanation never explains anything
this is why they call it good
the truth as always belongs
to those who govern
meaning those who continue to find holes in flowerpots
even though they don't like flowers
because when they bloom
they cry like newborn babies

Damn
ever since I stuck my head into this world
I knew life's meaning
resides far from here
As I was being born
I don't recall this moment clearly
a little while ago
as I was eating some pickled fruit
from the ancient Kosovar oak of dreams
at July 2, 1990 restaurant
I saw all three leaders of our parties on TV

addressing us with the words

> *ask not what your country can do for you*
> *but ask yourself*
> *what you can do for your country*
> for example the three of us and our close associates
> fertilize our dear land once a day
> and when we have diarrhea
> even more frequently

If they talk like that
even though they each have their own style
I agree with them
with the public
with you
and you
and if someone asks me how can this be
I agree with that person too
and of course
with myself
because
when I'm good I'm very good
but when I'm bad I'm better

The idea that a people who suffers
earns paradise
brings to mind memories of a time

when idiots walked straight to heaven

whereas politicians instead of entering history

took the long way round

toward forgetfulness

or jail

Our politicians walk in the footsteps of the one

who called himself Türkmenbaşy[16]

the father of all Turkmen

Saparmurat Atajevich Niyazov

the thirteenth prophet

eternal president of big reforms

who started

renaming months and days of the week

Famous for his humility

he named January Saparmurat

April took on his mother's name

he ordered the year to last a few months longer

so every member of his family would get their own month

       obviously because they all deserved it

Some months took on names according to titles of his books

the same thing happened with the names of schools

factories cities drinks

When a 300 kg meteor fell

---

16. The leader of Turkmenistan from 1985 until his death in 2006.

a newspaper reported that it fell bearing the inscription
long live Türkmenbaşy

He ordered all hospitals closed
because all the sick had to do
was approach him and they'd heal

Sculpture was one of the arts
Türkmenbaşy more or less supported
and so in every city square
every street every public building
you find his bust or statue
he was so handsome
that all coins bore his smiling face
Out of a great love for him
people hung his photo
on all four walls of their rooms
I don't like it that my image is everywhere
but the people's wishes must be respected

He decreed that doctors should take an oath on him
rather than the Hippocratic
and those who wanted to take a paddling test
had to recite his poetry from memory
Niyazov considered his opus so remarkable
he declared whoever read it three times over

would find spiritual wealth
would know the existence of God
and right away reach fucking heaven

When you landed at Türkmenbaşy airport
a taxi would take you to Türkmenbaşy Avenue
then drive by Türkmenbaşy stadium
from where it's impossible to not see
The Arch of Neutrality monument
a tripod
on which the tall golden statue of Türkmenbaşy stands
with a mechanism that moves in such a way
so that it always faces the sun
so the shadows of the clock's hands would never cover his face

By law he commanded the existence of a new cycle of life
in which childhood ends at 13
adolescence at 25
and after maturity
between the ages of 49 and 61 a prophetic phase begins
followed by the inspired phase from 61 to 73
ending with the arrival of old age at 85

In the same way he forbade by law
AIDS internet and rock music videos
When a journalist asked if he'd read Shakespeare

ha ha ha he responded
I dictated all the tragedies to him
but Will had a focus problem
so he lost it with Hamlet

Sir
they wanted to interrupt me
Don't interrupt me when I speak please
don't you see I'm trying to educate you
to make it all easy for you
so I continued

Since in Iraq the most popular song was
Ring of Fire by Johnny Cash
and in Lebanon Pink Floyd's Coming Back to Life
the people of Turkmenistan including the elementary
school children
used to sing every morning

> we are grateful to the sun for rising
> since it knew no other way
> to honor our president

[*One can hear the buzz of the mosquito again. The man first expresses
fear and then, annoyed, goes after it.*]

They call this life
man may be constantly frightened
but killed only once

Türkmenbaşy's life ended on a Thursday
the statue of him on a horse
placed that very day in the city square
honored the unwritten rules of cavalry
if the horse's front legs are up in the air
the hero has fallen in battle
if the horse lifts only one leg up
the hero has died from wounds in war
if all four of the horse's legs stand firmly on the ground
this shows the protagonist died a natural death
if the horse only has one foot on the ground
this shows the horse's ability to balance his weight
but if the horse's all four legs are up in the air
this proves the sculptor's ingenuity
and no one can do this
if they're not first of all a politician

A little before arriving at his own corner in the heavens
where Ali Baba and the forty virgin whores awaited him
he ordered his descendants
to build a pyramid on his grave

so that no one could ever
dance on it

His grave was spacious
there has to be enough space for my people
if without me they lose their reason to live
he'd said humbly

When a dictator dies
throw him in the toilet and flush him
you'll see that the sun himself
if there are no clouds
will shine a little brighter in his absence
it would be the perfect day to do laundry

We hadn't closed the door yet I and The Brave One with
Many Friends
when we heard the sound of the Witnesses mixed with
some other voices
it was the voice of a group of people half of whom were armed
dressed in a color I've always hated
the other half dressed in white uniforms
one of them carried a straightjacket in his hands
You're late I told them
I already solved the mosquito problem

They addressed me saying
you must come with us sir
In their eyes you could clearly see hate which
if it could transform into electrical energy
it would light up two Prishtinas[17]
or at least the road
that would take us straight to the future

What do you want
What do you mean come with us
three days ago
as I was walking on clouds
an airplane like one of those huge ones hit me
left me no time to measure its horsepower
it was foreign so it didn't recognize me
I died right there
my fall lasted all day long
I almost missed my own funeral
which was yesterday at 15 o'clock
so I'm not here
There's something unclear in all this
or is my tenth sense deceiving me

---

17. The capital city of Kosovo.

They insisted

    Sir

    we have a court order to arrest you

    based on your wife's statement

    and other witnesses

        in connection to what happened last night

Witnesses hmm

fuck those assholes

I put in way more effort than the brothers in *Chronicle of a Death Foretold*

so my neighbors should have stopped me

but they didn't even stick out their heads

so if there's been a crime

arrest them

besides

they wander the neighborhood deceiving people

parading falsely like Jehovah's Witnesses

What life has taught me

or what I read in the pages of a newspaper or book

which the wind from Malisheva[18] woods must have blown my way

is that when you find yourself in the middle of a hole

the first thing you must do

is to stop digging further

---

18. Malisheva is a town and municipality in the Prizren District of central Kosovo.

so I began to scream

watch out

a single word can kill

its absence even more destructive at times

killing the mosquito was an accident

I wanted to hit my wife and it came between us

it could have been this way or this is how it happened in fact

the woman wanted to hit me

but the mosquito tried to protect me

sacrificing itself for me

I wept for it

I tried to resuscitate it giving it mouth to mouth

it died trying to protect itself to protect us

but it was God's will and you can't interfere with that

even though you know only an idiot can be neutral

facing an act of violence

facing our tears

which are like petrol

in the absence of which politicians' vehicles

cannot move

Ah

Sometimes it's so hard to be a human

this terrifies me

I feel ashamed

it hurts

The Brave One with Many Friends is ready to sacrifice himself
he's always been my right eye my right ear
my right leg my right arm
whereas I have always been his right fang

Are you policemen politicians doctors or vice versa
I ask because you look so human
or let me say so revolutionary
that no mountain or hill in Kosovo would suffice
to shelter all these Che Guevaras
otherwise
The Brave One with Many Friends and I are inseparable
you may see us as two separate beings but we are one
two bodies and one soul
he is me and I am he and vice versa
I mean if you have to insist like a lot a lot a lot
ok
then take him

The dog looked at me a little annoyed
he barked outside then came inside
for a moment I wanted to imitate him
or at least close my eyes and scream
don't you see I'm not here

I wasn't afraid at all just felt fear

but I recovered quickly and fired up

look and hear me out

I hope your brain has moved from your ass to your head

the past doesn't exist here as such

here the past is the present and time comes first

In two hours I'll have company

no more no less than Bacchus

the king himself whose kingdom stretches

from where Our Esteemed Leader Bus Tour begins to where it ends

and it's not just any kingdom

the best wine is made from its grapes

exported throughout the world wrapped in a napkin

and I haven't even gone to the store yet to buy stuff

anyway the king will bring coca

and we don't need ice because he's cold himself

he acts coldly thinks coldly freezes with a glance

Here as in most places around the world

darkness comes straight from the summit of politics

chosen in a demoncratic way

altering the reality we live in

meanwhile nonstop producing long lines

sent with the speed of light

straight to Nowhere

testifying in this way that all democracies

are born somewhere between man's spilled blood and his
broken bones

while violence lives in every step we take

What would happen if on a Sunday afternoon

in a park or a stadium or a city square

while someone chews on pumpkin seeds

accidentally a man steps on his shadow

and so blood spills hair is pulled

heads fly

meaning

the past chooses

to break the future's legs

How terrible

the leader of this whole wonder has learned to read

but he never came down to be with the people

to see what's written in their eyes

I understand

he has a right to be an idiot

but not with so much dignity

because everybody's lives are at risk

even those of the children

of those

against whom we should never raise a hand

or raise our voice

or say even a single word

the kind

that weigh more than the cursed hand

which kills

in cold blood

I'm really upset with these visitors

These people instead of planning

to never find me here

have stuck to me like urine stains in my undies

Best I be patient a little longer

than watch them come close like birds

that approach a person

when he's dead

Because when reading garbage eating garbage

we become garbage

The worst is that

the children born and raised in this chaos

as a result of a quasimodoliterature

and quasimodointellectuals

believe that this state is normal

and so a majority of them while reading

blow on the commas thinking they're fallen eyelashes

and on periods

the twin brothers of the mosquito I killed a little while ago

Imagine life in your own country

where the corrupt politician's hands are as long

as the shadows of the morning

And what can we do

In the kingdom of the blind

the one-eyed man is king

If things don't change

this means

we don't need a democracy

but a good therapist

even if he's imported

Some of those who weigh more than air

in order to avoid hunger under this scorched egg in the blue pan

fled from here

others wasted away in foreign lands

others with broken hearts

continue to dream on earth

this makes them

             miserable

Those who resist

even though it's clear that something's not right

have no other choice

but to sell gum or cigarettes on the street

whereas those who are a little more able

can pierce four small holes
on one euro coins
and sell them like stamps
thirty cents one fifty cents two stamps
why not
it's better to be rich for a hundred years
than poor for five minutes

[*Takes another sip of raki.*]

I feel for our mothers
They're like old birds in our rib cages
who because of age
were not able to migrate with their own kind
and now are forced to eat
from the hands of these people
be they even criminals

Anyway
they took me
they threw me in a room
isolated me like the desert isolates an oasis
they read me some laws copied from those countries
where summer in the best-case scenario
lasts from three to five minutes
while

I kept on dreaming
eyes open
standing on my feet

They separated me from my dog with the excuse
that it's easy to count the teeth on a dead lion
but even dead a lion is still a lion
they say

This world belongs to all
to those who've gone and those yet to come
close the curtain
turn the lights off
the night is long and noble
and will forgive us all

Whatever happens nearly nothing will change
when the political situation fails
rejoice
because there has been worse
even though the actors were the same
playing the same roles
in the same theater
only the masks are different
or they will be the same but worn by other people
It may be that the band of musicians changes

but the music is the same

in the end

let those who want to clap clap

but the political stage will be nothing more than a stage

with the manager and his crew in the first row

until the real owners of the theater

those who forbid the public from spitting blood on the floor

will continue to sleep in VIP balconies

their faces glistening

from sweat or fat it doesn't matter

Always the law nothing but the law

by those who never even came close

to the Justice Department

After a brief procedure they brought me before the judge

you were drunk that day

Hmmm

thanks for asking

yes

Queen Elizabeth feels much better

Sir

you are drunk

he continued provoking me

Let it be clear and very clear
yes
but no

Then yes
said someone from behind my back

All I did was deny it
I responded cutting him off

Then no
it was the same voice again

For quite a while I've been saying yes
but I'm falling in an endless pit
or am I flying

They offended me with many more irrelevant questions
what's your name whose son are you where were you born
where are you from

Oh brother
how painful hearing
time's bells wailing in the wind
how painful understanding

that the world

the more it changes

the more it stays the same

Enough

they threatened me and continued

where were you born

All the while as the sun began to set

and the rooster from atop my country's manure hill

dropped feces while warning of a new night

I responded

where most of us are born

in a story by Gogol

[*You can hear the buzz of the mosquito which for a moment stops; the man launches in the direction of the wall and hits it; the wall falls; in the other room, his wife is making out with the neighbor.*]

My dear wife

so sorry to interrupt you

but did you see which way the tiger mosquito went

CURTAIN FALLS

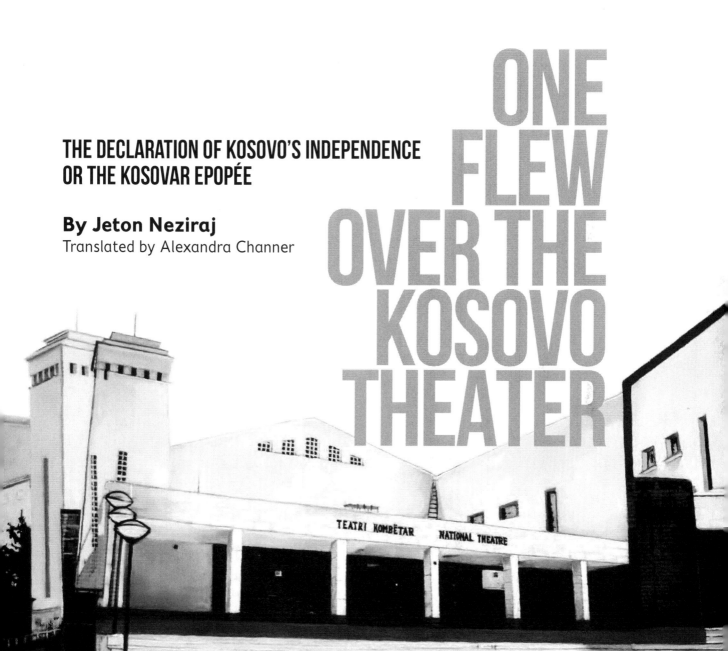

ONE FLEW OVER THE KOSOVO THEATER

THE DECLARATION OF KOSOVO'S INDEPENDENCE OR THE KOSOVAR EPOPÉE

By Jeton Neziraj
Translated by Alexandra Channer

CHARACTERS

Director

Dilo — actor

Rosie — actress

Secretary — the Secretary of the Ministry of Sport

James — stage technician and wannabe pilot

A PATRIOTIC COMEDY. SOME MIGHT ALSO CALL IT
AN "ANTI-NATIONAL PLAY." INSPIRED BY REAL EVENTS.

CHICKEN, COCKEREL

[*On stage at the National Theater of Kosovo. A day in January, 2008.*]

ROSIE. The story we're about to present happened a few years ago. It was cold, freezing. There was snow on the roof of the National Theater of Kosovo. The café was packed. Hardly any plays were being done.

DILO. Since it was very cold, and the theater had no heating, the café was selling raki.[1] A lot of raki. Everyone was drinking, the stage technicians and the actors. Even Vladimir and Estragon, the two heroes of the play we're about to present, were drinking.

ROSIE. Snow. Ice. The theater café. Raki. A director worn out by life's worries. An empty hall. Not a cent in the theater's account. Basically, the setup for a fairy tale.

DILO. Who are we waiting for?

ROSIE. Godot!

[*A long pause. Dilo and Rosie "freeze" and do not move for a few seconds.*]

DIRECTOR. Okay, let's move on.

ROSIE. Look, I really don't get this scene. Nothing happens.

DIRECTOR. Isn't it obvious? Well, what is *Waiting for Godot* all about?

JAMES. For me, what's clear is that I see this whole play as a protest, a protest against . . .

DIRECTOR. Exactly! This is the point. The play has to be seen in its entirety. [*To James.*] Next time, don't interrupt, just . . . worry about what you're doing.

ROSIE. So, since we've stopped, did you talk to the general manager about those contracts?

DILO. I did. He said he'd sort it out quickly.

---

1. Raki is a strong alcoholic drink made from grapes, popular in Albania, Kosovo, Turkey, and Greece.

ROSIE. I'm going to break down his office door one day.

DIRECTOR. Folks, we can talk about these issues after rehearsal. Let's concentrate on the work now. We'll continue with the cockerel's song and then start again from the scene where Vladimir and Estragon are looking at the moon.

DILO and ROSIE. [*They sing.*]

The chicken, the cockerel, were doing the "rokoko"

While the lovely egg was laid,

Oh, when will the egg be laid in the meadow

Rokoko, Rokoko
The chicken laid an egg

[*The Secretary enters.*]

JAMES. The Secretary!

DIRECTOR. We can see him.

SECRETARY. Go on, please. Go on. Don't interrupt the song. It was a lovely song.

DIRECTOR. Welcome, Secretary. What fantastic timing! We were just about to take a break. [*To Rosie and Dilo.*] Take a cigarette break.

JAMES. [*To Dilo.*] Do you want to play chess?

DILO. [*Acts as if he didn't hear.*] A glass of raki?

JAMES. No, no, chess. Come on, let me beat you again.

ROSIE. It's great that you're visiting us, Secretary. You can see what rotten conditions we're working in. It's January, and we haven't been paid since October.

DIRECTOR. Rosie, it's a cigarette break.

SECRETARY. Friends, this is why I'm here, to observe the conditions under which our artists create.

ROSIE. Enough talk. We're sick of it. Just give us our money, or I swear I'll go protest naked in front of the Parliament Building because that's the only way I can get your attention.

SECRETARY. You're very charming, you artists, even when you complain.

DIRECTOR. Rosieee!

ROSIE. Okay, forget it. I was just blowing off steam.

SECRETARY. That's fine; it's human.

[*Rosie goes out.*]

I completely understand. But, it isn't that we don't have money. We have money. We've always had it, and we have it now. We have money — for October's wages and for many other Octobers, but we've been saving it for something special. Something that for years and centuries we've all been waiting for. The Kosovo government is going to declare Kosovo an independent state.

DIRECTOR. Really?

SECRETARY. Yes.

DIRECTOR. This is big news. This is the news of all news. Congratulations!

[*The Director wants to hug him, but the Secretary avoids this.*]

SECRETARY. The Prime Minister's Office has ordered us to start preparations for this momentous day. We, at the Ministry of Sport, have been entrusted with organizing the cultural activities that will accompany this historic event. You must prepare theatrics which will be shown on precisely that solemn day. I know you can do it. You're a talented director. You've worked for the "national cause." You come from a patriotic family. Your works, *Kosova 1, Kosova 2,* and *Kosova 3,* are a guide for all freedom-loving generations.

DIRECTOR. Oh, Secretary, this is such a great honor! I feel privileged.

SECRETARY. But it is also a great responsibility. This will be an historic day, you know. And so, the theatrics should be a weaving together of all our history, depicting the crucifixion we've experienced as a people.

DIRECTOR. Oh, I can guarantee that it will be.

SECRETARY. It should be a . . . a . . .

DIRECTOR. A play? You are talking about a play, aren't you?

SECRETARY. Yes, a play, or theatrics. What I'm trying to say is . . . It should be something great . . . something heroic . . . No, no, not heroic . . .

DIRECTOR. Epic?

SECRETARY. Ah, yes. No, not epic. An épopée. The épopée of our people.

DIRECTOR. Oh, I can assure you that it will be something extraordinary. The ideas are already coming to me. We'll produce lots of smoke and the superhero will appear out of the smoke.

SECRETARY. Smoke? Out of the smoke comes the superhero?

DIRECTOR. Stage smoke. It makes the stage intriguing, mysterious.

SECRETARY. Good, good, but careful you don't burn down the theater.

DIRECTOR. There won't be any flames. Although perhaps we should have some flames. The flames of freedom. Out of the flames comes . . . comes . . . and then . . .

SECRETARY. Good, good. The play will be in the evening in honor of independence, and all the representatives of the diplomatic corps will participate. The Prime Minister will come. They will come from NATO, from the UN, EU representatives, the American Ambassador, etc.

DIRECTOR. The American Ambassador as well? So, this really isn't a game.

SECRETARY. It's not a game, and I have a request. I know it may seem strange, but it isn't. On the day that Kosovo's independence is declared, naturally the Prime Minister will give a ceremonial speech in Parliament.

DIRECTOR. He gives excellent speeches.

SECRETARY. I want you to put the speech into the play. In this way, the speech becomes part of . . . You know that famous speech of Martin Luther King? Artists made that speech famous.

DIRECTOR. An excellent idea. It makes perfect sense. The Prime Minister's speech will have symbolic meaning in our play.

SECRETARY. Yes, exactly! You've understood me very well. That's why you are artists.

DIRECTOR. The speech, could you email it to me?

SECRETARY. You can find it on the internet. Just go to www.google.com and type "Martin Luther King," and you'll find the complete speech.

DIRECTOR. I meant the Prime Minister's speech!

SECRETARY. Ah, but that speech doesn't exist yet. It's still being written. You'll get it on the day Kosovo's independence is declared.

DIRECTOR. What? But that means the actor will have to learn it by heart during the day, in order to perform it in the evening.

SECRETARY. He can read it. Why should he learn it by heart?

DIRECTOR. Oh no, you can't read on stage. It isn't artistic.

SECRETARY. Alright, alright. You know best about the theater!

DIRECTOR. We'll sort it out! We'll start immediately with preparations. But, when will independence be declared? In how many weeks?

SECRETARY. Oh, that's a state secret. It could be declared tomorrow, the day after, perhaps after a week . . .

DIRECTOR. Of course, it's a secret! How could something so important not be a secret? But perhaps we could know a little in advance, I mean, at least two or three weeks before. Since now we're . . . well . . . How to put it . . . We're part of the government, aren't we?!

SECRETARY. A secret that artists know isn't a secret anymore, is it? If artists know — the world knows.

[*The Secretary opens a file. He moves to one side and starts to look through various documents. He talks to himself.*]

Okay, now let me have a look at the financial file. Very good. Conceptual plan. The budget for "Flowers of Independence." The file on "Fireworks." [*He laughs.*] The project on "media support," naturally "support." Let's not forget to stress that pathetic title. "Corruption . . . Tenders . . ."

DIRECTOR. [*To himself.*] Oh, what a nightmare. What if independence is declared tomorrow! How to prepare a play for tomorrow! An historic play for an historic day! Goodbye to sleep, goodbye to everything. I'm frightened, and I feel insecure. Oh god, I know I'm going to have a fever tonight. What a huge task I'm being entrusted with. But it's an opportunity I must exploit. I'll show the Secretary, the Minister, and even the Prime Minister himself that I'm capable of being the General Manager of the National Theater, and even Dean of the Faculty of Arts. And I'll show these actors who behave like superstars.

[*The Secretary turns to him with the file in his hand.*]

SECRETARY. Did you say something?

DIRECTOR. Yes, I was just thinking about the play.

SECRETARY. Look, I have the financial file. It's the file called "Teater." Oh, it should be "Theater" — a computer error.

[*The Secretary leafs through some papers in the file.*]

SECRETARY. So, there are about two million euros.

DIRECTOR. Two million euros?!

SECRETARY. An extra million is for . . . While one million is for administrative services, decorating the capital's square with flags and for the fireworks . . . Okay, let's not add it all up. You artists will have a fund of about twenty thousand euros for the theatrics . . . the play.

DIRECTOR. Twenty thousand euros?

SECRETARY. That's enough money. Look, we must all contribute to this historic day, but that said, the government wouldn't want to exploit anyone.

DIRECTOR. Of course. Twenty thousand euros is enough. Right now, I'll pledge to forgo my honorarium. I'm grateful for the opportunity you're giving me — to be part of this historic day. I hope the General Manager will feel the same way.

SECRETARY. This is a state institution, not the General Manager's. He can decide the minor issues, but for this sort of grand affair, it's up to someone else. Don't worry about that. I'll issue an order to make it perfectly clear.

[*Rosie enters.*]

ROSIE. Are you closing down the theater, or what?

SECRETARY. Miss Rosie, I have great respect for you. I've watched those scenes of yours on television "*Mommy, Mommy, the house is burning.*" They were wonderful. And, on the contrary, we've just heard about a big project for which, naturally, you'll be paid. But the Director will explain it all. I don't want to bother you anymore. Good luck. Carry on. You have the government behind you.

ROSIE. Oh! With good news like this, come as often as you like!

SECRETARY. Of course, of course, from now on you'll be seeing me more often. And, that song at the beginning, it was lovely.

DIRECTOR. Which song?

SECRETARY. The one about the chicken and cockerel . . . Kokoko . . . How did it go?

DIRECTOR. Thank you. It was just a diction exercise.

[*The Secretary goes out.*]

SECRETARY. [*Off.*] "*Mommy, Mommy . . . the house is burning . . .*"

[*Dilo and James enter.*]

JAMES. Veni, vidi, vici.

DILO. So, what news did the herald bring?

DIRECTOR. Guys, we all face a great challenge. We're going to start a new play.

DILO. But what about the fate of Vladimir and Estragon of Kosovo?

DIRECTOR. We'll finish that play later. Now, we've been given an historic opportunity. It will be a play that has never before been seen in our theaters.

ROSIE. Every new play has never before been seen in our theaters.

DIRECTOR. I was speaking figuratively. It's expected that Parliament will meet soon and declare Kosovo's independence.

ROSIE. And on that day, we'll recite patriotic poems?

DIRECTOR. No.

JAMES. I don't want to interfere, but could it possibly be that instead of doing it in Parliament, they want to declare independence here on stage?

DIRECTOR. Why do you have to interrupt? Go on and paint those wooden boards for the play.

JAMES. What color?

DIRECTOR. No color. Oh, don't paint them. We don't need them. We're going to do a new play now, with new scenery. Something spectacular. We're going to do a "Kosovar Epopée."

DILO. We'll be paid?

DIRECTOR. Yes, yes. I saw the file. There is money for the play. There are two million euros.

ROSIE. Two . . . what?

DIRECTOR. Well, for our play there are ten thousand euros. I know it isn't much. But it's enough for a play with just two actors. What do you say?

ROSIE. That's fine. Just please don't make me play another mother.

DIRECTOR. Why, do you want to play a prostitute in a national épopée?

ROSIE. I'll play anything, but not another mother.

DILO. And me?

DIRECTOR. Naturally, you'll also be in it. It will be the same team.

DILO. And what will I play?

DIRECTOR. Slow down, slow down, the government only just informed me. I'll think about it tonight. I'll tell you more tomorrow.

JAMES. Shall I start working on the scenery?

DIRECTOR. How can you work on something when you don't know what it is? Idiot.

ROSIE. And when will the premiere be?

DIRECTOR. The premiere will be on the day independence is declared.

ROSIE. And when will independence be declared?

DIRECTOR. We'll find that out in time. We're going to work intensively. Nonstop, without a break. I'm going to ask for your utmost commitment. We start tomorrow morning at 9 a.m.

ROSIE. Can we start at 10? I've got a pedicure at 9.

DIRECTOR. I'm sorry, but no. The pedicure can wait; independence can't. Go and rest now. We'll meet tomorrow at 9.

SKY SONG

[*James, alone on stage.*]

JAMES. I'm called James, James Tafilaj. To be honest, my name's Bill, or the longer form is Bilall. Bilall Tafilaj, for short, James. That's what my father called me. I work as the stage technician at the National Theater of Kosovo. The other workers play chess, whereas I work. I like working. I do everything: paint, weld, clean, give suggestions to the directors, keep actors company when they drink raki — everything. For years I thought I should do something extraordinary to make my late father proud. He always told me he saw something in me he didn't see in other people. And it seems like now is the time to prove that my father was right. Father, my time has come.

[*He sings.*]

I know you can hear me
Father
My hour is here
Proud of me you'll be
Round the world I'll fly
Like an eagle so high
From Taipei to Chile, from Togo
To Turkey, from Poland to Papua
Father

FIRST REHEARSAL

[*On stage. The Director is deep in thought. Rosie and Dilo enter. They are still half asleep.*]

DILO. Good morning.

DIRECTOR. I put together some ideas last night. In fact, I worked all night.

ROSIE. Good morning.

DIRECTOR. Yes, good morning. Okay, these are the ideas, or images, that I think should be included in the play. Pandora's Box — out of which comes all the evil in the world. Our enemies will appear from there.

ROSIE. Are we doing a play or an animated film?

DIRECTOR. A play, naturally.

DILO. And how will we present this on stage?

JAMES. A box, out of which ants emerge. The public will understand the message, that they represent our enemies.

DIRECTOR. Excellent! Next time keep it to yourself. We'll find a way to stage it. Maybe we can use the ants. But don't interrupt me; let me get to the end of these notes. Another idea: the arrival of enemy hordes in our lands. We'll find a way to show this scene symbolically.

ROSIE. I have an idea.

DIRECTOR. Wait until I finish my notes.

ROSIE. No, no. Please listen to me. A beautiful woman, in this case, me, is planting flowers. A foreign soldier comes and tramples on the flowers, destroying them. Our eyes meet.

JAMES. *Beauty and the Beast.*

DILO. This sounds like a Turkish romance film.

DIRECTOR. In fact, it's not a bad idea, I'll note down "Beauty and the Beast." Thank you, Rosie. Let's go on with the outline. One after the other: the "Liberation War," a scene with Mother Theresa, to show the world that she is our daughter. And then, the coming of the enemies: The Romans,

Turks, Slavs, Germans, and at the end, the hordes of Serb barbarians. All of this can be sublimated in one scene.

ROSIE. Do they all rape me, one after the other?

DILO. You wish, but the enemies aren't interested.

DIRECTOR. Enough with the jokes. The last war in Kosovo will take up most of the play. Kosovo's liberation, then scenes of thanks for NATO allied forces, and gratitude for Bill Clinton and Tony Blair.

DILO. I have an idea. At the end of the play, Rosie takes out a breast — I'd say the left breast — and she invites the audience to come and drink milk.

JAMES. That's not a bad idea, the one with the breast. Shall we do a rehearsal?

ROSIE. Why don't you go paint the scenery?

DIRECTOR. No, there will be no breasts; neither on the left nor the right. The play will end with the Prime Minister's speech.

DILO. Nevertheless, I think that in the play we should also have . . .

DIRECTOR. What now?

DILO. Well, for example, a scene where Mojsi Golemi[2] betrays our national hero Skanderbeg?[3]

DIRECTOR. Absolutely not. To display our weaknesses to foreign diplomats? They'll say later, "*You see, they betray each other. They work behind each other's backs, and they don't deserve independence!*"

DILO. But . . .

DIRECTOR. There are no "buts."

DILO. But perhaps it would work if we had a ministerial official who, in a moment of weakness, asks for a bribe from someone?

DIRECTOR. I don't understand where you're going with this.

DILO. Well, for example, there could be a scene like this: A man applies for a tender and the official

---

2. The commander of the border guard during a fifteenth century rebellion against the Ottoman Empire, he joined forces with the Turks, betraying his commander-in-chief, Skanderbeg.
3. George Castriot Skanderbeg, 1405-1468, an Albanian nobleman who led a rebellion against the Ottoman Empire, a preeminent Albanian hero.

in question says, "*Yes, you could win the bid, but you must give me 30% of the total amount received.*" This will make the play convincing. We'll show that though we're angelic, there might be a devil here and there.

DIRECTOR. And then, all those who oppose Kosovo's independence will rise up and say, "*Do you see, even in their plays they concede that they are a corrupt society.*" Never.

DILO. Okay, okay, it was a just a suggestion.

DIRECTOR. Don't interrupt me. The play will be contemporary, but also complex, just as complex as our history. It will include monologues. We'll recite poetry, and we'll sing the national anthem, the anthem of Europe.

ROSIE. We will mock our enemies and praise our friends?

DIRECTOR. What's this now?

ROSIE. It's a stanza from some useless poem, but it stuck in my head.

DIRECTOR. A beautiful verse. But it needs work. Perhaps, "*We will forgive our enemies, but we will not forget their crimes.*" Like that maybe. But let's not forget something else. Somewhere in the middle of the play, in a scene where the characters are racked with suffering, enter Bill Clinton.

JAMES. I dream about meeting him.

DIRECTOR. Shut up. Okay, Dilo enters as Bill Clinton. He enters smiling. In fact, every time that you are on stage as Bill Clinton, you will be smiling, angelically.

JAMES. Have you thought about music?

DIRECTOR. Music . . . yes, of course. There will be selected music. A little classical music, perhaps an ode by Beethoven, but also some songs from our folklore tradition. The music must also support the concept of the play.

DILO. Maybe we're overburdening the play with metaphors, and symbols, and ideas?

DIRECTOR. Look, I still haven't crystallized the play as a whole, but — it will be wonderful. I just pray to God to give us a bit more time.

JAMES. Instead of God, you should pray to the Prime Minister, or better yet, the American Ambassador.

DIRECTOR. Stop with your pointless interruptions. But, perhaps it isn't such a bad idea to write to the Prime Minister. *"Dear Prime Minister, we are preparing something extraordinary for the great day, something that will make you proud. The rehearsals are going wonderfully. But please, delay the date a bit for declaring Kosovo's independence, so that we can finalize preparations."*

JAMES. Delay independence because of the play?

DIRECTOR. Absolutely not. And if the Prime Minister himself were to propose such a thing, I'd say, *"No. No, Prime Minister, declare it. Do it. We're ready. We'll be ready. We'll work through the night if necessary."*

ROSIE. We'll eat grass, if we need to.

[*The Secretary enters. He smiles at Rosie. Then he reads a letter.*]

SECRETARY. *In the face of this important historic process, which is, without a doubt, one of the most important in our history, the Kosovo government issues this instruction.*

Administrative Instruction Number 12

All public institutions in our country, which have duties and obligations relating to celebrations, which will be organized on the day that Kosovo declares its independence, are instructed that:

- *The use of national symbols is prohibited;*

- *The evocation and mentioning of national historic events is prohibited;*

- *The singing of songs with nationalist content is severely prohibited;*

- *The euphoric expression of national sentiment is prohibited;*

- *The driving of vehicles in convoys and the beeping of car horns is prohibited;*

- *Artists are encouraged to produce works of art with universal connotations;*

- *Various musical, theatrical, and dance groups, along with other artists, are encouraged to present works and artistic creations which display the multi-cultural, multi-religious and multi-ethnic tradition of our country.*

Signature:
Prime Minister

DILO. I don't get it. Are we doing a play or are we forming a political party? What has this got to do with us?

DIRECTOR. This is intolerable. We're being asked to be politically correct in the theater! How dare they restrict our artistic freedom? Artistic freedom is sacred. It cannot be negotiated. The great Goethe said . . .

SECRETARY. They called it an "instruction," but in fact it is a "guideline." It's drafted in collaboration with the "International Community."

DIRECTOR. Oh, it's clear. Now I understand. It's not a restriction on creative freedom because, naturally, art can sometimes be used in the service of society's objectives and ideals.

ROSIE. I like those instructions a lot. Enough of plays with war and blood. Why don't we do a play with love, with angels . . .

DIRECTOR. Rosie, this is a serious issue which must be addressed intellectually.

SECRETARY. Don't take it so seriously, Director. These measures are being taken in order to demonstrate European dignity and culture to the international community and to our friends, and especially our enemies, who are going to use a magnifying glass to examine every act of the new state that will soon be declared. All you need to do is to try to avoid a few words. When you talk about our enemies, for example, you don't need to mention their names, "Turks," "Serbs," . . . especially not Serbs. We don't need to compromise ourselves with our international friends. They'll say, *"See, now that they've become independent, their first instinct is to mistreat other communities."* We don't need this. Let's strengthen the state, and then we can sort out these issues, with Serbs, with Turks, with Romans, with Greeks, with the ancient Macedonians, and everyone else.

DIRECTOR. A wonderful explanation.

SECRETARY. Keep up the good work.

[*The Secretary exits.*]

JAMES STARTS TO CONSTRUCT THE PLANE

[*Play rehearsal. Dilo is dying. Rosie wipes his forehead.*]

DILO. *And when the dawn, with those rosy fingers*
Above the hills, its rays releases
Love will live, for your lips, for your eyelids
For sleepless nights, for my parched lips
For the enslaved homeland desperate for freedom
For me, for you, for our love.

ROSIE. *Please, don't die.*

DILO. *Goodbye. We'll meet in another world.*

[*Rosie caresses her stomach.*]

ROSIE. *You are dying, but the seed of our love is growing within me.*

DILO. *Now I can die happy. And know this. I loved you, and I will always love you.*

ROSIE. *As God is my witness, as God is my witness, they're not going to lick me!*

DIRECTOR. Rosie, we told you before, that monologue isn't in this play.

ROSIE. I know, I know, but it just came to me spontaneously. [*In a low voice.*] There's no need to lose it.

DIRECTOR. The rehearsal is over for today. Let's meet tomorrow, early. We'll work all day. We're doing well.

ROSIE. [*To James.*] Is it snowing outside?

JAMES. Yes!

ROSIE. I hate this snow. It makes me even more bored!

DILO. [*To the Director.*] Can I have the morning off?

DIRECTOR. Oh, come on, what kind of request is that? We're just about to hold the premiere.

DILO. We're not just about to premiere. No one knows when the premiere will be.

DIRECTOR. The premiere will be very soon. I can feel it. Haven't you noticed how deputies have started to go in and out of Parliament laughing?

DILO. I need to come in late tomorrow. Things are bad with my wife.

DIRECTOR. Again, with these stories about your wife? I have a wife too, but my wife understands the importance of this project. And until this project is over, I'm not going to have a wife, mother, father, child, or anyone. Don't you realize that this is an historic opportunity? A country declares itself independent only once in history. And only once in history does an actor have the chance perform in a play in honor of that declaration. What will you say if the American Ambassador really likes the play? Do you know what that will mean? He could easily send us to America. To Broadway!

DILO. Okay, okay, sorry.

DIRECTOR. Please, don't behave like this.

JAMES. Director!

DIRECTOR. Mmm?

JAMES. I have a question!

DIRECTOR. Speak up then, damn it, and don't keep us all waiting.

JAMES. For the play we're working on, will we use the stage?

DIRECTOR. Yes, of course we're going to use the stage. What, you think we're performing on the roof?

JAMES. I meant the part of the stage that rotates. Do we need it?

DIRECTOR. Maybe, why do you ask?

JAMES. Because the engine isn't working properly. The internal mechanism has begun to wear out, which turns the turbine, which moves the . . .

DIRECTOR. Oh, damn it to hell, it's always just before the important premieres that things start to break down. The spotlight bulbs flicker, the cables go missing, the toilet paper runs out!

JAMES. It isn't my fault. Talk to the General Manager.

[*The Director exits, and Rosie leaves after him.*]

DILO. [*To James.*] Do you still have that good raki we were drinking yesterday?!

JAMES. Yes, but I don't have time to drink it. I've got an important job to do.

DILO. Just a little glass.

JAMES. Oh, please, I've seen what you call a "little" glass!

DILO. I don't understand why no one gives a shit about me today! Not my wife, not this pathetic director, and not even you!

JAMES. Listen, I'm working on something important. It's a secret that no one can know, do you understand? So drink one glass of raki, that's it, no more.

[*James brings a bottle of raki and two glasses. They drink. After a little, from behind the scenery, James brings out an aircraft wing and some rusty parts of what once was an airplane. He starts to remove the rust.*]

DILO. What are these?

JAMES. They're parts of a German airplane that came down near our house in the Second World War.

DILO. The partisans shot it down?

JAMES. The partisans? It crashed because of engine failure. If it had been downed by the partisans, it would be in a museum in Berlingen in Germany. My father looked after it for years, as a keepsake. He always said to me, *"It's a German product; it'll stand us in good stead one day."* Before he died, he made a request. *"Use it in the interest of the homeland,"* he said. Now, I want to fulfill my father's last wish.

DILO. You want to use it as scenery in the play?

JAMES. No, for a flight. I want to fly in it. I just need an engine, like the one on the rotating stage, and then everything will be in order.

DILO. But you've never been to flight school, so how can you fly, James?

JAMES. In the army I was in the Air Defense Unit. I learned the basics about planes and piloting. You'll see who James really is. You've made fun of me long enough.

DILO. I've made fun of you?!

JAMES. All of you! Now you'll see. The world will know Kosovo through me.

DILO. You've really thought this out, but where are you going to fly?

JAMES. I'm going to fly across the entire world. Behind my plane there'll be a large banner which says, *"Please recognize Kosovo's independence,"* in English, of course. I'll release leaflets. I'll organize press conferences in international airports. I'll give interviews.

DILO. Be careful, James, the plane will crash in Africa, and the cannibals will catch you and eat you alive.

JAMES. Don't make jokes. And, please, don't tell anyone. No one's ever done anything like this before. The media will write about it. And not just our media, but from all over the world. *"What the Ministry of Foreign Affairs and what international chancelleries failed to do, one man is doing — James Tafilaj. He has turned the world's attention to Kosovo. He has encouraged all the states of the world to recognize us. Well done, James, star of Kosovo's sky."*

DILO. Wow, you're really serious about this!

JAMES. Yes, of course I am. I've made all the plans. Since the day I heard that independence would be declared, I haven't slept. The first symbolic flight, a sort of test flight, will be on the day of the declaration of independence. Then, I'm going to open a bank account and invite people to contribute.

DILO. The idea of the account is good. It's well thought out.

JAMES. You drank the raki, now go away. Go on, I need to work.

[*James starts working. Dilo exits.*]

VOICE EXERCISES

[*On stage. Voice exercises.*]

Protectorate
Freedom
Independence
Coexistence
Mission
EULEX
USAID
UNDP
UN
EU
OSCE
KFOR
NATO
UNMIK
ECLO
UNDP
World Bank
Peace
Corruption
Human Rights
SIDA
IOM
IDA
ICO
SFC
PFC
CCF
FF
C
CC

CIU
CIU CIU CIU

Ko-ko-ko
Ko-ko-ko
The chicken laid an egg

A new day is dawning

Ko-ko-ko
Ko-ko-ko

A new state is being born

Ko-ko-ko
Ko-ko-ko
The chicken laid an egg

We've waited long for this day

Roko-roko-rokoko

Kosovo is independent, sovereign and free
Ko-ko

Our hopes are high

Ko-ko-ko — a chicken laid an egg

Our dreams have no end

Ko-ko-ko
Ko-ko-ko
The chicken laid an egg

DIRECTOR. Okay, that's enough. Let's work on the Prime Minister's speech. To be honest, I'm still having trouble with this. How can we stage something that isn't meant for the stage? What if the speech is really long? Or perhaps it'll be very complicated, and Dilo will mess it up!

DILO. Why, do I look like an amateur?

[He recites from King Lear.]

> "Rumble thy bellyful! Spit, fire! Spout, rain!
> Nor rain, wind, thunder, fire are my daughters.
> I tax not you, you elements, with unkindness.
> I never gave you kingdom, call'd you children,
> You owe me no subscription. Then let fall
> Your horrible pleasure. Here I stand your slave,
> A poor, infirm, weak, and despis'd old man.
> But yet I call you servile ministers,
> That will with two pernicious daughters join
> Your high-engender'd battles 'gainst a head
> So old and white as this! O! O! 'Tis foul!"

You see, I can still remember the script of King Lear.

DIRECTOR. That doesn't matter. I'm talking about something else. This speech could change the entire concept of the play. But let's rehearse it anyway. We'll exercise intonation, the tone of the voice, sub-units, passages, pauses, energy . . . Let's go.

DILO. Today, I . . .

JAMES. Shouldn't you start first with, *"Thank you, America . . . ?"*

DIRECTOR. Exactly. [*To James.*] Don't interrupt any more. The speech has to start with, *"Honorable Ambassador of the United States of America . . ."* and so on . . .

DILO. Honorable Ambassador of the United States of America, honorable Joschka Fischer . . . Dear citizens, villagers, farmers, pregnant women, children in cradles, fields of Kosovo, rivers . . .

DIRECTOR. Don't be so banal.

DILO. I'm just improvising.

DIRECTOR. Improvise, but take it seriously.

DILO. Today, I am declaring Kosovo an independent state.

DIRECTOR. *"Today, we are declaring . . ."* in a more solemn tone.

DILO. Today, we are declaring it in a solemn tone . . .

DIRECTOR. I thought this part should have a solemn tone. It starts coldly, then solemnly, and then when he talks about sacrifice, obviously the tone should be longsuffering, and then finally, at the end, the tone should be a bit militaristic. Because, this way, we send a message to our enemies that now, after the declaration of independence, we're capable of defending our country. Do you get it?

ROSIE. No. I don't understand.

DIRECTOR. I'm talking metaphorically, Rosie.

ROSIE. [*Aside.*] *"Fuck your metaphors."* That's what I wanted to say, but they couldn't have handled it. Really, I've had it up to here with this. I'm going to leave this country. I'm going to marry Brugel Schmidt, and I'm going to go to Germany. And then, from there, to Broadway. Brugel is crazy about me. I don't care that he's old. I'm going to leave with Brugel and let them all go fuck themselves with their metaphors.

They don't deserve me. I've given all my talents to this public, to this stage, but I've had nothing in return. Apart from some cold applause, some wilting flowers, promises of roles, big plays . . . Just promises, nothing else. Oh, I'm so bored. Sad and bored. Like this boring winter snow. I want to leave, to go somewhere where they love me, where on stage all alone, I can open my arms, open my heart, and cry and pour out all my talent.

"As God is my witness, as God is my witness. They're not going to lick me . . . !"

Yeah, I'm going to marry Brugel.

EVERYONE KNOWS, NO ONE KNOWS

[*Morning. Dilo, dressed in the costume of King Lear, drinks and wanders around the stage.*]

DILO. Everyone knows, but no one knows. They say it will be declared tomorrow, but some say it will be the day after tomorrow. Some even say it won't be declared at all. Whereas others say that independence has already been declared, but we haven't heard about it yet. What about after becoming independent? Will our clothes dry faster on the wash line? Will the stoves keep us warmer this winter? Will Kumria open the door for me, even when I go to her late and drunk?

[*Rosie enters.*]

ROSIE. Don't tell me you've been drinking already?

DILO. Just a little, to wash away my many worries.

ROSIE. What worries?

DILO. My wife has left me, together with my daughter.

ROSIE. Again? Oh, she'll come back.

[*Dilo takes out the letter from his pocket and gives it to her.*]

DILO. Take it and read it. She seems serious this time.

ROSIE. I don't want to read your wife's letter.

DILO. Take it, take it and read it and tell me afterwards that I shouldn't kill her.

ROSIE. You're not the type to kill someone.

[*Rosie takes the letter and starts to read it.*]

ROSIE. *"Save that my soul's imaginary sight. Presents thy shadow to my sightless view."*

DILO. Wait, that's King Lear. He's not to blame.

[*Dilo takes out another piece of paper from his pocket and gives it to her. Rosie reads it.*]

ROSIE. *"You are a failed actor. You say you spend all day in rehearsals, but I know that all that time you're drinking and chasing tarts. The panties of . . ."* I can't read any more.

[*Rosie gives back the letter.*]

ROSIE. You do drink and chase tarts.

DILO. I don't drink, and I don't chase tarts. Tarts chase me, but I don't give a shit about them.

[*James enters.*]

JAMES. [*To Dilo.*] Did you sleep well? [*To Rosie.*] He collected all the costumes from *King Lear* and slept on them.

DILO. Better to sleep here than alone in the apartment, without my wife and daughter.

ROSIE. But how will you do the rehearsal, you poor thing?

DILO. I'm fine. I'm hurting spiritually, but my mind is sharp as ever.

[*The Director enters together with the Secretary.*]

DIRECTOR. Good morning.

SECRETARY. Good morning. Good morning, Rosie!

[*Rosie waves at him without looking.*]

DIRECTOR. A little discipline please. We have the honor of the Secretary's presence at our rehearsal. He can't stay for all of it, so we'll just show him one or two scenes.

DILO. Routine check-up.

SECRETARY. [*To Dilo, who has a cigarette in his hand.*] What are you planning to do with that cigarette?

DILO. Nothing for the moment, but I'm going to light it in a while, when the scene starts with the writer who works all night on our national anthem.

JAMES. He writes it in the day and erases it at night.

[*Everyone looks at James.*]

JAMES. I'm going to go and paint some wooden boards.

DIRECTOR. Yes, that is one of the most moving scenes.

SECRETARY. Don't even think about it. You know that smoking is prohibited in public institutions. We issued Administrative Instruction 2007/14VQE-KAQ to the General Manager.

DIRECTOR. But, Secretary, this is the theater.

SECRETARY. I know what a theater is. Why does it matter that this is a theater? It's a state institution and the rules apply the same to all institutions. What if there's a pregnant woman in the audience? Ask theaters in Europe if they dare to smoke cigarettes on stage! Never! If a cigarette is lit in a state institution in Holland, the Prime Minister immediately resigns.

DIRECTOR. Oh, I completely understand, but this is a very important scene. The character smokes a cigarette out of misery because the homeland has been so destroyed. He smokes and later, drunk, in a moment of delirium, he writes the anthem . . .

SECRETARY. Give him something else. Not tobacco. When he sees the play, I don't want the Prime Minister to think that my departments are not implementing government regulations. Please don't do it. I love the theater, but this is too much, too much. Give him something to drink which is more authentic. Cold water from our mountains?

DIRECTOR. Okay, okay, we'll find an alternative solution. But let's look at the scene now. It still isn't finished, naturally. In the beginning, you can hear thunder, then one flash of lightning and another, then some ravens cawing. Rosie plays a witch, and Dilo a poet. Let's go.

ROSIE. *Oh Sky, make thunder and shake this land*
Oh demons, come out of hell and tie up his tongue
Cut out the thoughts, confuse the mind
Of this man who wants to give words to his country.

DILO. *Get out of my sight, you old witch*
Oh Muses, are you listening to me, the poet
Bring me the magic words, warm my blood
With the old words of my ancient people.

ROSIE. *May you be cursed, Muses*
Accursed be those words that you will say.

DILO. Here are the anthem's words:
May the god be blessed who put us on this land
A nightingale's voice is singing in my ear
A rousing song of our ancestors
May it be raised up, the Albanian language, the last testament left to us by generations
We will exterminate the enemy, and the Homeland will be the victor.

SECRETARY. Wonderful.

DIRECTOR. You like it.

SECRETARY. Yes, a lot. I feel moved.

DILO. I felt moved too.

SECRETARY. Very good, very good. But I have a dilemma. What if Kosovo's anthem doesn't have any words at all, but is just music?

JAMES. May I?

DIRECTOR. No, you may not. That's a good criticism, Secretary. We never even considered that!

SECRETARY. It wasn't a criticism. Don't take it as a criticism. I meant it as a question.

DIRECTOR. And it's fine. We'll remove the text completely. Rosie, take it from: *May you be cursed, Muses . . .*

ROSIE. *May you be cursed, Muses . . .*

DIRECTOR. [*To Dilo.*] Now you want to talk, but because of the curse you can't get the words out.

DILO. [*Whispers nonsense.*] *Blablablablablabla!*

DIRECTOR. Excellent. Meanwhile, in the background you can hear music, which metaphorically symbolizes the music of our anthem. I think the audience will understand the message: Those evil forces can shut us up, but our free spirit, in this case the music, always triumphs. Thank you very much, Secretary, for such a beautiful metaphor.

SECRETARY. It's nothing. I didn't tell you, but as a child in nursery school, I was in the play *Red Riding Hood*. It was a wonderful play.

ROSIE. *Grandmother, grandmother, what a big nose you have?!*

SECRETARY. [*To Rosie.*] I like how you played the witch. You were very convincing.

DIRECTOR. Secretary, we have another request. We need a gun. How can we get one?

SECRETARY. A real gun?

ROSIE. Perhaps also a bomb, so I can throw it at the General Manager's office.

DIRECTOR. Rosie, I'm serious. [*To the Secretary.*] We need a training gun.

JAMES. We had a collection of different guns, but a few days ago some NATO peacekeeping soldiers came and took them. We tried to tell them, *"Hey, those are theater props, not real guns,"* but they didn't listen. They just repeated like parrots. *"NATO is in Kosovo for your security. NATO is in Kosovo for your security. NATO is in Kosovo for your security."*

SECRETARY. We'll work something out. I'll talk to the minister of internal affairs, and I'm sure we'll find a solution.

DILO. I can give you my Kalashnikov!

DIRECTOR. No, no, no. Let's not get involved in these kinds of adventures. We need a gun with a permit. Not a real gun, a training gun.

SECRETARY. I have a stash of weapons at home. But that's private. Here in the state institutions we have to behave according to the rules. The weapon you use must have a permit. Because, believe me, those foreign journalists are just waiting for something like this. Especially those rotten German journalists. If they see a child's toy gun anywhere in Kosovo, the next day the newspaper headline is "Kosovo is so full of illegal weapons, people sleep on them. Criminal groups . . ."

JAMES. *Kosovo schlafen im Kalashnikov . . .*

SECRETARY. You're right.

ROSIE. It sounds like we're preparing an assassination, and not a play.

DILO. Secretary, don't worry about her. Rosie is high-strung.

SECRETARY. Not at all. I like that she's straightforward. Please, keep going. It seems you're on the right track. We'll resolve this issue of the gun and any other problems you might face. The state is at your service.

DIRECTOR. Thank you very much for your encouragement. We value it.

SECRETARY. Good bye!

DIRECTOR. Good bye!

[*The Secretary exits.*]

DILO. They're lying. You know they're lying, but you want to believe, yet again, that they aren't lying.

DIRECTOR. Don't overdo it, he's a sincere man. Have you noticed how he looks you straight in the eye when he speaks?

JAMES. Yes, that's true. He especially looks at Rosie, deep into her eyes, and sometimes out of the corner of his eye.

ROSIE. Go paint some wooden boards.

DIRECTOR. He's a bureaucrat, but above all, he is also a man. He is incorruptible, transparent, and intellectual. He's read all three of my works, *Kosova, 1, 2,* and *3.*

SECRETARY'S SONG

[The Secretary sings.]

Rosie, my little Rosie,
In your gingham dress, with your girlishness
Mommy, Mommy, the house is burning

Chorus: *Careful Red Riding Hood*
Careful, my beauty

Rosie, my little Rosie,
In your gingham dress, with your curls
Soon, independence, my Rosie, will be yours

Chorus: *Careful, Red Riding Hood*
Careful, my beauty

SACRIFICING ROSIE

[*James cleans the stage after rehearsal. Tired, Dilo takes his jacket and gets ready to leave, but then remembers.*]

DILO. [*To James.*] Do you still have that good raki?

JAMES. No.

[*Dilo, desperate, goes out. Rosie gets ready to go out, but the Director stops her.*]

DIRECTOR. Rosie, can we talk for a minute?

ROSIE. Yes!

DIRECTOR. Remember I talked to you about that big project in England?

ROSIE. The one that fell through?

DIRECTOR. Yes, but no. It didn't fall through. It's actually going to happen.

ROSIE. Great.

DIRECTOR. Yes, yes. I got an email from them. They're interested. They even have some additional requests. Among them, they want the play to have an actor from Kosovo.

ROSIE. Don't bullshit me.

DIRECTOR. What do you mean? I'll show you the email.

ROSIE. And, have you decided who you'll take?

DIRECTOR. Not yet! But you're a candidate, of course! And I promise that in that project you can include your English monologue. It makes more sense there than here. Alright?

ROSIE. I wasn't thinking of insisting on the monologue. I'd given up.

DIRECTOR. You're an actress and a great friend. Rosie, what we're doing now . . . maybe it seems difficult to understand, but I want you to believe that we're on our way to achieving something great. The day they first showed *William Tell* in Germany was declared a national holiday. That could happen with our play too. It will be remembered every Independence Day. With the passing of the years, people won't know if the play was done for the sake of independence or independence was declared for the sake of the play. A good joke, eh. I exaggerated a bit.

ROSIE. I have to go home. I'm really tired . . . women's stuff. I almost didn't make it to the rehearsal.

DIRECTOR. Rosie, I need your help.

ROSIE. Why? What? Hurry up.

DIRECTOR. Listen. I have two problems. Everything else about the play has been resolved. Yes, there are details; there are questions; but that's to be expected. But there are two stumbling blocks: first, when will independence be declared — in other words, when will we have our premiere. And second, how to get a hold of the Prime Minister's speech. We have to have it early. I don't trust Dilo.

ROSIE. Okay, do I look like a Mata Hari or something?

DIRECTOR. No, but perhaps we could find this out from the Secretary. He likes you. Have you noticed how he looks at you?

ROSIE. See you tomorrow.

DIRECTOR. Please. All I'm asking is, go out and drink a coffee with him. One coffee. As friends.

[*Rosie exits. The Director remains alone.*]

DIRECTOR. It's not fair. No, Prime Minister, it isn't fair. You undervalue my work. I can't work under this pressure. I understand that this is an extraordinary case. Yes, I really understand, but please, I have to know when independence will be declared. This is torture. I haven't slept for days. I don't sleep at all. I wake up drenched in sweat. As soon as I close my eyes, the Secretary appears before me saying, "*Now it will be declared, two hours from now. Where is your play, Director?*" And I can't move, and then I wake up exhausted. It's like this every night. Oh go to hell, Prime Minister!

[*The Secretary enters.*]

SECRETARY. Did you say something?

[*The Secretary disappears into the darkness.*]

DIRECTOR. Secretary?

[*James enters with a part of the aircraft in his hand. He tries to hide it when he sees the Director.*]

JAMES. Why aren't you going home, Director? You look tired.

DIRECTOR. Was the Secretary here just now?

JAMES. You imagined it. No one was here.

DIRECTOR. I thought I heard a voice.

JAMES. It must have been a mouse. There are more this year. And they are much bigger.

DIRECTOR. That's it! Perhaps.

JAMES. Go home and rest. You wore yourself out today.

DIRECTOR. Oh yes. You're right. I am tired.

[*The Director exits.*]

ROSIE IN THE SECRETARY'S OFFICE

[*In the office of the Secretary at the Ministry of Sport. Rosie is looking at some files. After a bit, the Secretary enters with a bottle of wine and two empty glasses.*]

ROSIE. How did you like today's rehearsal?

SECRETARY. It was good. But about that anthem scene, find a quill. Don't write the anthem with that pencil.

ROSIE. The pencil is just for rehearsal.

SECRETARY. And those clothes don't go at all. He looks like a Russian.

ROSIE. Those were costumes from *King Lear*. There will be other costumes for the play.

SECRETARY. Find better costumes, so the characters don't look so shabby. They should belong to the middle class. Neither too rich nor too poor. And, in the end, in that scene, that actor can smoke a cigarette. Half a cigarette. But that's all, no more.

ROSIE. The cigarette in that scene is like the gun that Chekhov has go off at the end of the play.

SECRETARY. A very good idea. At the end, after the Prime Minister's speech, the gun should be fired. A shot, as a sign of a new start. But we must be careful that it isn't a Chinese or Russian gun. I'll get them a NATO gun, to imply that now, after independence we're aiming for NATO, for Europe.

ROSIE. Great idea. It's just missing a fart.

SECRETARY. Oh, how sweet it is when you talk like that. You know, it's made me very happy that you came to meet me.

[*A short silence. Rosie lights a cigarette.*]

ROSIE. When will independence be declared?

SECRETARY. Soon!

ROSIE. When?

SECRETARY. What do you mean, when? It's a state secret.

ROSIE. Oh yes, of course, secret . . .

SECRETARY. We as a people, we must learn how to keep state secrets. We must learn to behave like a state. Did you know that in Kosovo, there are over 324 foreign intelligence agencies? And just 3 or 4 of them want what is good for us. The majority want to see us humiliated, fall flat on the ground. What would you say if, for example, a Russian spy got hold of the information about the date of the declaration of Kosovo's independence? What then?

ROSIE. I don't know.

SECRETARY. Precisely. No one knows what the global consequences of such a thing might be. The Security Council, the UN, the G15 would meet. There'd be a Russian and Chinese veto, and endless resolutions, and who knows what else.

ROSIE. It seems very complicated.

SECRETARY. Nevertheless, you must work intensively. We prepared *Red Riding Hood* in a week. I didn't sleep for two days from joy. I played "the first tree in the forest" and there was just one sentence I had to repeat: "*Careful, Red Riding Hood! Careful, Red Riding Hood . . . !*"

[*Rosie takes off her coat.*]

ROSIE. Can you get me the speech the Prime Minister's going to read on Independence Day?

SECRETARY. I'm very close to him, but that's something I couldn't ask for. Ask for anything else, but just not this.

ROSIE. Anything else?

[*Rosie takes off her shoes. The Secretary removes his coat.*]

SECRETARY. I admire you. I have always admired you. When I saw you on television you seemed . . .

ROSIE. I haven't done much on television. I've had more roles in the theater.

SECRETARY. Unfortunately, I've only seen one play at the theater. It was *Red Riding Hood* and I was in it myself. The theater never attracted me. Our plays lack a message, an educational message.

ROSIE. They don't give me good roles. They always give me secondary ones, mothers, raped wives . . .

SECRETARY. From now on, it's going to be different. I'll show the General Manager who's in charge. If he doesn't cast you, I'll cut the budget. And not just the budget, I'll sack that drunkard. It's a state institution. He shouldn't dare to treat actors like that. What a shit.

ROSIE. After this play, I want to do another. A solo performance.

SECRETARY. Like this one . . . theatrics?

ROSIE. Yes, but just me acting. It won't be expensive.

[*The Secretary goes and locks the door.*]

SECRETARY. It can cost whatever you like. I'll finance it, Rosie.

[*The Secretary gets closer.*]

ROSIE. But listen, I want to do the premiere somewhere abroad. Not in Kosovo.

SECRETARY. No problem. After independence, we'll be opening up our embassies, and you can perform in all of them.

ROSIE. No, I want my premiere to be somewhere else. Broadway!

SECRETARY. Get me the Director's contact information, and we'll approach him officially. Maybe even the British Embassy would help us. Anyway, together with them we'll launch a program called "Cultural Diplomacy." This could be the first activity. Very good. Put the project on paper.

[*Rosie removes her sweater.*]

ROSIE. Ok, but Broadway is in America . . .

SECRETARY. So what if it's in America?

ROSIE. There are loads of theaters there.

SECRETARY. Okay, well you'll choose one of them. What's the big deal? Oh Rosie, Rosie . . . You are very beautiful.

[*The Secretary goes and closes the curtains.*]

ROSIE. [*Like Scarlett O'Hara / Vivien Leigh in* Gone with the Wind.] *"As God is my witness, as God is my witness, they're not going to lick me! I'm going to live through this, and when it's all over, I'll never be hungry again! No. Nor any of my folk. If I have to lie, steal, cheat, or kill! As God is my witness, I'll never be hungry again!"*

SECRETARY. What's that then?

ROSIE. I wanted to put it in the play, but the Director wouldn't let me.

SECRETARY. What? He didn't let you? I'll talk to him.

ROSIE. No, no, I don't want it anymore.

SECRETARY. Decide. And if you want, we'll put it in the Constitution of Kosovo.

[*The Secretary approaches her. He caresses her face.*]

THE DIRECTOR'S DREAM

[*On stage. The Director sits in a chair, looking tense. The Secretary is moving around him. The two hold a script in their hands.*]

SECRETARY. I understand completely, but you have no other option.

DIRECTOR. Okay.

SECRETARY. Scene 14. The anthem scene is too long. The actor makes an unnecessary pause. Shorten it.

DIRECTOR. The actor's pause makes that scene a masterpiece.

SECRETARY. Page 124, line 18. The word "enemy" must be replaced with the word "friend."

DIRECTOR. How? But, that changes the entire meaning of the scene!

SECRETARY. It's just a word, for God's sake. Don't you think you're overreacting?

DIRECTOR. No, I don't agree.

SECRETARY. What?

DIRECTOR. No, I don't agree. I cannot agree. That's too much. I'd rather not do the play at all than make that change. You're mutilating it. I'd rather give you a limb. Take a hand, or my legs, but don't make that change to my play. What am I saying? Nothing. I didn't say anything. I accept, of course.

SECRETARY. Scene 18.

DIRECTOR. What should we change here? This is a love scene.

SECRETARY. Exactly. Nothing should be removed from this scene, but you must add something. Make it longer, make it endless, and add more words of love.

DIRECTOR. That's the first thing I give you credit for in this whole rewrite you're doing.

SECRETARY. Why say "rewrite?" These are just friendly suggestions! Be careful with your vocabulary, okay?

DIRECTOR. Alright!

SECRETARY. Scene 34. It states, *"Albanians won their freedom with blood,"* and it should be replaced with, *"Death to fascism! Freedom to the people!"*

DIRECTOR. Okay.

SECRETARY. Page 316. Take out this monologue completely.

DIRECTOR. Oh no, please no. Rosie will go crazy.

[*Rosie, Dilo, and James enter.*]

ROSIE. No one should dare to remove that monologue.

SECRETARY. Erase the monologue. The content isn't suitable, and even stylistically it isn't anything special. Monologues don't allow the play to develop.

DIRECTOR. Rosie, do it for me.

ROSIE. Never ever, not even with a state decree.

DILO. Rosie, give up that monologue, like I gave up alcohol.

ROSIE. No.

JAMES. Rosie, that monologue is a trap. Forget that you ever knew it.

ROSIE. No. I'd sooner die than agree to such a thing. That monologue is my fate. My career is linked to that monologue.

SECRETARY. Director?

DIRECTOR. I removed it. It's gone.

ROSIE. I'm leaving this play.

SECRETARY. Big deal. Good bye.

[*Rosie exits.*]

DIRECTOR. We must find another actor. Fast. We don't have time?

SECRETARY. We have time. There's no reason to rush.

DIRECTOR. But won't independence be declared soon?

SECRETARY. No. And besides these changes to the script, they've ordered me from the top to make some other changes.

DIRECTOR. What other changes?

SECRETARY. The play's not going to be directed by you, but by James. He's the Prime Minister's choice.

DIRECTOR. What?! But he isn't a director. He's a stagehand. He's a failure. How dare you do such a thing? Don't you know who I am? My family and I contributed to this country's freedom. I'm going to talk to the Prime Minister. I have lots of friends in government. They wouldn't allow such a thing. No, don't do this. Mother, do you see what they are doing to me? Mother, help your son!

SECRETARY. Independence was declared yesterday. Can you prepare the play for yesterday?

DIRECTOR. Yesterday?! But that isn't possible.

SECRETARY. James can.

[*The Secretary, James, and Dilo go out. The Director falls to his knees, his soul defeated.*]

DIRECTOR. Mother . . . mother . . .

[*James enters.*]

JAMES. Director! Still here?!

DIRECTOR. [*Recovering from the dream.*] What? Where am I? James?

JAMES. Go and rest. You're very tired.

DIRECTOR. Are you going to direct the play?

JAMES. I beg your pardon?

DIRECTOR. Was the Secretary here before?

JAMES. No, no one's been here. It's two in the morning.

DIRECTOR. So, it was a dream, was it? Oh god, what an awful dream.

JAMES. You look sad.

DIRECTOR. Have you ever thought of being a director?

JAMES. Never, not even in my dreams. I don't have that kind of ambition. I like my job.

DIRECTOR. And how fantastic you are at it!

JAMES. You really mean it?

[*The Director goes and embraces James. James is amazed by the Director's warmth.*]

DIRECTOR. Oh god, it was a terrible dream.

[*James exits. The Director sings.*]

My fate and the fate of this people are bound
This play, this great work of art
I dedicate to Kosovo, a gift from the heart

My name will be engraved in gold
In poetic verse, in rhapsodic song
In lectures, in choirs, in folktales
My name will forever resound

Upon anguish, our Kosovo was founded
Upon martyrdom and love
My name will forever be written
In unforgiving blood.

NEWS ABOUT INDEPENDENCE

[*The Director is on stage with a bunch of papers. James enters.*]

DIRECTOR. What have you been up to now. Where are the actors?

JAMES. They're coming now. They're getting coffee in the café.

DIRECTOR. They should come earlier if they want to drink coffee. Rehearsal starts at 9. We don't have time to lose.

JAMES. True, there isn't time. Ten days, at the most two weeks.

DIRECTOR. Oh, James, if that was so, I'd be the happiest man in the world. But, James, independence could be declared tomorrow.

[*Enter Rosie and Dilo.*]

DILO. Good morning.

ROSIE. Independence will be declared in two weeks. A secure source.

DIRECTOR. Who told you, Rosie?

ROSIE. I know a girl who works for the Prime Minister as a senior photocopying official.

DILO. I heard it would be declared in a week.

ROSIE. In two weeks, Dilo. It's certain.

DIRECTOR. Oh, if only it were, then you'd have given me good news. Just one more week or ten days of rehearsal?! Wonderful. Nothing could be better. Let's get started.

DILO. From the beginning, with Pandora's Box, or from the end, with the speech?

DIRECTOR. No, since we have time, go and get the black costumes. We'll return to those 12 scenes of suffering and misery. Rosie plays "suffering," and Dilo "misery."

[*Rosie and Dilo exit.*]

DIRECTOR. Hey, James, what do you think? The man who works sincerely never fails, regardless of the challenges. Work and faith in what you are doing are the key pillars of success. What do you say?

[*The Secretary enters.*]

JAMES. I say . . . The Secretary is coming!

DIRECTOR. I can see him!

SECRETARY. I bring you good news. It is officially confirmed. Independence will be declared tomorrow.

DIRECTOR. What?! No, oh god!

[*The Director loses it. He almost faints. The Secretary holds him up, so he doesn't fall.*]

SECRETARY. I beg your pardon?

DIRECTOR. I meant, oh god, what happy news. Tomorrow will be the happiest day of my life. But . . . !

SECRETARY. But what?

DIRECTOR. We aren't ready. We need at least another 10 good rehearsals!

SECRETARY. Shall we just delay declaring our independence?

DIRECTOR. Are you joking?

SECRETARY. Of course.

DIRECTOR. No. No way.

SECRETARY. I don't understand?

DIRECTOR. I said — what did I say? No, I didn't say that. What was I saying? Tomorrow. Okay, then, tomorrow is independence; tomorrow is opening night. Fantastic. We have enough material. Excellent material. We've done a lot of work.

SECRETARY. I hope so.

DIRECTOR. Oh, you can be sure. Tonight, we'll make the final adjustments, and we'll be ready. I'm sorry about before. But I was shocked. Out of delight, naturally. I should be more optimistic.

SECRETARY. I understand. You have a difficult craft. But after the premiere tomorrow, I believe you'll feel better. Much better, even. You'll make the Prime Minister happy. He likes you.

DIRECTOR. Really?

SECRETARY. Naturally. When I told him about the project, he smiled. He even described you with a word like . . .

DIRECTOR. Maestro?

SECRETARY. No, no. Something else!

DIRECTOR. A great artist?

SECRETARY. No. A word that he said he'd called you when you were together at school.

DIRECTOR. Tiny?

SECRETARY. Yes!

DIRECTOR. Oh, how happy you're making me. Everyone called me Tiny at school. He remembered me.

SECRETARY. Of course. He has an extraordinary memory.

DIRECTOR. He's always been like that. Extraordinary memory and intelligence. And brave. Which reminds me, when can we have his speech?

SECRETARY. Tomorrow, as soon as he reads it in Parliament. Okay?

DIRECTOR. Fine. I apologize, but I must go and inform my team. I'm a bit stressed.

SECRETARY. Please go. That was all. See you tomorrow.

DIRECTOR. Good bye.

[*Rosie and Dilo enter in black costumes.*]

ROSIE. We're ready!

[*The Director faints. Dilo and Rosie try to help him.*]

SECRETARY. Everything will go well. The Prime Minister will feel proud. He'll be surprised when he hears his own speech on stage. He'll be amazed. I can just imagine, how after the play, he will leave the group of foreign ambassadors and come over to greet me. *"Well done, Secretary,"* he'll say to me. *"It was a wonderful concert. All the foreign ambassadors are amused. It was an artistic creation entirely appropriate for this great day."* *"Prime Minister,"* I will say, *"congratulations to us on independence. May you live as long as the mountains of Kosovo. I'd lay down my life for you, let alone organize something as small as these theatrics."*

[*The Secretary extends his hand as if he were greeting the Prime Minister. He closes his eyes and enjoys his fantasy.*]

INDEPENDENCE DAY

[*Final rehearsal. The Director is covered with a blanket. He has a fever. Outside, there is shouting and the sound of exploding petards and fireworks.*]

DILO. If you won't go to the doctor, how about the doctor coming here? I can call.

DIRECTOR. No way. We don't have time. We need to keep rehearsing.

ROSIE. The fever will kill you. At least drink a glass of raki.

DIRECTOR. We'll continue with rehearsal. Damn, what the hell is the time?

ROSIE. One o'clock!

DIRECTOR. Why haven't they brought the Prime Minister's speech yet! What's going on? Oh god!

DILO. Shall we go to the café to watch the assembly session on TV? They're broadcasting live.

DIRECTOR. No, we don't have time for television. We need to rehearse.

JAMES. How long will the whole play last?

DIRECTOR. About two hours.

JAMES. That's a bit long.

DIRECTOR. Look, who the hell is making the decisions around here?

JAMES. It's just my opinion.

DIRECTOR. I'm not interested in your opinion. What, did you imagine we'd tell our entire history in less than two hours? What do you think? Should I have put on a mini-play of 50 minutes, and then those cynical foreigners would have said, "*See, they don't have any history. They just have some fog, but no battles, no heroes, except a few wimps who looked askance at the enemy. That's why the play is so short.*" Is that what you wanted? Huh?

JAMES. No, but . . . everyone has the right to say what they think.

DIRECTOR. You know what, why don't you go do something? Do your job.

JAMES. What should I do? I've painted all the wooden boards.

DIRECTOR. Get out of here, out of my sight. Go find the Prime Minister's speech.

JAMES. Me?

DIRECTOR. Go to the top, to the General Manager's office, to the Kosovo Assembly, to the café . . . break a neck somewhere.

[*James exits.*]

DILO. Perhaps we should take it out completely?

DIRECTOR. Take out what?

DILO. The Prime Minister's speech.

DIRECTOR. Friends, let us now focus on the other scenes which are still totally unfinished. As for that speech, let them go to hell. If they don't bring it, they don't bring it. I don't care about it. We won't do it at all. Let them put me in prison for it. Let them persecute me and do whatever else they want. That's it. It's over. I can't wait anymore.

ROSIE. He's right.

DILO. Who?

ROSIE. The Prime Minister, of course! He's right to have that speech in the play. In the end, it's an historic day.

DILO. Oh, Rosie, how innocent you are.

[*The Director talks as if delirious.*]

DIRECTOR. Beloved actors, today we are facing a great challenge, but we must not allow ourselves to surrender to fear. We have waited so long for this day. Do not doubt that it finds us ready.

ROSIE. You have to go to the doctor. Don't you see what's happened to you?

[*Enter James.*]

JAMES. Here's the speech.

[*James gives an envelope to the Director.*]

DIRECTOR. Who gave it to you?

JAMES. A man I met in the hallway.

ROSIE. Don't open it; maybe it has some kind of poison powder.

DIRECTOR. Who the hell is that "man?" What did he say when he gave it to you?

JAMES. I don't know who he was, but he said to me, "*Here's the Prime Minister's speech. Give it to the Director.*"

DIRECTOR. Whoever wants to can open it. I don't want to do it.

JAMES. Neither do I.

ROSIE. Get it away from me.

DILO. Give it here. I'll open it.

[*The Director gives the letter to Dilo. Dilo starts to open it, while the others move away out of fear. Dilo reads the letter.*]

DILO. "*Follow the instructions precisely, and you will find the Prime Minister's speech. Go to the left of the stage, and below, in the corner, there is a small box.*"

[*They can all barely get orientated.*]

DIRECTOR. "Left," but from which side?

[*Dilo finds the box. He opens it and finds another letter. He opens it and reads it.*]

DILO. "*In the Director's bag, in the first pocket, there is another letter.*"

[*The Director goes and opens his own bag and takes an envelope out of it.*]

DIRECTOR. Oh, to hell with this. What's going on? Who put this envelope in my bag?

[*He gives the envelope to Dilo. Dilo opens it and reads it.*]

DILO. "*Now you are very close. Open Rosie's lipstick, not the new one she bought today, but the other that she threw yesterday to the right of the stage, below the big spotlight.*"

ROSIE. I threw away that lipstick the day before yesterday!

[*They look everywhere and then go toward the "big spotlight" below where they find the lipstick. Dilo opens it and takes out another letter.*]

DILO. The Prime Minister's speech.

DIRECTOR. Its authenticity must be verified.

DILO. It's the Prime Minister's signature. See, those lines that only he knows how to make.

ROSIE. I don't get it. What on earth has my lipstick got to do with all this?

[The Director takes the speech and gives it a once over.]

DIRECTOR. It seems short. Very good, just four pages. We'll do it. Dilo?

DILO. I can, but on one condition!

DIRECTOR. What condition?

DILO. I need to be alone, so I can learn it by heart. I just need some silence.

DIRECTOR. Oh, of course. Go home; learn it; and we'll meet here 30 minutes before the play. But promise me that you won't drink even one glass of raki.

DILO. I promise.

DIRECTOR. Not a single one!

DILO. Nothing.

ROSIE. Promise!

DILO. I promised you, damn it. I'm going to learn this shitty speech. Do you understand? There are four whole pages.

[Dilo exits.]

JAMES. They've started giving out free raki in the square.

DIRECTOR. And what do you mean by that?

JAMES. I just hope he doesn't walk that way.

ROSIE. Free raki will put him in a trance, like the sirens did to Odysseus.

JAMES. Free raki will make his heart tremble, just as a kid makes a mother's heart tremble.

DIRECTOR. Enough! Do you want to make me crazy?!

[The Director starts to tremble. He faints. Rosie takes his head to her chest and strokes it. The Director regains his consciousness.]

DIRECTOR. I'm fine. I'm fine.

SECRETARY'S SPEECH

[*On stage at the National Theater of Kosovo. Outside, the cheers of the crowd can be heard, the noise of fireworks, and celebratory music. The Secretary speaks to the public.*]

SECRETARY. Honorable Prime Minister, honorable U.S. Ambassador, honorable representatives of the diplomatic corps, dear members of the public:

Today, on this historic day, when the Parliament of the Republic of Kosovo has just declared Kosovo an independent state, our theater troop, with its wonderful actors, has prepared a solemn play which we will enjoy watching tonight.

For many years in this theater, the dramas of our nation have been performed in the midst of the suffering and sacrifice that has accompanied us on our journey to independence.

Our artists have kept alive the spirit of the nation in our worst days.

This play is further proof that our state is being built on the rich cultural values of an ancient tradition.

Now, it is my honor to introduce the Prime Minister of Kosovo who will say a few words.

FEAR AND MISERY BACKSTAGE

[*Backstage. Rosie is smoking. The Director, to one side, is crying silently.*]

DIRECTOR. Why? Oh god!

ROSIE. I knew this would happen! You shouldn't have let him go.

DIRECTOR. I made a mistake; I lost my mind. How could I have trusted him! He promised. Oh, damn him.

ROSIE. How many more speeches are there?

DIRECTOR. The Prime Minister's speaking now. After him, it's the American Ambassador, and then the play should start.

ROSIE. Maybe you should go out and explain the situation to them. Of course, you can say that Dilo's uncle or aunt died, or something like that.

DIRECTOR. Of course I can't do that.

ROSIE. But what will we do?

DIRECTOR. I'll act.

ROSIE. What?

DIRECTOR. Yes, I'll act. There's no other option. Bring me the costume. James?

JAMES. Immediately!

DIRECTOR. [*To Rosie.*] Never again. He's never again going to act in my plays. His career as an actor ends tonight.

ROSIE. Don't get carried away by emotions.

DIRECTOR. But how can I not, Rosie?

[*Enter James.*]

JAMES. He's coming. He's coming.

DIRECTOR. There is a god.

JAMES. He was sleeping in the wardrobe. He's stone drunk. He can barely stand.

[*Enter Dilo, dressed in a King Lear costume.*]

DILO. What's kept you all until now?

DIRECTOR. You've been drinking, haven't you?

DILO. Just a little glass.

DIRECTOR. Have you learned the speech?

JAMES. Of course. Do I look like an amateur actor to you?

DIRECTOR. Well done!

[*The Director kisses Dilo on the forehead and then Rosie.*]

ROSIE. He's going to act in that costume, is he?

JAMES. Hasn't anyone told him that tonight we're not performing *King Lear*?

[*Dilo looks at his costume. He realizes he's got the wrong clothes on. He wants to take them off.*]

DIRECTOR. It's too late now. Leave them. We'll discuss it later. Concentrate now. This is the last speech. We have to start soon. [*To Dilo.*] Do you remember the scenes?

ROSIE. Come on, King Lear, or has your memory been wiped clean?

DILO. I remember, of course.

JAMES. The box . . .

DILO. Pandora's Box — I play the Box. The coming of enemies to our lands — I play the Monster, then I play Bill Clinton smiling, and then come the six scenes of "suffering." After that the scene with the anthem, and at the end, the Prime Minister's speech.

DIRECTOR. Especially the last, don't forget.

ROSIE. I hope you won't confuse the scenes.

JAMES. We start in thirty seconds. Lights, music, and action.

[*Rosie and Dilo go on stage. The Director and James remain alone.*]

DIRECTOR. When does this hell end?

JAMES. It started well. "Break a leg," as the English say.

DIRECTOR. Do you think everything will go okay?

JAMES. Oh, of course. I'm convinced of it.

DIRECTOR. You don't have a pain killer, do you? I finished mine.

JAMES. I have pills for dizziness.

DIRECTOR. For dizziness?

JAMES. Yes, pills for flying. Take one. It will help.

[*James offers him a pill. The Director takes one and swallows it quickly. Clapping is heard from the front of the stage.*]

DIRECTOR. [*Whispers.*] They are clapping at the first scene — a miracle. I'm a genius.

MY LAND

[Darkness. Then out of the darkness come Dilo and Rosie.]

ROSIE. *This is my land*
These are my rivers
Fields, gardens, and forests.
And these are the flowers I have watered with my tears.
I, the mother of this earth that was reborn from the scent of these flowers.

DILO. *This is not your land*
Nor are these rivers yours
Nor the fields, nor the gardens, and not even the forests belong to you.
And these flowers that are said to give life,
Are not your flowers.

ROSIE. *What?*
You want to take even the flowers from me?
You, the enemy of my people.

DILO. *Yes, and later I'm going to rip out your eyes*
I'm going to yank out your hair
I'm going to violate your honor
And I'm going to chop off your limbs.

ROSIE. *Leave me but one eye*
So that I might see how my boy grows up
Leave me but one breast so that I might feed him
And leave me one hand to cradle him when he cries.

[Dilo takes out a knife from his belt and he "kills" Rosie. She dies theatrically. Dilo, the victor, chuckles quietly. The stage goes dark again.]

THE FIRST AND LAST FLIGHT OF JAMES TAFILAJ

[*The roof of the National Theater of Kosovo. James, with goggles and a pilot's cap, stands proudly in front of what looks like a primitive aircraft. He looks at the town where fireworks can be seen, and the happy noise of people celebrating can be heard. Then he looks at his watch.*]

JAMES. Alright, the moment has come. Father, wherever you are, I know you're listening to me. I'm fulfilling your dying wish. I said that one day you'd be proud of me. No Father, I'm not frightened, not frightened at all. In a little bit, I'm going to be high up, up there, where you always wanted to see me. People will wave at me. *"See that good-for-nothing from the National Theater, the one who painted the wooden boards! Look! He's flying! He's contributing to the homeland."* I'm going to throw out leaflets saying, "Please, recognize Kosovo." They'll fall everywhere, in town squares, in forests, on the balconies of homes, in children's playgrounds. And perhaps one of them might flutter to the open window of the Prime Minister's office. He will see it the next day. *"Where did this letter come from? What is happening?"* the Prime Minister will ask, frightened. But his advisors will quickly calm him. *"They are James's leaflets,"* they'll say to him. *"He's going to fly around and about the world, to every corner of it, asking countries and continents to recognize our independence."* *"Is he?"* the surprised Prime Minister will ask. *"Give him a diplomatic passport. Give him as much money as he needs. That boy has my blessing."* Yes Father, this is what's going to happen. The Prime Minister is watching the play now. Can you hear the applause? But it's a boring play, Father. It's too long and very disconnected. It's a national play, so perhaps that explains it.

[*James looks at his watch once again.*]

Now, it's time. I'm going to get Kosovo a seat at the UN. This is my modest contribution to independence. See you up there, Father.

[*James puts on his glasses and cap and climbs into the aircraft.*]

THE PRIME MINISTER'S SPEECH

[*On stage, Rosie is dancing to the rhythm of the Kosovo anthem. After a little, she starts to withdraw, while Dilo enters the stage, in the role of Prime Minister. Dilo pulls from his chest a new flag of Kosovo and he gives it to Rosie who leaves the stage, enveloped in the flag. A thin cloud of smoke covers the stage. Then, a deep silence.*]

DILO. *"This day has been long in coming. So many have given so much to make Independence Day a reality. I welcome all those who have sacrificed so much and are here with us today, and for those observing us, I express my deepest appreciation on behalf of my people. At last this day has come, and from this moment on, Kosovo is proud, independent, sovereign, and free. Our hopes have never been higher. Our dreams are infinite."*

[*Dilo gets the hiccups. This catches him by surprise. After a short pause, he starts again.*]

"Dear fellow citizens, today marks the end of a long process. Belgrade's threats are in the past, and this is the end of the delusion that it will ever rule Kosovo again."

"Our pledges will be embodied by three key elements:

First, the strong and irrevocable guarantee by law of the equal rights of all the members of every community in Kosovo.

Second . . ."

[*He can't remember. He goes on.*]

"Third . . ."

[*He pauses, takes out a piece of paper from his pocket, looks at it for a long time, unbelievingly, but then starts to read from it.*]

"I'm going to leave my torn panties hanging at the entrance to the apartment. I'm leaving home, together with my daughter."

[*Dilo looks away from the letter, at the public. He is not sure what to do. The hiccups continue. Then, he puts the letter in his pocket and takes out another letter, which he also puts back into his pocket. He looks again at the public, realizing that something is not going right.*]

You can never believe letters. Let's forget about them completely.

Second . . .

So that you're not confused, that was an old letter from my wife. She goes off like this all the time, but she always comes back.

[*The Director slowly enters the stage, trying to gesture to him to stop, but Dilo doesn't notice.*]

Second . . .

I'll carry on where I left off. A bit earlier, while coming back from drinking raki with friends, happy about this great day, we were reminded of our friend, Hasim, who two months ago fell in a big hole in the middle of town and died. It was that hole that no one has bothered to fix, I don't know why. Maybe Hasim would be alive if they had made space for him in the hospital that night, but poor Hasim didn't have any money. But who has money today, huh? Yes, businessmen, politicians, and the mafia have it. For some months now, we haven't received our salaries. Isn't that right, General Manager? Greetings, General Manager! You must be here in the audience. I really am not interested in trivia, but well, I'm asking myself, what sort of a shitty state are we creating like this? How is it possible that a deputy has a salary that is ten or twenty times bigger than mine, though I've been an actor for thirty years? Have you seen my plays? It isn't fair, Mr. Prime Minister. I know you're here in the room. I order you . . .

Second . . .

[*Dilo looks round about, as if he is seeking help from someone. Then, he is sick from anxiety. The Director faints. The Secretary comes on stage.*]

SECRETARY. He is drunk. Mr. Prime Minister, please stay, don't go. He is an agent working for a foreign government. I have precise information. He works for the Russian secret service. It is part of a conspiracy. Please, Prime Minister, stay. About now, a gun will be fired. Where is the gun? Please, give me the gun. Damn it, give me a gun. It is a NATO gun, Prime Minister, not a normal gun.

[*Rosie gives him the gun. The Secretary takes it and shoots it high above.*]

Please, stay. Dear members of the public, this is part of the play. It's a symbolic shot. Please don't abandon the hall. Prime Minister, honorable ambassadors . . . Why are you leaving?

[*He searches for Dilo.*]

Here's the bastard. I'll put him in his place.

[*When Dilo realizes that the Secretary means it, he runs. The Secretary pursues him. From above the stage, James's leaflets begin to fall. Rosie takes one and looks at it curiously. Then, a small sound is heard, like a crack, and then a bigger noise. James, hanging in the ropes of a parachute, falls upside down in the middle of the stage. He remains hanging, swinging. Meanwhile, Rosie, who is confused, repeats her monologue like a parrot.*]

ROSIE. "*As God is my witness, as God is my witness, they're not going to lick me! I'm going to live through this, and when it's all over, I'll never be hungry again!*"

JAMES. Please . . . recognize . . . Kosovo.

[*Everyone gathers around him. The Director recovers from his delirium and approaches James.*]

JAMES. Hallo, hallo . . . I am from Kosova. Kosovo. NATO. Newporn. My playne . . . eet crashed. Help meee.

ROSIE. Call the ambulance . . .

DILO. A horse, a horse. My kingdom for a horse.

[*James faints. The Secretary turns toward the audience, wanting to attract attention.*]

SECRETARY. *Mommy, Mommy . . . the house is burning!*

Careful Red Riding Hood . . .

Mommy, Mommy, the house is burning!

Careful Red Riding Hood . . .

DIRECTOR. Stay, dear members of the audience. Everything is going according to the script. This is a modern play. See, now we're going to sing a song. A song, we'll sing a song.

[*Rosie and Dilo start singing, and the others then join in: the Director, the Secretary, and James.*]

DILO and ROSIE

The chicken, the cockerel, were doing the "rokoko"

While the white egg was laid,

Oh, when will the egg be laid in the meadow,

[*Everyone joins in the song.*]

Ro-ko-ko
Ro-ko-ko
The chicken laid an egg

[*The stage goes dark slowly.*]

WHERE ARE THEY AND WHAT ARE THEY DOING

[*The five actors line up before the public, as if to greet them.*]

EVERYONE TOGETHER. Where are they, and what are they doing?

DIRECTOR. Where are they, and what are they doing?

DILO. That night James, the stage technician, wanted to fly with that aircraft of his, but it didn't work. He flew, but not for long. The engine failed, and he fell on the roof of the National Theater of Kosovo. He spent some months in the hospital and then some months in prison. Yes, yes. In prison! They accused him of wanting to use his aircraft to strike the Parliament Building. Now, he lives in Prishtina. He is unemployed, but some days he can be found in Mother Theresa Square selling balloons to children.

JAMES. The director of the play . . . He disappeared without a trace on the night of what the media called "the great failure." There were so many rumors: that he had committed suicide, that he had fled to America, that he was living in the mountains, far from people, that he had dug his own grave among the martyrs and had buried himself alive, etc. But he amazed everyone when after a year he appeared in the media presenting a mega film project: *God is Albanian*. The Kosovo Government allocated four million euros to it.

DIRECTOR. The actor, Dilo. They sent him to the hospital in shock. The analyses showed that the level of alcohol in his blood was twice as much as a man's body can stand. But Dilo survived. They didn't imprison him. They say that Rosie is credited for this. Dilo continues to act still. Recently, he did a street play called *King Lear and Father Christmas*. Since that time, his wife has left him another three-hundred-and-forty-five-times. They continue to live together.

ROSIE. The Secretary of the Ministry of Sport? He continues where he was, in the same job. They accused him unjustly of stealing a million euros dedicated to the celebration of Kosovo's independence, but he made it seem like the money was spent just as it should have been, and the court believed him. He fell in love with Rosie, the actress from the theater, and he even separated from his wife. In memory of Rosie, he started the construction of an opera and ballet theater in Prishtina.

SECRETARY. Rosie, the actress from the play? She broke the Secretary's heart. She never starred on Broadway. She married the former head of the United Nations in Kosovo and went to live with him in the Swiss Alps but, in a matter of days, they separated. After a painful divorce, she returned to Kosovo and became a human rights activist. For a while, she founded and directed the "Let's Bury Violence" organization. But she's best known for one unique performance — appearing nude in front of the Parliament Building. She was recently appointed Kosovo's ambassador to Papua, New Guinea.

DILO. And the Prime Minister? He continues to be Prime Minister.

END

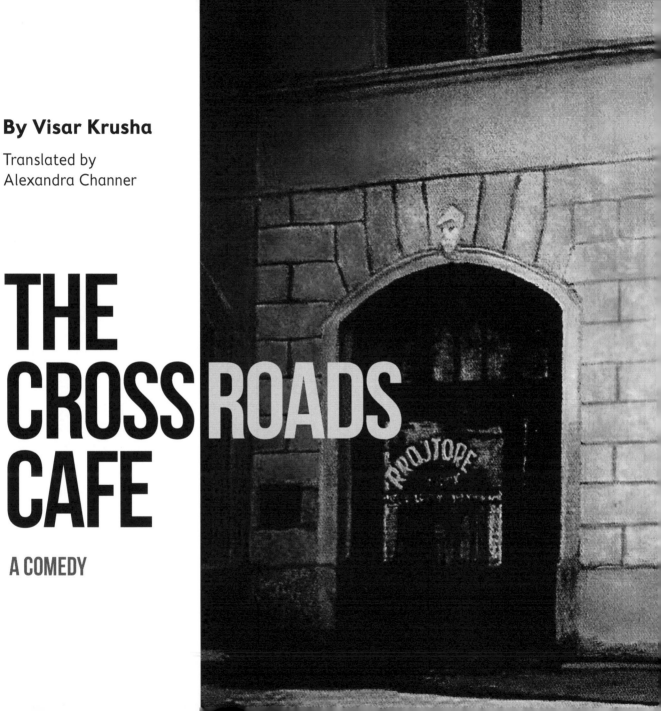

By Visar Krusha

Translated by
Alexandra Channer

THE
CROSS ROADS
CAFE

A COMEDY

CHARACTERS

Sokol — a café owner

Sara — Sokol's wife

Mom — Sokol's mother

Xhevdet — Sokol and Sara's son

Enkela — a waitress from Albania

Mejremja-Meri — a waitress

Ahmet — a customer of Sokol's

Gazi — a customer of Sokol's

Dragan — a Serbian policeman

Nebojsha — a Serbian policeman

Zhut[*] — a Serbian security inspector

Drita — a political activist and a friend of Sara's

Betim — a customer of Sokol's

Participants in the Congress

A Guest

An American Journalist

Man in Disguise — a guerrilla

Groom and Wedding Party

A Refugee

A Wounded Fighter

A Man (along with other visitors to the refreshment tent)

[*]The Serbian word for red.

ACT I

Scene One

[*The interior of a café. Upstage is a bar with barstools. Downstage is an assortment of tables and chairs. Behind the bar is a door that leads to the kitchen. There is another door stage right that leads both to the street and to the second floor where the café owner and his family live, together with the wait staff. Stage left is the café entrance. Sara and Drita enter from the door on the right.*]

DRITA. Oh, Sara, I just made it! Go outside and see if anyone's coming.

SARA. What happened? There's no one there.

DRITA. I'll tell you in a minute, but first I need some water.

[*Sara brings her water from behind the bar.*]

SARA. There's no reason to worry. No one is in the street. No police, no people. What happened?

DRITA. A police patrol followed me all the way up to the turn onto your street, and then I don't know where they went.

SARA. Well, that's good. Then you're safe. Don't worry so much.

DRITA. You never know. [*A boom is heard from above.*] What was that?

SARA. It's nothing. I think Mom's just woken up and started her exercises.

DRITA. I'll need a change of clothes when I leave, so I can slip past the spies.

SARA. Alright. I'll give you some of Mom's things. But what's up? Tell me why you're here.

DRITA. Sara, listen very carefully. You know, I never say things more than once. I can't spare the time, and, in any case, it's in keeping with my doctrine and my duty.

SARA. I know, I know. Go on, tell me what's happening.

DRITA. Now, listen very carefully. The situation is escalating. [*She looks around in case anyone is listening.*] The movement needs to call a party congress, and because you've been wanting to prove yourself, I thought we might hold it here in the upstairs room. Do you agree? Any objections? Anything to add?

SARA. Well of course I agree. That won't be any problem. We'll hold it in Mom's room. Drita, have I ever said no to you or to the movement? When I joined, I took my decision very seriously. I'm ready to sacrifice anything for this country's freedom.

DRITA. I know, you've always come through, but will Sokol agree to it?

SARA. Yes, of course. Don't you worry about that. I'll sort it out. But tell me what we actually have to do.

DRITA. I have a plan. Let's go somewhere private.

SARA. Alright then. We'll go to Mom's bedroom. We can talk and find you some clothes.

DRITA. Okay.

Scene Two

[*Sara and Drita exit by the door on the right. Sokol enters through the door behind the bar, wearing an apron. He unlocks the café door and hangs an OPEN sign, then goes back to the bar, cleans up a bit, and arranges the tables. Mejremja-Meri walks in through the café entrance.*]

SOKOL. Hey, where have you been? We left the house door open all night. Do you know how worried we were about you?

MERI. Don't even ask. Oh God, people have become so rotten. Everyone's looking out for themselves. No one cares about talent. Talent is withering on the vine because no one has any exposure.

SOKOL. What happened, Mejremja?

MERI. Sokol, my name is Meri. How many times must I tell you?

SOKOL. Oh alright, "Meri." Why are you fretting so much? You're like a chicken with its head cut off. You struck out again, huh?

MERI. I sang all night, and at the end he said, *"I'm sorry, dear, but we need something else for the album."* Idiot, stupid idiot! I'll show him! Look what's happened to my legs. My veins are bulging from all those hours on my feet.

SOKOL. Do you have to stand?! Why don't you sing lying down?

MERI. *"Sing like this singer,"* I got to my feet. *"Sing like that singer,"* I got to my feet. And in the end, nothing. Look how raw my throat is. Look at the dark circles around my eyes from sheer exhaustion.

SOKOL. What are you doing to yourself?! It's better to get to work. It'll calm you down. You will become a famous singer. You will! Oh Meri, Meri.

MERI. [*Throws herself into his arms.*] Oh Sokol, don't look at me with such longing. It breaks my heart. Come on, let's go away. Leave Sara. What are you doing with that old Hungarian? Take me instead. You won't regret it. Oh, I love you so much. Let's go abroad somewhere. We'll start a new a life. You'll open a hotel, and I'll sing and be the main attraction. Everyone will be jealous.

SOKOL. I know, Meri, I know how much you love me. And I love you too. Now, it's better to start work before anyone comes in. I've put out the sign.

MERI. Oh Sokol, nothing could extinguish the fire of my love for you.

SOKOL. Go on now, go. Go and get ready. You're going to become a great singer.

MERI. I can't tear myself away from your gaze, from your claws, my handsome tiger. I'll be back again, to be near you, to come to life.

[*Meri exits though the bar door.*]

Scene Three

[*Mom's bedroom. She's practicing ballet.*]

SARA. That's good, that's good. Not like that. Hold your head high. That's it. Chest forward. Hold onto the table tight. Imagine a mirror in front of you, and you can see your reflection in it. No, no, don't lean over. Like this, like this, straight.

MOM. I can't do it without music. If you put on the music, I'll dance. Who dances without music?!

SARA. No, no Mom. First you have to learn the steps. The music comes later. Now turn around.

MOM. How do I turn around?

SARA. Once, twice. There, like that. That's it. Now left. On tiptoes. Slowly, slowly.

[*Mom falls over*]

MOM. I'll break something in a minute. It will be your fault. I tell you to put on some music, but you won't do it. [*Drita enters dressed as an old woman.*] Hamide, my sister, where did you come from?

SARA. It isn't Hamide, Mom. It's my friend, Drita.

DRITA. Can you tell it's me?

SARA. Not at all.

MOM. Why is your friend wearing my slacks?

SARA. They aren't yours. You aren't the only one with slacks.

MOM. Oh, what's the world coming to? They steal the clothes off your back, and no one bats an eyelash.

DRITA. Sara, be careful. I'll be back later, just as we planned.

SARA. Wait, let me come with you. Mom, I'll be right back.

MOM. What about me? Are you leaving me?

SARA. I'll be right back, and we'll go on with the lesson.

MOM. Oh Sara, Sara. At least put some music on. [*Sara and Drita exit.*]

Scene Four

[*In the café, Sokol is cleaning something. Enkela enters from the stage right door and throws herself into his arms.*]

ENKELA. Oh Sokol, you are the best Kosovar I've ever seen. Listen, listen to how my heart beats: THUD-THUD, THUD-THUD!!

SOKOL. Mine beats for you too: BOOM-BOOM, BOOM-BOOM!!

ENKELA. Why should I go out with all these bastards who promise the world and give you nothing, like the one last night? Why, when I have you, my love? But I'll take revenge on them all. They'll explode with rage when they find out I've married you. You're the one for me.

SOKOL. Enkela, my darling, I love you, but I'm married. What can I do?

ENKELA. Leave that old thing. Let's go to Italy. We'll start a new life there.

SOKOL. Why run away with me when there are so many young guys out there?!

ENKELA. I don't want those boys. I want you. We'll take a speedboat to Italy.

SOKOL. Don't hold me so close. Someone might come. We're open for business.

ENKELA. And my heart is open for you. I'm going to swallow you up in it.

SOKOL. I think I can hear someone coming.

ENKELA. Let them come. I love you. I'm not frightened of anyone. You shouldn't be frightened of love.

SOKOL. I'm not frightened of love, just crazy love. Enkela, don't go wild.

ENKELA. Oh, how wussy!

[*Enter Ahmet, a 60-year-old.*]

AHMET. Morning Sokol, morning everyone . . . Oh, oh Sokol, how lucky you are not to be alone.

[*Sokol and Enkela end their embrace. Ahmet sits by a table.*]

SOKOL. Ahmet, how are you? Did you sleep well? How's your head?

AHMET. I slept a little. My head's okay, thanks.

SOKOL. Ah, I know what you need.

AHMET. And I know what I need, but it can't be ordered.

SOKOL. Come on, there's an answer for you too.

[*Meri enters with a tray and brings Ahmet a glass of water.*]

AHMET. Let Enkela serve me. She knows how I like things.

MERI. Look, look, he's choosing his own waitress.

AHMET. It's not me that's choosing. It's my heart.

ENKELA. Why should I come over there? You can order from where you are.

AHMET. I want you to come over and wait on me. Sokol, are you listening?

SOKOL. Enkela, wait on Ahmet. Don't be difficult, my dear. The customer comes first.

ENKELA. Did you hear what he said?

SOKOL. Don't pay any attention.

[*Enkela goes over to Ahmet and takes his order.*]

AHMET. Well, finally, finally. Coffee and a raki.[1] And whatever you want for yourself.

ENKELA. Thank you, but I don't need your bribes. Ugh, dirty old man.

[*Betim enters, a 14-year-old, holding a newspaper. He sits down at a table.*]

BETIM. Sokol, what's with all this dust?

SOKOL. But I just cleaned the tables.

BETIM. It's not right. A man comes to relax, to have a drink, but it's too filthy to sit anywhere. But you don't care about that. You just care about making money.

[*Meri goes over to wipe it off.*]

SOKOL. Uh, we try our best to keep things looking good.

MERI. Now it's clean. What would you like?

BETIM. Coffee and an orange juice.

[*Enkela brings the drinks to Ahmet, ignoring him. Betim reads the newspaper.*]

AHMET. Ah Sokol, when I was in Germany, I had loads of women, and now even waitresses tell me to get lost. I'm a nobody.

---

1. Raki is a strong alcoholic drink made from grapes, popular in Albania, Kosovo, Turkey, and Greece.

SOKOL. If you whine, you won't have luck. With patience, you'll find someone. Anyway, things aren't that bad. You'll get your pension, all those German marks. But here I am, working all day long like a horse, and I can barely make ends meet.

BETIM. People are dying of hunger, and you gripe that you don't have enough. You are under occupation, Sokol, occupation.

[*Gazi enters. He sits at a table.*]

GAZI. Greetings! How is everybody? You always take good care of us, Sokol. I'm in a rush today. I need coffee right away.

SOKOL. You never have any time. You're doing important work!

GAZI. Uncle Ahmet, have you met anyone?

AHMET. Well, sort of . . .

[*The waitresses serve. Betim watches Gazi suspiciously. Nebojsha, a member of the Serbian police force, enters.*]

NEBOJSHA. How are you, neighbors? How are things?

SOKOL. Good to see you, Nebojsha.

GAZI. Come and sit down, Nebojsha.

AHMET. Good, good thanks. How are you? How's your dad?

NEBOJSHA. Well, thanks.

AHMET. Ah, he's a good man.

GAZI. Sokol, bring Nebojsha something to drink.

[*Sokol comes to serve Nebojsha. He greets him obsequiously.*]

SOKOL. How are you, Nebojsha? Are you well?

NEBOJSHA. Yes, thanks, and you? I'll have a raki.

SOKOL. Of course, right away. For you, anything.

GAZI. Did you pull it off?

NEBOJSHA. I just managed. If you weren't my friend, I wouldn't have taken the risk.

GAZI. Ah, Nebojsha, there's no one like you. I know who can get the job done and who can't.

[*Nebojsha takes a passport out of his pocket and passes it to Gazi under the table. Gazi gives Nebojsha some money in return. They clink glasses. Betim watches Gazi and Sokol.*]

NEBOJSHA. And here's to you, neighbor.

[*Dragan, a member of the police force, enters.*]

DRAGAN. Good to see you, friends. Never have I seen so many people just hanging out all day in a café.

SOKOL. What else is there to do? You have to pass the time somehow.

DRAGAN. And what about honest labor?

SOKOL. You can't work all day. You have to take a break at some point. How are you, Dragan? Is everything okay?

DRAGAN. Fine. Any news?

SOKOL. No, nothing. What will you have to drink?

DRAGAN. I'm in a rush, so just a small raki. I have to get to work. [*To Nebojsha.*] What are you doing here?

NEBOJSHA. Just hanging out with Gazi.

DRAGAN. You better get a move on because the boss is on his way from Belgrade. We've got to go meet him.

NEBOJSHA. Which boss?

DRAGAN. It's Zhut. What a dumb question!

NEBOJSHA. Alright, I'm ready.

[*Nebojsha downs his raki. Dragan gestures to Sokol to come over. Sokol approaches him smiling, bringing the raki.*]

DRAGAN. Sokol, I have something to ask you, "officially."

SOKOL. At your service.

DRAGAN. Do you know anything about a congress that's supposed to be held today?

SOKOL. What kind of congress? I haven't heard anything about it.

DRAGAN. The kind your politicians, with their fake parties, organize.

SOKOL. Oh, I don't know anything at all about that stuff. Dragan, I just mind my own business and take care of my family. I'm not that kind of a guy. I've never wanted to get involved.

DRAGAN. Yes, but you run a café, so maybe you hear things. I want you to let me in on what you hear.

SOKOL. No, I swear, I haven't heard a thing.

DRAGAN. Okay, okay. Don't worry. I believe you. But there's something else, Sokol. Listen: You must serve a luncheon at one o'clock.

SOKOL. Well, of course, why wouldn't I?

DRAGAN. I mean a good lunch — fine dining. I'll come with Nebojsha and our boss, Zhut. You know him!

SOKOL. Mr. Zhut, huh? Of course, I know him! He always stops by when he's in town.

DRAGAN. Well, you know how he is. He's a bit of a gourmet.

SOKOL. Don't you worry. I'll prepare a lunch like you've never had before. From the soup to the dessert.

DRAGAN. And something else. [*Takes out a cell phone from his jacket.*] Keep this. If you see or hear anything about that congress, call me. Just call this number. See, it's already in the phone.

SOKOL. I'm telling you, I don't know anything about that kind of stuff. I'm always taken by surprise. I never spot the criminals, let alone the politicians. Maybe I'm too goodhearted to mix with bad people.

DRAGAN. Call, like I said, if you see something, okay? If not, I'll come pick up the phone. [*Sokol takes the telephone.*] Nebojsha, come on, let's go.

[*The police leave.*]

SOKOL. Well, that was bad luck.

GAZI. [*He leaves a passport on the bar.*] Sokol, a friend of mine will come to collect this passport. He's tall and dark. If he asks for me, give it to him.

SOKOL. Oh, for God's sake, I'm sick of all these favors.

GAZI. I know, but this isn't that hard.

[*Gazi leaves.*]

AHMET. Bring me a raki, Enkela. Those dogs upset my stomach.

BETIM. So Sokol, you're hanging out with the cops these days?

SOKOL. What can I do? I can't throw them out. I don't do anything for them.

BETIM. Ah well, soon the day will come when we'll all know who did what.

[*Meri serves Ahmet.*]

AHMET. Ah Mejremja, you're so lovely.

MERI. Are you kidding? And my name isn't Mejremja, it's Meri.

AHMET. Well, congratulations! When did you change it?

MERI. Oh, who cares, it's not a big deal. Anyway, what do you know about music?

[*Sokol enters the kitchen and sees a death notice for his mother.*]

SOKOL. [*Shouting.*] Sara, come down here right now!

[*Sara comes downstairs.*]

SARA. What's going on?

SOKOL. What's this nonsense?

SARA. It's nothing.

SOKOL. It might be nothing to you, but she's my mother! Who would do this to Mom?

SARA. It's nothing, Sokol. Xheki did it on the computer. He was just fooling around. Your mom thought it was funny.

SOKOL. Come in here. [*He tears the poster down from the wall and reads it.*] "Today, our dear old mother died. The burial is scheduled for three o'clock, accompanied by ballet music. We would be delighted if you could join us." Idiot. Xhevdet!

SARA. Life is full of problems. Oh, don't shout like that. Please, you're putting me in a bad mood.

SOKOL. Your mood? What about my mood, huh? [*Xhevdet comes downstairs.*] What's all this?

XHEVDET. Nothing, It was just a joke.

SOKOL. So, my mother's some kind of a gag. Get out of my sight! You're a disgrace.

[*Sokol throws the piece of paper in the bin.*]

VOICE OF MOM FROM ABOVE. Sara, come here! I'm stuck on my tiptoes!

SARA. I'm coming, Mom. Leave Xheki alone. Didn't you see how beautiful the colors were? He's going to be an artist. We have to send him abroad to study.

XHEVDET. Yes, yes, I'm going abroad.

SOKOL. He can go if he earns some money and doesn't just mess around.

XHEVDET. But that poster was my homework.

SOKOL. Use your own mother for your homework!

SARA. Sokol!!!

SOKOL. Oh, go on now. Get out of my sight.

[*Xhevdet goes outside onto the street.*]

SARA. Let it go. It doesn't matter.

SOKOL. How can it not matter!

[*Sara takes Sokol to one side.*]

SARA. I need to tell you something.

SOKOL. What?

SARA. We have important work to do today.

SOKOL. What? Tell me.

SARA. You know I'm a party member. Well, they've called for a special congress, and they're going to hold it here.

SOKOL. What?! No. Over my dead body! I knew, from the first day you joined, you'd do something stupid. Are you crazy? Do you want us to go to prison? I told you, *"Sara, don't do it. You're not made for that kind of work,"* and you said, *"No, I have to do something for these good people."* You want to be more Albanian than I am. No, and that's the end of it.

SARA. You remember, Drita, my friend from the movement? Well, she came to see me today and begged me, and I said yes.

VOICE OF MOM FROM ABOVE. Ballet, ballet! Sara come quickly!

SARA. I'm coming, Mom.

SOKOL. Tell Drita no.

SARA. It will all be clandestine. They'll come in disguise. We'll put them in Mom's room.

SOKOL. Are you listening to yourself? Go and tell her no.

SARA. Sokol, it's all arranged. They're already on their way. They're coming at one o'clock.

SOKOL. At one? At one o'clock, three policemen have reservations for lunch, and you expect me to welcome these politicians, so then, we can all go to prison together??

SARA. Police?!

SOKOL. Yes. Dragan and Nebojsha, and they're coming with that inspector from Belgrade.

SARA. The redhead?

SOKOL. Who cares if his hair is red or blonde? What matters is that we're in trouble.

SARA. We'll pull it off somehow. I can't turn Drita down, and think of what will happen when all the police have gone. How will you make a living? How will you finance the hotel?

SOKOL. This is no time for hotels.

SARA. Not now, but it will be.

SOKOL. So, you've gone ahead and decided without consulting me?

SARA. Please, darling. Now is the time for action. Drita is coming soon, and she'll let us in on the plan.

SOKOL. Here is the first problem: How are all those people going to enter without anyone getting suspicious?

SARA. I'm sure it will all be fine, darling.

VOICE OF MOM FROM ABOVE. Sara, where are you? We were supposed to practice ballet, but you never showed up.

SARA. Okay I'm coming, Mom.

[*They panic. Sokol takes the "death notice" out of the garbage.*]

SOKOL. Xhevdet!

SARA. Xhevdet left.

SOKOL. Let's pretend Mom has died, and that's why we have so many visitors. Tell Xhevdet to print out more death notices. What do you think?

VOICE OF MOM FROM ABOVE. Sara!!!

SARA. Good idea. You get hold of Xhevdet, and I'll go to Mom. [*Kisses Sokol.*] It will all be fine.

[*Sara leaves.*]

SOKOL. Ahmet, go and find Xhevdet, please, and bring him here right away.

[*Ahmet leaves.*]

BETIM. Sokol, be careful. The day of reckoning is coming.

[*Betim leaves. Enkela – since she and Sokol are alone – throws her arms around him.*]

ENKELA. Oh Sokol, come feel how my heart is pounding because it misses you. I can't go ten minutes without holding you.

SOKOL. You couldn't survive for half an hour?

ENKELA. No, and I'd like shorten the time and squeeze you every few minutes.

SOKOL. Oh Enkela, my love. I'm so busy. Let's start to save up minutes, and then we can hug for a whole hour.

ENKELA. Uhm –

SOKOL. Two hours!

ENKELA. Uhm –

SOKOL. All day!

ENKELA. Uhm –

SOKOL. All night!

ENKELA. Uhm –

SOKOL. You're still not happy. What else?!

ENKELA. I want you for all my life. I want to bask in your manliness whenever I feel like it.

[*From the door on the right, Drita, dressed as an old woman, enters with Sara. Drita coughs. Enkela darts away from Sokol.*]

SOKOL. Sara, darling, where were you?

SARA. Drita came, so we could finalize things.

SOKOL. Drita?! What happened to you, Drita?

DRITA. Nothing. What's wrong with you two?

SOKOL. Oh, I . . . I wanted to . . . Enkela had something in her eye, and I was trying to help her with it.

ENKELA. Yes, Sara. You've no idea how painful it was.

SARA. Let me have a look, dear . . . Go and rinse it with chamomile tea.

ENKELA. Don't worry, it's fine now. Sokol got it out.

SARA. Oh, he does the same for me when I get something in my eye. He's an expert.

ENKELA. Yes, he is.

DRITA. Sara, are you ready?

SARA. Yes, of course. Sorry, dear, go on.

DRITA. Can I speak freely in front of her?

SOKOL. Yes, it's fine. Enkela can help us.

DRITA. Okay, call her and the other one too.

SOKOL. Mejremja. Meri.

[*Meri enters. Everyone gathers around Drita.*]

DRITA. Listen very carefully! Listen very carefully! I will speak but once, in keeping with my doctrine and my duty. And don't waste time looking over my clothes. Duty calls. Sara told me about the death notice. I think it's a good idea. You need to behave as if nothing unusual is happening. The participants will pass for mourners. Sokol, take this phone. [*She gives a mobile phone to him*.] The number is here. If something doesn't seem right, just call me. Say, "Nightingale on the verandah." The participants will use this password too, and that's how you'll recognize them. Let's go. There's no time to waste. [*Drita begins to leave but comes back.*] Once again. Don't forget, be discreet, be natural, be relaxed. Do you understand?

ALL. Yes. [*Drita leaves with Sara. Sokol and the waitresses clean the tables.*]

SOKOL. Weep for Mom, so they don't realize we're faking it. [*Ahmet enters with Xhevdet.*] Xhevdet, run upstairs. Print five, or six, or ten of those death notices.

XHEVDET. Why?!

SOKOL. Don't ask any questions. Just go upstairs. Your mom will explain everything.

[*Xhevdet goes.*]

AHMET. What happened, Sokol? Why are you upset?

SOKOL. This is what comes of having a crazy wife. Don't worry about the death notices. Loads of people are coming for some kind of party congress, at the exact same time that the police have reservations for lunch, so I have to pretend that my mom has died, and a whole crowd is coming to pay their respects.

AHMET. Ah . . . I didn't know you were mixed up in all that business.

SOKOL. Help me greet the mourners.

AHMET. But how can I help? What do I know about that sort of stuff?

SOKOL. You don't need to know anything. I'll tell you what to do.

AHMET. But if the police catch on, then what?

SOKOL. You're scared, huh?

AHMET. I'm not scared. I was just saying . . .

SOKOL. If the police find out, I'll take responsibility. They won't bother with you. You just need to stand with me and greet the mourners. "You don't have a clue about anything else."

AHMET. Alright then, I'll help. Don't worry.

Scene Five

[*Mom's room. Mom is sitting by the table, singing something. Meri enters with a tray in her hands.*]

MERI. Time for lunch, Grandma. Today we have soup, meat, and potatoes. You like that, don't you?

MOM. Where did you come from, young girl? Why is it you serving me and not my daughter-in-law?!

MERI. Sometimes it's me, and sometimes it's her. Whoever can spare the time.

MOM. Who are you then?

MERI. Meri, Grandma. How can you not recognize me?

MOM. Did you come to steal my clothes, like the other girl did today?

MERI. No, Grandma. I'm Meri, Sokol's waitress. [*Mom tastes the soup.*] Do you like it? [*The old lady throws the plate at her.*] Why did you do that?

MOM. Thieves! Thieves! You've poisoned the soup, you bitch. You want me to die, so you can steal my clothes and steal my house. You can't trick me, see. Thieves! Thieves!

MERI. Oh, you crazy old bat, look what did you did! Look at what you did to me!

MOM. Thieves! Thieves! Sokol! Sara!

MERI. I put on a clean shirt today. Now the grease will stain it. I bring you food, and you call me a thief!

[*Sara enters.*]

SARA. What's going on?!

MERI. Mom!

[*Meri gathers the dishes and leaves.*]

SARA. Mom, Mom, why are you acting like this?

MOM. Catch her, catch her, before she gets away! She wanted to poison me and then rob us. The bitch!

SARA. Don't talk like that! She's our waitress.

MOM. You leave me alone with all sorts of riffraff. I can't bear it.

SARA. Can't you be nice for once? Don't shout. We have company coming. You need to behave properly with them.

MOM. Why are they coming? To look for me? To make me marry someone!

SARA. Don't be ridiculous! They're coming to visit.

MOM. Then they must be looking for Zadja. She is the eldest!

SARA. I'm going to bring you some lunch. Now listen. When the guests come, you have to behave yourself.

Scene Six

[*Below in the café. Xhevdet comes down with the death notices.*]

XHEVDET. Here, there are ten copies.

SOKOL. Great. Wait, let me see if you wrote them properly. Just in case you made another joke?

XHEVDET. No, no, I changed the text, just like Mom told me.

SOKOL. They're fine. Ahmet, take these, and post them around the café. [*To Xhevdet.*] You take some too.

[*Sokol, Ahmet, and Xhevdet put them up around the café. They post one at the entrance. A man in a leather jacket and sunglasses comes in and sits at a table. Everyone looks at him suspiciously. Enkela serves him, weeping.*]

ENKELA. Can I help you??

GUEST. Some orange juice.

[*A congress participant enters through the café door, dressed as an imam.*]

PARTICIPANT 1. Nightingale on the verandah. Condolences for your mother.

SOKOL. Thank you. Go up through that door.

[*Another participant enters dressed as a woman.*]

PARTICIPANT 2. Nightingale on the verandah. Condolences for your mother.

SOKOL. Thank you. That way.

GUEST. Excuse me, what's going on here?

ENKELA. We're having a wake.

GUEST. A wake?

SOKOL. Yes, my mother died. People are coming to pay their respects.

GUEST. My condolences!

SOKOL. Thank you.

GUEST. Am I disturbing you?!

SOKOL. No, no, we're at your service, sir. We're still open for business. [*To one side, Sokol takes the telephone from his apron pocket.*] Nightingale on the verandah. There's someone suspicious in the café.

[*Sokol notices that the two telephones are identical and gasps. A woman enters.*]

PARTICIPANT 3. Nightingale on the verandah. Condolences for your mother.

SOKOL. Thank you. Right through that door.

[*Another four congress participants enter and go through the stage right door. Sokol exits by the door behind the bar.*]

Scene Seven

[*Mom's room. Seven congress participants and Sara are sitting around a table.*]

PARTICIPANT 1. The Serbian-Slavic-Chetnik, fascist, communist monster, as you know, has stifled the life of the majority, autochthonous Albanian community who, from time immemorial, has lived in the ancient Dardanian lands. We have gathered here, to review the progress of our struggle to counter the Carpathian witch, who feeds insatiably on noble Albanian blood. I take this opportunity to thank our hosts, and particularly our honorable colleague, who with her tireless work and sacrifice, always succeeds in achieving the impossible when it comes to our vital national question. She, who has been a mote in the occupier's eye, who has proven once again that, in moments of great crisis, our movement and the Albanian people can count on her. In other words, I thank the unique, the industrious, activist, artist, and intellectual: Sara.

SARA. Oh, thank you very much. I am so moved by your kind words, by your generosity. You are always welcome here.

ALL. Thank you . . . Thank you, Sara . . . Well done!

PARTICIPANT 1. And now, honored guests, we declare that our congress will come to order. [*Clapping.*] Let's go over the agenda.

PARTICIPANT 2. I think it would be good, at the start, to condemn the violence to which we are being subjected by the racist, Nazi policies of the occupation.

PARTICIPANT 3. I agree.

PARTICIPANT 4. I think that . . . as a prerequisite, we must first review the progress of our movement from its inception until the present, in order to then determine our future activities.

[*Enter Sokol.*]

SOKOL. I apologize for interrupting, but I need to speak to Sara about something.

SARA. Sorry, I'll be back soon.

SOKOL. [*To one side.*] How long are they planning to stay here?

SARA. We only just started!

SOKOL. Just started! Tell them to get on with it!

SARA. That's all you wanted to say?

SOKOL. Didn't Drita tell you that someone suspicious is down in the café?

SARA. No.

SOKOL. Oh God!! Look. [*He shows her the phone.*] Her cell phone and Dragan's are exactly the same model.

SARA. What?!

SOKOL. I must've taken out the wrong phone. I rang to say that someone suspicious had come into the café, but I seem to have called the police.

SARA. But you think the suspicious person might be a policeman himself?

SOKOL. I don't know. But it does seem like that. He has on a leather jacket and dark glasses. He doesn't say a word but just sits there, watching. And now reinforcements are coming, and we'll all go to prison. Tell them to save themselves!

SARA. Maybe you did call Drita. But even if they come, don't worry. Keep cool, Sokol. Work it out.

SOKOL. Work it out?! Tell them to save themselves.

SARA. Okay, okay, I'll tell them now.

SOKOL. Hey, where's Mom?

SARA. Sleeping?

SOKOL. Be careful she doesn't find out. Make sure she stays in her room.

SARA. Alright.

Scene Eight

[*Dragan, Nebojsha, and Zhut enter the café. They read the death notice for Sokol's mother.*]

DRAGAN. Where's Sokol?

AHMET. He's coming now. His mother died, and mourners have come.

DRAGAN. Uh huh. Listen, can you give us your best table? Our boss is the top brass.

MERI. At your service. This is the table for guests of honor.

[*The police sit down. Sokol enters.*]

SOKOL. Oh, good day, welcome. Welcome, Mr. Zhut. We haven't seen you for ages. How was your trip?

ZHUT. Fine, thank you. How are you? I hear your mother has died.

SOKOL. Yes, the poor thing has passed. What can be done?

POLICE. Our condolences for your loss.

SOKOL. Thank you. Thank you very much. Lunch isn't quite ready, but as you can see, we have company and . . .

ZHUT. But why did you stay open?

SOKOL. Well . . . the poor thing was up in years, and I still have to make a living, and I promised Dragan that I'd make you a fine lunch.

ZHUT. There was no need, but thank you.

SOKOL. I'm someone who keeps their word. But Dragan, you said you would come at one o'clock, what brought you so early? If I'd known, the lunch would be ready.

DRAGAN. Sokol, you must be kidding. You sent for us. You said there was someone iffy in the café. Who is it?

SOKOL. Gosh, I've been so distracted lately. And I can't figure out how to work these new phones. I'm so sorry, but I meant to . . . I was calling . . . my wife's cousin from Hungary. You know my wife's Hungarian? Well, her cousin sent me a coffee machine. Since so many mourners have come, I thought I'd serve them some extra good coffee to thank them for paying their respects, but I can't make it work . . . And . . . I was calling him to say that the machine didn't function properly, that it was iffy, but it seems I called you instead. I'm so sorry, sir. You've rushed over here by mistake. No one iffy has been in the café. It's just the usual customers and my guests. No one else has come.

DRAGAN. What's that word, nightingale, nightingale? . . .

SOKOL. Nightingale?! Huh?! Oh, that's what I call my cousin. He sings like a nightingale. [*Sokol's phone rings.*] Look, my cousin's calling now. "Nightingale, how are you? What's the story with the coffee machine?" Excuse me, I have to consult him quickly. Lunch will be ready soon.

[*Sokol exits using the door by the bar and bumps into Sara who is coming out.*]

SARA. [*To one side.*] Mom has woken up. She's having a tantrum and keeps shouting at the congress to leave her room. She says she can't breathe, it's so crowded.

SOKOL. [*To one side.*] Go entertain the police and that spy. I'll go calm her down.

SARA. But is lunch ready? Won't it be late?

SOKOL. It'll be ready in half an hour. [*Loudly.*] Sara, dear, look after the guests.

SARA. Sure, why not? [*Sara approaches the police.*] How are you gentlemen? Welcome! [*Zhut kisses her hand.*] Oh, you're so charming.

ZHUT. You're the most elegant woman in the country. It's a crime that you live here and not somewhere else – a place where you could really express your talent.

SARA. Thank you for the compliment. Enkela, bring our guests some drinks on the house, as lunch isn't quite ready. Please make yourselves at home. [*Sara approaches the man with the leather jacket.*] Welcome, sir. How are you? Is everything okay?

GUEST. Great, thank you.

SARA. Meri, can you bring our guest some wine on the house? Please make yourself comfortable, sir.

GUEST. Thank you.

SARA. Sokol will be coming shortly, gentlemen. So many mourners have come. That's why lunch is a bit late.

ZHUT. Ah, yes. Condolences for your mother-in-law.

SARA. Thank you, thank you. Please make yourselves at home, gentlemen. We're at your service.

DRAGAN. This Sokol is an odd man. His mother has died, but he's still on the job.

[*Sokol enters with a large tray in his hands.*]

SARA. [*To one side.*] What did you do with Mom?

SOKOL. [*To one side.*] I calmed her down a bit. You go to her now and make sure that she doesn't act up.

[*Sara goes into the kitchen. The waitresses tend to the customers. Ahmet is there among them. Sokol serves the police.*]

SOKOL. At your service, gentlemen. This should be everything.

ZHUT. Forgive us for disturbing you when you're mourning.

SOKOL. Not to worry, it can't be helped. What is one to do? The dead are with the dead, the living with the living. Please don't give it a thought, just make yourselves comfortable.

ZHUT. You're right. The living with the living.

SOKOL. Enjoy your lunch.

[*Betim enters, sits down somewhere, and reads the newspaper. He surreptitiously follows the goings-on in the café.*]

NEBOJSHA. Here's to the chef.

SOKOL. I'll be back with dessert later. I know Mr. Zhut likes his sweets.

NEBOJSHA. Very, very tasty.

DRAGAN. Let the boss talk. You're not here to have opinions.

ZHUT. Oh, the lunch is really delicious. Thank you, Sokol. I'm sure the dessert will be just as good.

SOKOL. No worry there. You'll see. [*Sara enters.*]

SARA. Excuse me, but I need Sokol for a moment. Come here, dear, just a moment.

SOKOL. [*To one side.*] What's going on?

SARA. [*To one side.*] The conference was adjourned because of strenuous objections – meaning Mom's – but the members don't dare to leave with the police and that spy around.

SOKOL. Let them stay up there until the police are done with lunch.

SARA. Yes, but Mom's in a rage. She can't bear them, and they can't abide her.

SOKOL. Again, huh? I can't do anything. Have them wait upstairs. Maybe I can get them all drunk. Then it'll be easier.

SARA. I'll go up and tell them. You keep them company down here.

[*Sara leaves. Sokol sits at the table with the police.*]

SOKOL. Women's work. But how are you all? Did you enjoy lunch? Enkela, bring us another bottle.

POLICE. Lunch was excellent . . . It's been a long time since I ate such a good lunch . . . You have wonderful wine . . .

SOKOL. Cheers!

POLICE. Cheers!

SOKOL. How are things going in Belgrade, Mr. Zhut?

ZHUT. Fine, but I have to come here too often. There are so many problems.

DRAGAN. Over my dead body, will there be problems.

SOKOL. Oh, I see. How is your family, sir?

ZHUT. Good, good thanks.

SOKOL. Come on then, another toast!

POLICE. Cheers!

[*From the right-hand door, Mom appears. The police, Betim, and the guest with the leather coat are stunned when they see her.*]

MOM. Sokol, aren't you ashamed to tease your mother like this in her old age. How could you have put up a photo announcing that Zadja is dead. Zadja is getting married in a week. Oh, what man will take her? What great place will she go to? One day I'll marry too. That's what Dad said. Oh see, her friends have started to sing. Oh Sokol, where's your father? Where's Xhevdet? Why doesn't he come home? When he has a new wife here . . . It's shameful . . .

[*The police stand up.*]

ZHUT. What's this, Sokol?

DRAGAN. What's this, Sokol?

ZHUT. [*To Dragan.*] Shut up. Everyone sit down. Who's this? Is this your deceased mother?

SOKOL. Oh Mr. Zhut, don't be alarmed, please.

ZHUT. Hell, I'm not alarmed. I just want to know what the meaning of this is.

SOKOL. This is my aunt, my mother's twin sister. Look at the photo. They are identical. She suffers from dementia. That's why she's a bit confused.

MOM. Oh, shame on you. You put pictures up here too. Oh, oh, what's the world coming to? What was I saying? Where's Xhevdet?

SOKOL. Oh Aunty, go on, don't bother us. Go and sit with the guests. Xhevdet died 18 years ago. Go back upstairs.

MOM. You're calling me Aunty? Me, who raised you. Oh, what a disgrace. Shocking!

SOKOL. Do you even know what you're saying? You did raise me, Aunty, but go on now and stop disturbing the customers.

[*Sara enters.*]

SARA. Mom, come on, let's go upstairs.

SOKOL. Sara, take Aunty upstairs.

SARA. Aunty?! . . . Oh, of course. Come on upstairs, Aunty?! . . .

MOM. Hamide, is that you?

SOKOL. Sara, take Aunty upstairs.

SARA. Mom . . . Aunty . . .

SOKOL. She likes being called Mom. The poor thing had no children of her own. Sara always calls her Mom.

SARA. Excuse us, gentlemen. Come on, Mom, let's go. [*Sara leaves with her.*]

ZHUT. Now, Sokol, will you explain what the hell is going on?

SOKOL. Like I said, this is my aunt, my mother's twin sister. She has dementia. Today, my mother died, and it looks like my aunt has taken a turn for the worse. Twins grieve for each other more than others do. It's one of those strange phenomena. Did you see how she thinks I'm her son?!

NEBOJSHA. Yes, I did. In our village, there were once two twins and . . .

ZHUT. [*To Nebojsha.*] Shut up, idiot. Sokol, there's something going on. I'll be looking into it. But since I can't figure it out just now, I won't break up the mourning. We'll be back, and then we'll get to the bottom of it.

SOKOL. [*Calling after him.*] Inspector, there's nothing going on, I promise you. It was just my crazy aunt. What can I do?

DRAGAN. We'll be back.

[*The police exit.*]

SOKOL. Gentlemen, you didn't finish your lunch. Come back, please, come back.

GUEST. Excuse me, can I use the toilet?

SOKOL. Yes, it's over there.

BETIM. Listen, Sokol, the more you pander to them, the more they'll make you suffer. I've told you before, don't get too close.

[*Betim exits.*]

SOKOL. [*He calls after him.*] Sort yourself out first.

SOKOL. Ahmet, go upstairs and tell them to leave before the police come back and while that character is in the toilet. Quick. Oh, we're done for. Now they're going to come and imprison us all or kill us. Enkela, Meri, go and watch from the windows in case the police turn back. Is anybody coming?

MERI. No.

ENKELA. And I can't see anyone here either.

SOKOL. Enkela, if the spy with the dark glasses comes out of the toilet while party members are leaving, try to distract him. Slow him down.

ENKELA. Slow him down?

SOKOL. Slow him down.

MERI. I can do that too, Sokol.

SOKOL. Okay, if you need to, you can slow him down too.

MERI. I can do that.

[*Sara, Ahmet, and the participants enter through the upstairs door.*]

SARA. Have they gone?

SOKOL. Yes.

SARA. How did it go?

SOKOL. I hope to God they believed that fairytale about my aunt.

SARA. It's all fine. At least they didn't come upstairs.

SOKOL. I think Mom's dementia saved us.

PARTICIPANT 1. We give thanks to your mother. She merits the title, "Mother of the Nation."

SOKOL. Oh, that's enough. Get out of here as fast as you can because I'm done for. Hurry, before that guy comes out.

[*Meri slaps one of the participants. He speeds up.*]

MERI. Stupid idiot.

SOKOL. Mejremja, have you lost your mind? Hasn't today been bad enough?!

MERI. That was the producer who tricked me.

[*The participants exit. As they leave, the stranger returns from the bathroom, and looks curiously at the participants running off. Enkela gestures to Sokol, but he can't stop them.*]

SOKOL. Ah sir, as you can see the mourners have gone. They leave me alone in grief.

[*Gazi enters. He approaches the guest.*]

GAZI. Bujar, what are you doing here? Why didn't you get your passport from Sokol?

GUEST. But you told me, "*Sit at a table. Sokol will come with the passport.*"

SOKOL. Wait . . . so you aren't?!

GAZI. No way! I said, when you see Sokol, ask for the passport. He'll understand. And I told Sokol about you. Sokol, why didn't you give Bujar his passport? Didn't I tell you what he looked like? I said he had glasses, a leather jacket . . .

SOKOL. Oh, did you?! You never told me what he looked like. You just said, "*He'll come and tell you I sent him.*" Do you know how much trouble you caused me today?! Go on, get out of here. "*He has glasses, a leather jacket.*" Get out now. Quickly, out of my sight!

GAZI. Wait a minute, Sokol, don't get cross. Hold on, it's not my fault. Give me the passport, and then we'll go.

SOKOL. Get out of here, out. . .

[*Gazi and Bujar exit. The stage goes dark.*]

ACT II

Scene One

[*The same place. Sokol, Ahmet, Betim, and an old man are in the café. Sokol has his head bound up with a bandage.*]

BETIM. Oh, come on, Sokol, you get what you ask for. I told you so. There's no point. The more you grovel, the more you suffer. I warned you, so don't be surprised.

SOKOL. Phew! I made it. This is nothing compared to what could have happened. In the end, they believed that it was my aunt and not my mother, so things are all right. Gazi sorted out the documents. I registered my mother's death. I changed her identity card, so now she's my aunt. I paid a huge bribe, and that's that. For the rest of my life, I have to call her "Aunty" in front of strangers. I created a twin for my own mother.

AHMET. Don't worry about that, Sokol. They could have imprisoned you and never let you go. Did they beat you?

SOKOL. What kind of question is that? Don't you see my head? They beat me black and blue. But okay, as you say, they could have killed me. It would have been nothing to them. I was this close to the barber's razor.

BETIM. Prison is for real men, Ahmet. They held me for five years, and I've never forgotten it. They don't lock up just anyone, and not one of their own.

SOKOL. Let people say what they want. God knows what's in my heart.

AHMET. They have no shame. They'll be back tomorrow. They'll eat, drink, and kid around with Sokol like brothers.

BETIM. But Sokol pandered to them. Do they ever ask me to serve them? No. Why? Because I never even look at them.

[*From the customer door Xhevdet enters with a journalist.*]

XHEVDET. Dad, this is an American journalist. She's come to interview you.

SOKOL. How on earth can we communicate? Don't be stupid.

XHEVDET. I'll translate.

SOKOL. Alright, alright. [*Sokol sits at a table with the journalist and Xhevdet. The journalist speaks English. Xhevdet translates with mistakes.*] Good day.

JOURNALIST. Miredita. [*She says "hello" in Albanian.*]

SOKOL. Wow, she speaks Albanian.

GAZI. She knows a little.

JOURNALIST. So, you're from here, aren't you?

XHEVDET. She said, are you from here?

SOKOL. Yes, of course! I've been here for 50 years. My father was born here and all my ancestors. I've done business in Romania and Hungary, and now I'm married to Sara, and at some point, I returned to run this café.

XHEVDET. He say, yes, how, no? He 50 years here, his father here and all.

JOURNALIST. His father is alive?

XHEVDET. No, no. His father alive here, before.

SOKOL. What did she say?

XHEVDET. [*To Sokol.*] Nothing, be quiet, don't worry. [*To the journalist.*] He sell in Rumania, Hungaria. He marry my mother, Sara, in Hungaria. He come back here, job in caffe. You look.

JOURNALIST. I understand. Do you know people around here?

XHEVDET. She said, do you know people around here?

SOKOL. Of course, I know everyone, and everyone knows me, even the children, because my dad also ran this café. Ask anyone you want, and they'll all know Sokol.

XHEVDET. Dad, don't talk so fast because I can't keep up with the translation. It's not like speaking Albanian.

SOKOL. Okay, okay.

XHEVDET. She know everybody. Everybody she know. His father work . . . ah, how to say it . . .work here in caffe. And . . . question everybody, know my father, Sokol.

JOURNALIST. I understand, I understand. That's good. Do you know any of the guerrilla fighters?

XHEVDET. Gerilla? What is gerilla?

JOURNALIST. Guerrilla. The people who fight in the mountains.

XHEVDET. Yeah, yeah. She said. Do you know the people fighting on the mountains?

SOKOL. No, I swear I don't know anything about them. I mind my own business. I work in a café just to make a living. I don't know any of them.

XHEVDET. If you cut him, he don't know. He took his job, his job in caffe, to make money. She don't know everybody.

JOURNALIST. But he just said that he does know everybody around here.

XHEVDET. She says, you just said you know everyone. How come now you say you don't know anyone.

SOKOL. I know my own age group, but not these young guys. But what was I saying . . . It has become dangerous. Look at what the police did to me. Just for fun. They came to the café and said, "*Sokol, come with us,*" and look what happened. I help them as much as I can. I help. Look, I've taken in that old man who's fled the war zone. I don't have enough room here for myself and my family, but I'm sensitive. I have a sensitive heart.

XHEVDET. Slower dad, don't talk so fast. He say, he know old, but no boys, young. Police, my father . . . POW-POW.

SOKOL. POW-POW. They hit me as hard as they could.

JOURNALIST. Really? I'm sorry to hear that.

XHEVDET. They come and take him, just for fun. This old man is refugee. She stay here. We don't have place, but this is his heart.

JOURNALIST. That's kind of you.

[*Sara enters.*]

SARA. Hello!

SOKOL. This is my wife, Sara. She was a ballerina.

XHEVDET. This is my mother, ballerina.

JOURNALIST. Oh, really?

SARA. Yes, but I don't do ballet now. You know, you can't do ballet here. There are no studios, nothing. You can see what that's done to my body because I haven't exercised for ages.

XHEVDET. She is no now ballerina. She say, we don't have . . . place for ballet. She is . . .

[*He gestures to show that she is fat.*]

JOURNALIST. No, on the contrary, you look beautiful.

XHEVDET. She says, you are beautiful.

SARA. Oh, thank you. Why have you come to see us?

XHEVDET. Why we have you . . . friend today?

JOURNALIST. I would like to contact the guerrilla fighters. Does she know anything about them?

XHEVDET. She asks, do you know any of the men who are fighting?

SOKOL. No. Sara knows nothing. She is here with me all day in the café . . .

SARA. I could say something if, of course, you keep it secret.

XHEVDET. She will say something. You don't tell everybody.

JOURNALIST. Yes, sure. Thank you very much.

SOKOL. [*Aside.*] What?! Sara wants to show off. [*To Xhevdet.*] Tell this journalist that Sara knows nothing. She's just showing off.

XHEVDET. I can't do anything. She understood.

SOKOL. She understood?! Why are you translating?!

SARA. Please come with me.

[*Sara, the journalist, and Xhevdet approach the old refugee, who is sitting alone at a table. They motion for him to go through the door that leads upstairs. All three follow, but Sokol stops Sara.*]

SOKOL. Sara, have you gone crazy? What ties do you have to those people?

SARA. Sokol, I'll tell you later. Don't interrupt me.

SOKOL. No, not later. Tell me what ties you have to them. Why are you troubling that poor old man?

SARA. He isn't an old man. He's a young man in the armed resistance, and he needs to stay here for a while.

SOKOL. He's a young man?! That old refugee?!

SARA. He's in disguise.

SOKOL. You're mad! He's going to get us killed.

SARA. No one will recognize him. See, even you couldn't tell. Sokol, please don't panic. I'll just be upstairs for a minute.

SOKOL. How dare you bring that man here without my knowledge. You think you're so clever. You and that escapade with the congress, and now with the "armed resistance." Wasn't my beating bad enough? Now you want them to kill me?

SARA. They won't kill you. Don't be stupid. Look at you shouting. Everyone will hear. Calm down. No one will know. He'll stay for a little while and then leave. Now let me go before anyone notices.

[*Sara goes.*]

SOKOL. Crazy woman. [*Sokol looks out the door to see if anyone is coming. Enkela enters from the kitchen and embraces him.*] Ah, cut it out. You're making me dizzy.

ENKELA. Oh, Sokol, there's no need to be frightened. No harm can come to you while you're in my arms. Just stay here for a moment. Love me a little, darling.

SOKOL. Ahmet and Betim are here. They'll see us. Betim's just waiting for something to gossip about.

ENKELA. Don't mind what that idiot says.

SOKOL. Enkela, I'm a family man.

ENKELA. Oh, you don't know how much I love you. You don't know what happened to me today.

SOKOL. I know, my love, but I'm so tired right now.

ENKELA. Do you know what happened to me?

SOKOL. I know that you love me.

ENKELA. Oh, Sokol, I was supposed to be a bride today, but instead something awful happened. I was supposed to get a ring, but instead I found out that my boyfriend is getting married. Oh, I'm so unlucky. It gets even worse. He's marrying someone else. Without telling me. Come on, let's run away somewhere together.

SOKOL. Oh Enkela, you'll find your soulmate. You're just looking in the wrong place. Look at Betim. He's young. He's not a bad chap. Bring him some raki. Say something sweet to him.

ENKELA. Betim?! That idiot?! Sokol, don't break my heart. You Kosovars are such fuck-ups.

AHMET. Sokol, what's going on?

SOKOL. Oh, Enkela was straightening my tie. [*To Enkela.*] Go to Betim, go.

[*Enkela goes over to Betim with the raki.*]

BETIM. Enkela, you look so pretty today.

ENKELA. You think so?! Look at my skin, how soft and smooth it is.

BETIM. Yes. Like a seashell.

ENKELA. And this skin . . . you . . . will never touch it.

[*Enkela moves away. Betim quickly downs his raki and exits angrily.*]

BETIM. Spoiled brat! Sokol, control your waitresses.

SOKOL. Enkela, Enkela, you're going to chase all my customers away. Ahmet, can you go outside and see if the police are coming?

AHMET. Why, what's going on? Don't be frightened, Sokol. They've finished with you.

SOKOL. Don't ask me now. I'll tell you later.

[*Ahmet leaves.*]

Scene Two

[*In the police station. Dragan and Nebojsha are sitting at a table playing cards and drinking raki. Zhut enters with a suitcase.*]

ZHUT. Long live our great country!

NEBOJSHA, DRAGAN. Hooray! [*They get to their feet and salute.*] Long live our country!

ZHUT. What's this?

DRAGAN. Nothing sir, we didn't know you were coming!

ZHUT. You didn't know. So that means you only work while I'm here. Where is your loyalty to the country that sustains you? Where is your patriotism?

DRAGAN. We are loyal to the country.

ZHUT. Shut up you idiot. You forget that I'm your boss.

NEBOJSHA, DRAGAN. No, we haven't forgotten.

ZHUT. Well, take this suitcase then.

DRAGAN. Nebojsha, take the gentleman's suitcase.

[*Nebojsha takes the case, and Zhut sits.*]

ZHUT. You demonstrate your loyalty with raki and cards. I have to do your work for you.

DRAGAN. But we wanted . . .

ZHUT. Shut up, idiot. I didn't ask you anything. You couldn't capture a fistful of terrorists.

NEBOJSHA. We are trying.

ZHUT. You are trying?! It's people who try like you do that brought this crisis on. Go out and investigate right now. In the streets, the cafés, wherever you spot suspicious people and report back to me immediately. Then I'll decide what to do.

NEBOJSHA, DRAGAN. As you wish, sir.

[*Dragan and Nebojsha push off.*]

ZHUT. Wait, wait, where are you going?! Do you know why I came here?

DRAGAN. Yes, sir. You came to catch terrorists.

ZHUT. No. You?

NEBOJSHA. You came to kill terrorists.

ZHUT. No. I came to "celebrate my girlfriend's birthday." Do you get it?

NEBOJSHA. Yes, why not. That's great.

ZHUT. No, you idiot. I came for the terrorists, but only you need to know it. To anyone else, "I've come to celebrate my girlfriend's birthday." Later the truth will come out. Get it?

NEBOJSHA. Ah, now I understand. You're so clever, sir.

DRAGAN. Really, sir, you're so clever. I'm proud that our country has people of such brilliance.

ZHUT. Now, get going.

[*Dragan and Nebojsha exit.*]

Scene Three

[*In the café. Sara, the journalist, Xhevdet, and the man in disguise enter from the kitchen.*]

SARA. Please come again

XHEVDET. Come again.

JOURNALIST. Thank you. Good luck to you.

XHEVDET. She says, thank you. She wishes you good luck.

MAN IN DISGUISE. And to you too.

XHEVDET. And you, and you.

JOURNALIST. Bye bye.

SARA. Bye bye.

MAN IN DISGUISE. Bye bye.

SOKOL. Oh, Bye bye.

[*Nebojsha and Dragan enter. Sara and the man in disguise slip into the kitchen.*]

SOKOL. How are you, Dragan? How are things, Nebojsha?

DRAGAN. [*To the journalist.*] Just a moment, madam.

XHEVDET. She say, one moment.

JOURNALIST. Yes, certainly.

XHEVDET. Yes, yes, she says. How can I help you?

DRAGAN. Your documents please.

XHEVDET. Document.

JOURNALIST. Yes, of course.

XHEVDET. Here are her documents.

DRAGAN. Yes, I can see. I can see. What are you doing here?

XHEVDET. She's a journalist.

DRAGAN. I didn't ask you. I want to hear it from her.

XHEVDET. As you wish her. What you do here?

JOURNALIST. I'm a journalist.

XHEVDET. She says she's a journalist. She said so earlier. Ask anyone else if you don't believe her.

DRAGAN. Search her.

[*Nebojsha searches the journalist.*]

DRAGAN. Okay, its fine. Our apologies, madam, but we have to enforce the law.

XHEVDET. She say, I'm sorry, but this country is law . . . order . . .

JOURNALIST. I understand, I understand. It's OK.

[*The journalist and Xhevdet exit. The police sit down.*]

SOKOL. How are you? You look busy, huh? What would you like to drink?

NEBOJSHA. Yes, a bit busy. Two beers.

SOKOL. Coming up.

DRAGAN. Sokol, what was that American doing here?

SOKOL. Who?! Oh, the journalist. Oh, I don't know, Xhevdet has learned English on his computer, and she asked him to help do an interview with Sara.

DRAGAN. With Sara? But why?!

[*Sara enters.*]

SARA. Good day, how are you, gentlemen? You look well.

POLICE. Good, thanks. You look well too.

SOKOL. As I was telling you, Sara was a ballerina, you know, and this journalist was interviewing her about the ballet here, asking about studios and what sort of work is done.

SARA. Ah, yes. Believe me, gentlemen, as soon as she saw me, she knew I had been a ballerina. She was very cultured.

NEBOJSHA. She came all the way from America for ballet. Doesn't she have anything better to do?

SARA. But it's worth it, sir. Ballet is worth the effort.

[*Ahmet rushes in from outside without noticing the police. Meri enters from the kitchen and begins to serve.*]

AHMET. Sokol, don't worry, there are no police out there.

SOKOL. Ah, Ahmet, that's okay, Dragan and Nebojsha are here.

DRAGAN. What's going on? Was that some kind of warning?! Sokol, is something going on . . .

SOKOL. Oh Dragan, I've had such a day. A guy came here and parked his car in front of the café, blocking the entrance. I told Ahmet, *"Go and find Dragan and Nebojsha. Ask them to come and sort it out."*

[*Ahmet sneaks outside.*]

DRAGAN. Where is the car? I'll have it removed immediately. Who would dare break the law like that?

SOKOL. No, no need, it's all resolved. Just after Ahmet left to find you, he drove off. Do you want some snacks with your beer?

DRAGAN. No, we don't have time.

NEBOJSHA. No, we can't be late.

[*The police drink their beers quickly and leave.*]

SOKOL. [*After them.*] Good day. [*To the others.*] Look how they're behaving. I'm sure they've realized something's going on.

SARA. Sokol, don't panic. They don't know. If they did, they would have arrested us or searched us.

SOKOL. You're so cool and calm about this. Didn't you see how they watched our every movement, like traffic cops.

SARA. I said I'd explain later.

SOKOL. No, not later, now.

[*The sound of knocking from above.*]

SARA. Mom!

SOKOL. Oh, take it easy, Mom, or the roof'll come down.

SARA. Mom is coming.

[*She enters.*]

MOM. Sara, why are you being so selfish? You didn't dance with me today or play any music. You should be ashamed.

SARA. Let's go up, Mom.

MOM. No, don't ask me. There are just two weeks to Selman's wedding, and I'm not ready. That old man you brought me won't leave me alone. Let him go back to his own house. He's hammering night and day, BANG-BANG, BANG-BANG. I can't sleep.

SARA. Come on, let's go.

[*Sara takes Mom upstairs.*]

Scene Four

[*Mom's room. Sara and Mom enter.*]

SARA. Mom, sit down and don't cause any trouble. I'm a bit busy. We'll practice ballet later.

MOM. You should be ashamed. I wait for you all day. You're like a stranger.

SARA. But what can I do? I have my work.

MOM. Your work is so important, is it?

SARA. Please be quiet and don't come down to the café.

MOM. Why shouldn't I go down? It's my husband's café. Xhevdet left it to me. If you don't like it, you should go away.

SARA. I didn't mean it like that, Mom. You can't go down because there are strangers around right now, and they might make fun of you.

MOM. Why would they make fun of me? I'm not naked, and I'm not eating.

[*Drita enters.*]

DRITA. Sara, I'm so glad I found you. Where is that friend of yours?

MOM. Eh, she came again. Did you come to steal more clothes? If it's the last thing I do, I won't let you.

SARA. No, Mom, this is my friend, Drita. Which friend are you talking about?

DRITA. Yes, *"Which friend are you talking about?"* Sara, please, I don't have much time. I've come about "the old refugee."

SARA. Aha. He's in the other room, busy with something. He just did an interview with an American journalist.

DRITA. A journalist?! Oh, God. I told him not to speak to any journalists. It's too dangerous.

SARA. She was very nice, very well-meaning.

DRITA. Please go and get him.

[*Sara leaves. Drita wanders around the room.*]

MOM. Hey, are you waiting for me to fall asleep so you can steal from me? You'll do it over my dead body.

DRITA. Mom, I'm very nervous. Please don't upset me.

MOM. Who cares! You won't get away with it. I'll stay here all day and night without budging. I'm not closing my eyes. Enough is enough.

DRITA. Oh Mom, I didn't come here to steal from you. I'm Sara's friend. Why don't you trust me? I have business here.

MOM. I don't trust anyone anymore. I told you, it's no use talking . . . Hey, are you Hamide? Hamide, my sister? What are you wearing? I hardly recognized you. How is your husband and your children?

DRITA. Oh, I don't have a husband or children.

MOM. Why, did they die?

DRITA. Oh . . .

[*Sara and the man in disguise enter.*]

MAN IN DISGUISE. What's going on, Drita?

DRITA. What do you mean, what's going on? I came to see how you're doing, and I found out you've been talking to a journalist. You know the rules. We don't talk to journalists.

MAN IN DISGUISE. I didn't use my real name.

DRITA. That doesn't matter. We cannot have any contact with the media.

MAN IN DISGUISE. Look, I know the rules, but . . .

DRITA. Okay, okay. End of conversation.

MOM. Phooey, phooey, this place is a madhouse.

DRITA. Sara, please can you take the old woman away?

SARA. Yes, of course. Mom, let's go to Xhevdet's room. You wait for me there, and I'll come, and we'll do some ballet.

MOM. What do you mean? If I leave, she'll steal all my things!

SARA. She won't steal them. I'll be here.

[*Sara and the Mom exit.*]

DRITA. Look, I don't have much time. [*Drita crosses her legs uncomfortably.*]

MAN IN DISGUISE. I know, I know.

DRITA. Did you do what you came to do?

MAN IN DISGUISE. Not quite.

[*Enter Sara.*]

DRITA. Sara, I will speak but once about the operation we are engaged in.

SARA. There's something else you need to tell me?

DRITA. Now listen. We'll have to let Sokol know.

SARA. Okay.

DRITA. In keeping with my doctrine and my duty, but now I really mean it. We really must discuss this only once.

SARA. Okay, okay, but why are you wriggling so much?

DRITA. I can say it only once, because . . . I have to go to the bathroom!

SARA. Oh Drita, why didn't you tell me? Go on, and then we can really talk.

DRITA. I tried to go, but it was occupied.

SARA. Come on, let's go. Then we'll talk.

[*They exit.*]

Scene Five

[*In the café. Meri throws herself into Sokol's arms.*]

MERI. Sokol, darling, Sara's gone. Please God, may she never return. What are we waiting for? Let's get married. Let's escape this prison and live life as it should be lived . . .

SOKOL. Meri, I'm tired. Let's talk about it another time.

MERI. Can't you see that Sara doesn't care for you? She spends all her time with Drita, and journalists, and those sorts.

SOKOL. What can I do? She's my wife. I can't control who she spends time with.

MERI. She puts you in danger, without consulting you at all. Wasn't what the police did enough? You'd be better off with me. I wouldn't put you in danger, just here, in my heart.

SOKOL. She wants to help people. Her heart's in the right place. I can't do anything about it. But, she *has* put me in danger. I won't let it happen again.

MERI. You're right. You can't do anything about it. So why bother with that old thing? Let's go abroad. Let's get rich and famous. I'll be your lover and headline at the largest restaurant in the world, and you'll be Robert De Niro. Everyone will be dazzled by my evening gowns. I'll sing nothing but love songs and be thinking of no one but you.

SOKOL. Wake up, Meri. There's no way that could happen.

MERI. But I was always thinking of you – in every song I sang.

SOKOL. Oh, Meri, I'm really so busy today.

MERI. Darling Sokol, sharpen your claws, make me your prey.

SOKOL. My claws have been clipped. I can't do it anymore!

MERI. Can't do it?! Take off your shirt, and let's go inside and get comfortable!

SOKOL. No, no, Meri, I meant I can't do my job. My shirt's fine, don't worry. [*From the right-hand door, Drita enters, and her knock interrupts their embrace.*] Oh sorry, Drita, Meri isn't feeling well.

MERI. I was wiping Sokol's shirt. He got it dirty.

SOKOL. Yes, she was cleaning my shirt. I don't know how it got so dirty, like everything else around here.

MERI. I think I've got it out.

SOKOL. Yes, yes, leave it, it's gone.

DRITA. Sokol, I need to tell you something important. Let's wait for Sara. Sara! Sara! [*Sara comes down, and Enkela follows.*] I will say this only once, in keeping with my doctrine and my duty. The situation is dire, and it's getting worse by the day. Now listen. Zhut, an inspector from Belgrade, is coming today to celebrate his girlfriend's birthday. Doesn't he usually eat here when he's in town?

SOKOL. Yes.

DRITA. Then you must present him with a cake for her.

SOKOL. A cake? Why a cake?

DRITA. A cake-bomb, prepared by my friend, whom you've sheltered as a refugee.

SOKOL. A cake-bomb?! Sara, will you please explain what's happening, or should I wait for a bomb to explode in my head?! Sorry, Drita, but no, I won't go along with this.

SARA. Sorry, Drita. [*Sara takes Sokol to one side.*] Now that we've gotten into this, we can't back out of it.

SOKOL. You can't back out of it, but I can back out very easily. No. Haven't you noticed how they spy on us, how they questioned that journalist? Do you want to blow the house with everyone in it sky-high? And where would we go afterwards?!

SARA. We won't get blown up. It won't explode until after they leave. There won't be any evidence left to show whether the bomb was in the cake or not.

SOKOL. They will figure it out. Of course, they will!

SARA. If we're in danger, we'll go to my family in Hungary.

SOKOL. If we're in danger! Doesn't this already seem like danger?

SARA. Yes, it's a bit dangerous, but not as bad as you think.

SOKOL. You want to blow up a policeman, and you want to do it with a cake. And you think this is *"a bit dangerous?"*

SARA. I told you already. The bomb will explode later. How will anyone guess it was in the cake when they'll all be turned to dust?

SOKOL. Dust? Are you crazy? You sound like a bomb expert. You think they won't work out where the bomb came from? They're the police, dear. They'll work it out.

SARA. We'll go to my family before they do.

SOKOL. How will we go? They'll stop us at the border.

SARA. We'll leave the house for a while. Then Gazi can sort out some passports so we can escape.

SOKOL. Where will we stay until then?

SARA. Drita will find us a place.

SOKOL. No.

SARA. No?! Think of the future, darling. Tomorrow, the day after tomorrow, our countrymen will still be here. How will we survive? Who will back the hotel?

SOKOL. When I save enough money, I'll back it myself.

SARA. But if you don't take any risks for the people, who will come to stay? No one! Who will give us a permit to build it? No one! Think about it, dear.

SOKOL. It's too great a risk.

SARA. We'll do it somehow.

SOKOL. We can't do it.

SARA. Believe me when I say, we'll get through this. Come with me. [*Sara takes Sokol by the hand. She approaches Drita.*] Drita, everything is arranged.

SOKOL. Arranged? Fine, fine, alright. But on the condition that the bomb explodes far away from the café.

DRITA. Of course. You have the phone. Any problems, call me at the same number, me or my friend here. And one more thing. Listen carefully. You must tell Gazi that once the operation has been concluded, he must get our man out of the country. I wish you success.

[*Drita exits.*]

SOKOL. Oh God, oh God, help me! What to do with the money? Enkela, Meri, be careful. Behave as if nothing has happened. [*Xhevdet enters.*] Xhevdet, go quickly and find Gazi, tell him that it's an emergency.

XHEVDET. Gazi just passed by. Didn't you see him?

SOKOL. A stroke of luck! Go find him. Quick.

SARA. Tell him not to delay. I'm going up to tell the bombmaker that everything is arranged.

[*Xhevdet exits. Sara goes upstairs. Enkela and Meri go into the kitchen.*]

SOKOL. Everything is arranged. Nothing was ever arranged so well, thanks to my lovely wife.

[*About 35 guests enter, dressed formally.*]

CUSTOMER. Good day.

SOKOL. Good day. How can I help you? Please take a seat.

CUSTOMER. No, thank you. We've come for something else.

SOKOL. How can I help?

CUSTOMER. Can you make me a wedding cake for later today?

SOKOL. Ah, a cake. Yes, why not? Come in the afternoon, and we'll have it waiting for you.

CUSTOMER. Thank you.

[*As the customer leaves, Enkela enters and sees him leaving.*]

ENKELA. Sokol, what did he want here? Was he looking for me?

SOKOL. No, he came to order a wedding cake.

ENKELA. That means there's no hope!

SOKOL. What's wrong?

ENKELA. Sokol, that was my lover, and he's getting married today. [*She cries and embraces Sokol.*] Oh Sokol, I've lost all hope. Listen to my heart beating. Come on, let's go away and leave these idiots in Kosovo.

SOKOL. I'd love to if it were that easy. Things will get better, my dear, don't be sad.

ENKELA. I'll show him who I am. He'll remember me forever.

SOKOL. He wasn't very special. Someone better will make it up to you.

ENKELA. You're the only one for me. All I need is you to comfort me.

SOKOL. Enkela, my dear, don't be a baby. Can't you see the situation we're in?

ENKELA. How can a little love hurt?

SOKOL. Let's get through these hard times, and then we can comfort each other. Now let me go . . .

ENKELA. I don't ever want to let you go. Every minute without you seems like eternity. I can't go on without my arms around you, not till I survive this tragedy.

SOKOL. Enkela, my dear, let me go.

ENKELA. I can't, Sokol. I can't.

[*Xhevdet enters with Gazi, worn out from running.*]

XHEVDET. I just managed to find him. I'm so exhausted. Gazi, you walk so fast. Didn't you hear me running after you, shouting, *"Gazi, Gazi."*

SOKOL. Enough Xhevdet, that doesn't matter. Come inside quickly.

GAZI. Sokol, what do you need?

SOKOL. Gazi, we need your help. Wait while I call Sara. Sara! Sara! Come down. Gazi is here.

[*Sara comes down*.]

GAZI. Talk, Sokol.

SOKOL. Gazi, I've never asked you for anything, but today, I'm in big trouble. Can you do something for me?

GAZI. I'll do it if I can. Tell me.

SOKOL. We have a guest here that we need to transport.

GAZI. To transport how?

SARA. By you getting him a passport or sneaking him across the border.

GAZI. It will be a bit difficult.

SOKOL. I know, and you'll need to do it fast.

SARA. Now or never.

GAZI. But when do I need to move him?

SOKOL. Today.

GAZI. Today? But why didn't you tell me earlier?

SOKOL. I didn't know earlier.

SARA. That's how it is, Gazi. We've never asked you to help us before. We'll be so grateful.

GAZI. Okay, I'll try. It will be very difficult, but . . . we'll see.

SOKOL. Not we'll see. You need to make it happen.

GAZI. Okay, Sokol, that's what I meant. Now, I'm going. When I've arranged it, I'll be back.

SOKOL. As fast as you can.

[*Gazi starts to exit. Nebojsha and Dragan enter.*]

GAZI. Nebojsha, I need to talk to you.

[*Nebojsha nods at Dragan.*]

NEBOJSHA. I haven't got any time. We're here officially.

GAZI. Okay, let's catch up later.

[*Gazi exits.*]

SOKOL. Welcome, gentlemen. What would you like to drink?

DRAGAN. Sokol, we don't want any drinks. We need to see your guest, that "refugee." We need to talk to him.

SOKOL. Oh, he isn't here. I think he left.

SARA. Yes, yes, he left.

DRAGAN. Where did he go?

SARA. He didn't say, I think off to some relatives.

DRAGAN. Let's go and search upstairs!

SOKOL. But why are you doing a search? There's no one there except Mom . . . my aunt. She's a bit sick, and maybe she'll . . .

DRAGAN. Sokol, get on with your work.

SOKOL. Alright, alright, whatever you want.

[*Dragan and Nebojsha go through the door that leads upstairs.*]

SOKOL. Now we've had it. Are you satisfied, my darling activist?

SARA. No jokes, Sokol.

SOKOL. I wasn't joking. We've had it.

SARA. But what should we do?

SOKOL. I don't know what to do. I can't think.

SARA. Take out your phone.

SOKOL. Ah yes, the telephone. [*He takes out the phone.*] Nightingale on the verandah, nightingale on the verandah. The police have gone upstairs. Hide somewhere if you can, or all of us are through. [*To Sara.*] They're getting close. They'll catch him, and then they'll take us. They'll kill us.

SARA. Let go of the negative thoughts. Pray to God. He'll help us.

SOKOL. No, Drita will help us. She'll say it only once, and it will all be sorted out, in keeping with her doctrine and her duty.

SARA. He'll get away somehow. He's experienced.

SOKOL. I had a business. I had the hotel and educating Xhevdet. Oh Xhevdet, I only hope he survives.

Scene Six

[*Mom's room. Mom is lying on the bed, reading the newspaper.*]

MOM. Look, look, that old man died! "*Today, it is the tenth year of mourning and grief since our unforgettable husband, father, grandfather, father-in-law, brother, beloved, and uncle died.*" Those ten years went so fast. It seems like just yesterday when I last saw him. Look, look what they wrote: "*How to explain to young Qendresa, who misses her grandfather's loving hugs. How to accept the fate that is ahead of us.*" Oh, you wretch, you wretch! See what they wrote. [*She starts to cry.*] "*You were my wise dad, my dignified husband, my wonderful father-in-law, my laughing grandfather, beloved by all.*" Oh God, oh God, thank you. "*It was a gloomy day, overcast, the day when you left us forever. Oh death, why did you take our friend at the time when we needed him most. Death, you are so cruel to have taken our friend.*" How they must have loved him. How they loved you, you wretch, you wretch. I can't bear it any more. Look what they wrote: "*May the earth of Kosovo be soft, martyr. With a great longing, that keeps growing, we remember you. Your wife, Sevdija; sons, Remzi, Xhemal, Sefedin, Shefqet; daughters, Minirja and Hajrija; daughters-in-law . . .*" and so on. Their wives didn't really care. Their husbands put their names there. [*Dragan and Nebojsha enter.*] Come on, come on, you're the last thing I need now.

DRAGAN. Grandma, we're just doing our job. Don't be frightened.

MOM. No, you can't frighten this grandma. Why should I be scared? They stole from me. I wasn't the one who stole. I never killed anyone. This grandma has no reason to be frightened. Oh, how they stole from the house of my brother once. All the gold, the bride, the television, everything in the house . . .

DRAGAN. Grandma, where is that refugee who's staying with you?

MOM. Refu-what?

NEBOJSHA. The old man who had fled the war.

MOM. That old man with the long beard and moustache, who stopped me from doing ballet?

DRAGAN. Yes, yes, him.

MOM. Why, what did he do?

NEBOJSHA. We need him for something.

MOM. Ah, that old man. There's no point looking for him. He died. Look at the newspaper. They reported it so well. I cried, I cried. Oh, oh, it broke my heart.

DRAGAN. Which one was he?

MOM. There, this one, do you see? He would never let me be. He only caused me pain, the wretch.

NEBOJSHA. It's him. Just like him.

DRAGAN. Shut up, don't talk rubbish.

NEBOJSHA. Why, doesn't it look like him?

DRAGAN. Look at the date of death, idiot. It was ten years ago. Grandma, who told you to tell us he had died?

MOM. Don't you see? Don't you believe me? Do you think I'm stupid? [*The police search the bedroom.*] What?! Did you come to steal my clothes? Why are you all so obsessed with my clothes? Sara, Sara. No, she isn't coming. She leaves her mom all alone, and people come to steal.

DRAGAN. Grandma, don't shout. We're not stealing anything. We're just searching.

MOM. Why are you searching my house? Go to your own homes. Search them as much as you want. I know, I know, Sara sent you. *"Go, take my mom's slacks. She's got too many."* That's all very well, but a stranger won't launder and care for my clothes.

NEBOJSHA. Grandma, we don't need your slacks.

MOM. Go off then. Why are you still here?

DRAGAN. There, we're going now. He isn't here. Let's search the other rooms.

NEBOJSHA. Perhaps he's hidden under the old woman's bed?

DRAGAN. Shut up, idiot. Where could a person hide in that tiny space?! Where?! Let's go.

[*The police exit.*]

MOM. Oh, Hamide, oh sister, look. Whoever wants to can come right into my home and wander around. My home has become a bazaar.

Scene Seven

[*The police go downstairs to the café. They search under the chairs and under the tables.*]

DRAGAN. So, he's gone.

SOKOL, SARA. Yes, he's gone. We told you.

DRAGAN. But I sense he is somewhere nearby. We'll find him.

SOKOL. No, he isn't. If he were, I would have told you.

DRAGAN. Where do his relatives live?

SARA. He didn't say.

DRAGAN. Okay, let's go.

[*The police leave.*]

SOKOL. Thank God, we escaped. I wonder where he hid?

SARA. Let's go up and see where he is.

[*Enkela and Meri enter from the door behind the bar.*]

ENKELA. Sokol, did we escape?

SOKOL. For the moment, yes.

MERI. Where is he?

SOKOL. We don't know. Let's go upstairs to see where he hid. Come on.

[*They all exit and return after a while.*]

SOKOL. It looks like he got away.

SARA. But what happened with the cake?

SOKOL. Who knows?

SARA. Did you check the toilet?

SOKOL. Yes, but he wasn't there. He wasn't in any of the wardrobes.

SARA. And the attic? Did you check the attic?

ENKELA. Yes, yes, I went up to the attic. He wasn't there.

SARA. Maybe he's in the kitchen, in the fridge, and now he can't get out?

MERI. I checked the kitchen but not the fridge. I didn't think of that.

SARA. What?! Then he must still be in there.

[*They all scream and set off for the kitchen. The young man in disguise descends, bumps into the others. His beard is falling off and his face has lines on it – the imprint of wire.*]

SARA. Hey, where were you? Are you okay?

MAN IN DISGUISE. I escaped. You're all okay?

SARA. Yes, we made it, too.

SOKOL. For now, yes. Where did you hide?

MAN IN DISGUISE. Do you have to ask? I slid under the old woman's bed while she was away. When the police came, she lay down, and then her weight and the wires of the bed squashed me. After the police left, I could barely move.

SARA. Oh God, I'm sorry about my mother, but you know what she's like. What can we do?

MAN IN DISGUISE. It's fine. She saved me. When the police saw her lying down, they wouldn't look under the bed.

SOKOL. That's just like her. She's lucky when it counts.

MAN IN DISGUISE. Oh well. I've taken care of the cake. Now I have to make my getaway.

SARA. We spoke to Gazi. He should be here soon to get you out.

[*Gazi enters.*]

GAZI. Sokol, I'm ready.

SOKOL. Here's Gazi. I'm so glad you're here. This is the guy we told you about.

MAN IN DISGUISE. So, we can go?

GAZI. Yes.

MAN IN DISGUISE. Goodbye and good luck.

SARA. You too.

SOKOL. Safe journey. [*Gazi and the man exit.*] Now we're in great danger.

SARA. Don't you see how well things are going?

[*Betim enters and sits down.*]

BETIM. Oh Sokol, I think you'd report for work on your dying day.

SOKOL. There's always work to be done, Betim, until the bitter end.

BETIM. Don't you comprehend the situation?

SOKOL. Life doesn't stop because of a situation. [*Dragan, Nebojsha, and Zhut enter, and sit somewhere.*] Oh, good day, Mr. Zhut. Are you tired? How was your trip?

ZHUT. Fine, thank you.

SARA. Oh sir, we're honored to have you here.

ZHUT. How could I not come, when there is such a beautiful woman to wait on us.

SARA. Oh sir, you're so charming. What can I get you to drink, on the house of course?

ZHUT. Nothing, thank you.

SOKOL. No, Mr. Zhut, we insist. What would you like?

ZHUT. Alright, a bottle of wine.

SARA. Meri, some wine for the guests.

SOKOL. So, Mr. Zhut, what good news has brought you here? You look very happy to me.

SARA. You look snazzy.

SOKOL. I know, I know.

ZHUT. Sokol, don't embarrass me in front of the ladies. But I suppose it doesn't matter, I'll tell you. It's my girlfriend's birthday today, so I wanted to come to celebrate.

SARA. You're so thoughtful.

SOKOL. Sara, let's give the gentleman a cake for his lady. That kind of love is rare.

SARA. Yes, why not?

ZHUT. Please don't go to any trouble.

SARA. It's no trouble at all. We'll get it ready.

ZHUT. Thank you very much.

[*The American journalist enters.*]

SOKOL. Ah, here is that journalist. Sara, your friend's here. Xhevdet, come down. [*Xhevdet descends. The journalist, Xhevdet, Sara, and Sokol sit together at the table.*] Mr. Zhut, this journalist has come to do an interview with Sara, about having been a ballerina. You know, women's stuff.

ZHUT. Very good. [*To one side.*] Is this journalist the one you searched?

DRAGAN. [*To one side.*] Yes. We checked her out. Her documents were in order.

ZHUT. [*To one side.*] But did she say why she came?

NEBOJSHA. [*To one side.*] Yes, Sokol told you. She came to do an interview with Sokol's wife.

ZHUT. [*To one side.*] And you believed that?! What idiots you are.

DRAGAN. [*To one side.*] But we didn't find anything suspicious.

ZHUT. [*To one side.*] She didn't come to do us any good! Sokol and his wife are up to something. But we'll find them out. We'll catch them like mice in a trap. How did Sokol know why I'd come?

DRAGAN. [*To one side.*] But you told us to spread the rumor that you'd come for your girlfriend's birthday. He must have heard it in town.

ZHUT. [*To one side.*] Well, everything's under control. And I can handle a cake.

SOKOL. [*To one side.*] Tell this journalist that she has come at a bad time.

XHEVDET. [*To one side.*] She say, you come bad moment.

SOKOL. [*To one side.*] Now that the police have seen us with her, we'll be on their radar.

XHEVDET. [*To one side.*] He say, because police see you with me and he, we will be bad.

JOURNALIST. Oh, I'm sorry. I understand, but maybe it's better to stay and keep up with the pretense that I'm doing an interview with Sara. To leave might be more suspicious.

XHEVDET. She says that it is better to stay here to . . . talk with Mom . . . because if she leaves, the police will suspect her. And she says sorry, but what can she do?

SOKOL. Okay, Sara, pretend to do an interview.

SARA. Okay fine. Excuse me for a moment, madam. [*She speaks to the guests.*] What can I do for you, gentlemen?

SOKOL. Leave the guests to me. I'll look after them.

[*The customer who ordered the cake enters.*]

CUSTOMER. I came earlier and ordered a cake.

SARA. Enkela, bring the cake for the gentleman. [*Enkela quickly goes inside, so her lover cannot see her. Then she passes the package with the cake to Sara through the kitchen door.*] Here you are, sir.

CUSTOMER. Thank you.

[*The customer pays and exits.*]

ZHUT. Sokol, come here for a minute.

SOKOL. Yes, yes of course. At your service, Mr. Zhut.

ZHUT. Was your wife such a well-known ballerina that she does interviews all day?

SOKOL. Yes. She was famous in Hungary, which is where she was born. Journalists often come here. Sometimes three or four are waiting to interview her. It's irritating, but I don't like to interfere.

ZHUT. You mean that journalist came all the way from America to interview your wife? I never knew she was that famous.

SOKOL. Well, what can I do? This journalist is writing an article about how women have progressed here.

ZHUT. I heard you had a guest, a refugee who has left.

SOKOL. Yes, yes, he left. He never even said thank you. No one saw him leave. We just suddenly realized he'd gone.

ZHUT. Are you sure, Sokol?

SOKOL. Ah, Mr. Zhut, you know I never lie to anyone. Least of all to you.

ZHUT. Fine, Sokol. We're going.

SOKOL. Stay a bit longer, gentlemen.

ZHUT. Thanks, we're off.

SOKOL. Sara, bring the cake since Mr. Zhut is leaving.

[*Sara enters the kitchen and returns with the cake.*]

ZHUT. Oh, Sokol, there's no need.

SOKOL. Please, Mr. Zhut, we promised.

SARA. At your service, gentlemen. Peace and long life to you and your lady.

ZHUT. Oh, thank you, thank you so much. You've wrapped it so beautifully. Goodbye.

SOKOL. Goodbye.

SARA. Goodbye.

[*The police exit.*]

SOKOL. Xhevdet, tell the journalist to leave because we have to close the café. We're in a dire situation, and we have to get out of here quickly.

XHEVDET. He say go, because situation not good, and we go.

JOURNALIST. Okay, okay, I'll be off.

XHEVDET. She said, she will leave.

SOKOL. Say that if the police come here again and find her, it will be bad for all of us.

JOURNALIST. What?

XHEVDET. Okay, okay.

[*A loud explosion is heard. Everyone in the café is terrified, and they look at each other.*]

SOKOL. We've had it. Did you hear that? We're finished. Now, Sara, what do we do? Where do we go?

SARA. Sokol, no one will find out. Trust me, just as you always have.

BETIM. What was that?

ENKELA. We don't know. You're the clever one. You should know.

[*Ahmet enters.*]

AHMET. Ah, Enkela, it was your boyfriend's car. He went out to buy cigarettes. Then the car went BOOM. It's fine. He survived. I asked you to marry me. You wanted him because he had a car. Now look at that car.

SOKOL. What?! What are you saying? Enkela's boyfriend's car exploded?

AHMET. Yes.

SOKOL. And how did you know it was him?

AHMET. I know him. I know him. I've seen him a few times with Enkela.

ENKELA. Shut up, you old fool.

SOKOL. Shut up, Enkela. Sara, was he the customer that bought the cake?

SARA. Yes.

SOKOL. Who gave it to him?

SARA. I did.

SOKOL. Who gave it to you?

SARA. Enkela gave it to me.

SOKOL. Oh God, the cakes were switched. Enkela, are you mad? You could have killed an innocent man.

SARA. So that means all our work was for nothing. Enkela, how could you do this?

ENKELA. I don't care about him.

SARA. What should we do now?

SOKOL. Nothing. What can we do? Enkela, this isn't a game. You could have . . .

[*A stronger explosion than the first is heard. Everyone in the café gets under the table. Mom comes down the stairs and crawls under the table, frightened.*]

MOM. Sokol, son, you forgot your mom.

SOKOL. Don't shout, Mom. Come here. What was that?

BETIM. Hey, perhaps NATO is bombing. The newspaper said they might start today, but . . .

[*The sound of an airplane is heard.*]

SOKOL. Listen, listen.

MOM. What's going on, son? What were those booms? Is Germany firing at us?

SOKOL. Keep calm, Mom. Everything's okay. I think it really did start.

ALL. Hooray! Hooray!

[*Zhut, Dragan, and Nebojsha enter. They are covered in mud and cake, and they point their weapons at everyone.*]

POLICE. Get outside!

SOKOL. Where are we going, Mr. Zhut?

ZHUT. Go wherever you want. You can't stay here.

SARA. Sir, come and relax a bit. Why are you so upset?

DRAGAN. Shut up. Get out.

SOKOL. [*To Sara, aside.*] Go down to the cellar. Take the safe with the gold.

NEBOJSHA. Where are you going? Don't move.

SOKOL. To get some clothes for my mom.

DRAGAN. You're not taking a thing. Outside.

SOKOL. Okay, Dragan, I leave my café and my home in your hands . . .

DRAGAN. Don't say Dragan to me. Do you understand? What do you mean, you leave me your café? This belongs to us from today on. Outside!

[*Sokol takes his mother by the arm, and everyone goes outside with only the clothes on their backs.*]

ACT III

Scene One

[A road in the mountains. Sara, Enkela, Meri, and Sokol, who is carrying Mom on his back.]

SOKOL. Mom, I have to put you down. I can't carry you anymore.

MOM. What, you're going to leave me on the mountain for the wild animals to eat?!

SOKOL. We're all going to rest for a while. Sara, Enkela, Meri, stop. Let's take a break.

SARA. Mom, hang in there. We'll be there soon.

SOKOL. But can I hang in there? Mom's fine. It's like she's riding a horse.

MOM. What do you mean, I'm fine? It feels like my body's been beaten black and blue.

SOKOL. I'll see if they're coming.

ENKELA. Sokol, don't leave us alone. We're scared without you.

SOKOL. I won't leave you alone. I just want to see if the two of them are coming with that cart.

MERI. Please, Sokol.

SOKOL. I still can't see them.

SARA. I'm worried they might catch Xhevdet.

SOKOL. You don't need to worry. That villager said there are no police in these parts. They'll catch up soon.

MERI. Oh, God, I'm covered in mud. If anyone sees me, my image will be destroyed, and it was so hard to build.

ENKELA. Me too. Look at my hands. It looks like I work in the fields.

SOKOL. Forget your image. Just pray to God you survive. No one has time to focus on your image.

MERI. But I still care about it.

SARA. Girls, be more reasonable. Don't you see the situation we're in?

MOM. Sokol, will you tell me something? What are those shots? Is it war? Could it be an earthquake, or is it the end of the world? What's happening?

SOKOL. No, Mom, things are fine. It's just the army doing exercises. They're firing for no reason.

MOM. But why did we go to the mountain?

SOKOL. We went for an outing. They advised us to go, for practice. We need to train too.

MOM. I've never seen such dirty work in all my years. We've become grubs.

[*Xhevdet and Ahmet enter with a handcart.*]

SARA. Come and hug your mom. I've been so worried about you.

SOKOL. Ahmet, are you tired? Where did you find the cart?

AHMET. In the yard of an empty house. A villager took us there and let us have it.

SOKOL. Well done! Come on, Mom, up you go.

MOM. I can't get up there.

SOKOL. You can, you can, slowly, slowly. Ahmet, help me. And you, Xhevdet, don't just watch. Come and help me.

SARA. Let the boy rest a while. He's exhausted.

SOKOL. Okay, you come here then.

SARA. Get up, Mom. Not like that. As if you were doing your ballet. That's it.

MOM. Oh, fools! I'm going to fall over! I'm going to be blown to pieces!

SOKOL. Mom, hold on. We're going. Ahmet, which direction should we take?

AHMET. The ones who were ahead of us went that way.

SOKOL. That way?

AHMET. Not that way, this way.

SOKOL. That way?

AHMET. Yes.

SOKOL. Let's go then. Hang on, Mom. And the rest of you hang on too. Let's wish ourselves luck.

OTHERS. Amen.

Scene Two

[*Scene Two takes place, roughly, in the same café set, but the inventory is stacked overhead in a UNHCR tent with a large sign that has "Refreshments" written on it. In front of the bar, Sokol, dressed in tight clothing. The other characters are also wearing clothes that are not their style – donations from the refugee camp. Xhevdet enters.*]

XHEVDET. Dad, I'm going out.

SOKOL. Where are you going? Go look at the lists in case your name's come up.

XHEVDET. I took a look this morning. It hadn't come up.

SOKOL. Go again. Don't you want to study abroad? Do I have to go for you?! You can see how busy I am. Go on.

[*Xhevdet exits. Ahmet enters, dressed in a rock 'n roll leather jacket.*]

AHMET. Well done, Sokol, well done with the café. You've gotten lucky.

SOKOL. No, Ahmet, it isn't my café. UNHCR opened it. The drinks are free. I get a small wage. It was hard to negotiate even that.

AHMET. It's little but enough. I'm left with nothing but aid. I can't get my pension. They don't know how to get it to me. I want to go to Germany, but my name isn't coming up on the list. The ones who arrived after me have already gone. I don't understand the system.

SOKOL. Talk to them on the phone.

AHMET. You're right.

SOKOL. Here's my mobile. [*He gives him the telephone.*] Just so you know, the phone isn't free. It isn't aid. It's mine, and I have to pay for calls. I'm sorry, but I have to make a living somehow. I'm planning to send Xhevdet abroad for school, and I need the money.

AHMET. Okay, okay, do what you have to do.

[*Ahmet sits down and speaks on the phone. Sokol brings him a drink. Betim enters.*]

BETIM. Sokol, it's great to see you. You're made for this world. Even in this camp, you manage to do business.

SOKOL. At least I'm working. You exhausted me with all your analysis and jingoism, and now both of us have ended up in this camp.

BETIM. The day is coming when everyone will know exactly who did what.

SOKOL. Why don't you pick up a gun instead of just talking about it? Say the word, and I'll follow. I know that the day is coming when we'll all know who did what . . .

BETIM. Don't worry, you're not the only one left. You don't need to grapple with these problems. I have other friends.

SOKOL. Okay, boast in front of them and not in front of me. [*Sara enters with the badge of a humanitarian organization.*] Sara, how are you? Come and help a little.

SARA. Sokol, I don't have time. I'm about to go with Drita to give a talk to traumatized women in the camp.

SOKOL. Fine, and what do I do, left on my own?

SARA. Don't be sad. Why, are you worried that people will leave without paying? You don't need to serve them. Let them take the drinks themselves.

SOKOL. Hey, see if your organization can do something for Xhevdet. Let's get him out quickly because he'll never have this chance again.

SARA. Don't worry, I know. I'll see what I can do.

[*Mom enters in sports clothes.*]

MOM. Don't ask; don't ask. It's the end of the world. I'm dying from the flies, the lice, the dust. Sokol, why don't we go home? Why do we stay here in this field? Our house was so much better.

SARA. Mom, don't worry. We'll go home again.

MOM. And you should be ashamed. We don't practice our ballet or play music, and you spend all day with Drita.

SARA. I've just been busy.

MOM. I want to rest a bit, to lie down properly, but when I do, either a louse crawls all over my body, or a wasp gets inside, and it takes me hours to get it out, or it pours with rain, DRUM, DRUM, DRUM, or it's so hot that you can't stand to be in it.

SARA. Come on, Mom, I'll sort the place out. If you shut the tent, no one will disturb you.

[*Sara and Mom exit. Xhevdet enters.*]

XHEVDET. Dad, my name wasn't on it.

SOKOL. What are you saying?! Alright, then go and sign up for Sweden. Don't hang around. No one will just go up to you and say, *"Hey, come with us."* Go on, off you go.

[*Xhevdet exits.*]

AHMET. [*After he finishes the telephone call.*] Nothing can be done for now. They tell me to wait a bit longer. How much do I owe you?

SOKOL. Twenty marks.

AHMET. Gosh, that's a lot!

SOKOL. You talked for a long time, Ahmet.

BETIM. He can even make money with a phone. Heh, heh, heh . . .

[*Gazi enters dressed in a suit.*]

GAZI. How are you, gentlemen?

SOKOL. What happened to you, Gazi? You look like a bridegroom!

GAZI. I got these clothes by chance. Look at Ahmet! Ahmet, let's trade? I'll give you the coat, and you give me that leather jacket.

AHMET. No, son, they gave this to me.

GAZI. But that's for a young guy.

AHMET. What does that matter? At night, when I'm cold, it's great. It keeps me nice and warm.

GAZI. Sokol, bring me some juice.

SOKOL. Come and get it. Gazi, are you doing something about sending Xhevdet abroad?

GAZI. I don't know what to say, Sokol. It takes money.

SOKOL. What money? We're refugees! We don't have money. I've tried myself. You try too —
do something.

GAZI. I'll see.

AHMET. Gazi, see if you can do something for me too.

GAZI. Like I said, Ahmet. It takes money.

AHMET. I don't have any here, but I promise you. As soon as I get back there, I'll have my pension and send something to you.

GAZI. And let's exchange coats.

AHMET. I'll give you the jacket right now. [*They change jackets.*] You'll try, won't you?

GAZI. I'll do what I can.

AHMET. Alright, I'm off. See you later.

[*Gazi exits. Enkela enters with a package in her hands.*]

SOKOL. Enkela, darling, I'm so glad you're here.

ENKELA. Sokol, you've opened a café!

SOKOL. Yes, and I need someone to help me. It's great that you've come.

ENKELA. Sokol, I can't stay. I'm going to my boyfriend, that Kosovar I told you about.

SOKOL. Where are you going?

ENKELA. We're flying to Holland today. I came to say goodbye. Here's something to help you, but you don't need me anymore. Sokol, you're the best Kosovar of anyone.

SOKOL. Oh, Enkela, don't talk like that.

ENKELA. I mean it.

SOKOL. Anyway, where did you say you're going? To Holland?!

ENKELA. Yes. Where's Sara? Where're the others?

SOKOL. Sara will be back later.

ENKELA. I'll wait to see her. Then I'll go.

AHMET. Ah Enkela, Enkela. It would be better if you'd flown to Holland with me.

ENKELA. Oh, you dirty old man, even the war hasn't cooled you off!

[*Ahmet exits. Another refugee enters, carrying a bag.*]

REFUGEE. Can I use the phone?

SOKOL. Yes, why not.

REFUGEE. If anyone wants to go and get the daily stipend, they've started to distribute it.

[*Betim exits. The refugee talks on the phone.*]

SOKOL. Enkela, do you love that Kosovar?

ENKELA. Yes, a lot.

SOKOL. And he loves you?

ENKELA. He's crazy about me.

[*Meri enters.*]

MERI. Hi Sokol, hi Enkela.

ENKELA. Meri, it's great to see you.

SOKOL. Meri, you came too. Slowly, slowly, the café is becoming like it was in Kosovo. Come and get an apron.

MERI. I don't have time.

SOKOL. You don't have time either?!

MERI. Fate has started to smile on me. I'm singing for the children in the camp. Later, all the singers here are going to perform for the diaspora on a two-week tour. I'm sure I'll find a producer for my album there. [*To Sokol, aside.*] As soon as I get somewhere, I'm going to send for you, my Sokol.

[*After he finishes his call, the refugee pays and exits.*]

SOKOL. Forget it, Meri.

MERI. I'm on my break now, and I used it just to see you.

[*Drita and Sara enter.*]

SARA. How are you, my dear?

MERI. Great, and how are you?

ENKELA. You look so good, Sara. . .

DRITA. How are you? Sokol, I need to talk to you.

SOKOL. What's up, Sara? Have you come to send me on another operation?!

SARA. Yes.

DRITA. But not a hard one.

SOKOL. Fine, my wife, since you've decided to get rid of me, I'll do whatever you want. Tell me, Drita.

DRITA. Now listen, Sokol, you know I'll speak but once, in keeping with my doctrine and my duty. One of our fighters has been injured just over the border. You can cross the line more easily because you're older and don't look suspicious. You're to bring him here for treatment.

SOKOL. How will I get there? How will I know where to go? How will I know him?

DRITA. I'll tell you. Take this flashlight. When you reach the rendezvous point, you'll flash the light three times. He'll see the signal and approach. When he's near, you give the password, "nightingale on the verandah." Sokol, you need to leave now. It's almost sundown, and the operation can only take place at night.

[*Sokol takes off his apron and says goodbye to Sara, Meri, and Enkela.*]

SOKOL. Goodbye, Sara. Take care of Xheki and make sure he goes abroad to study and tell Ahmet to look after the café till I get back.

SARA. Goodbye, my love. I'll pray for you.

SOKOL. Goodbye, Enkela, good luck.

ENKELA. Oh Sokol, all the best.

SOKOL. Meri, sing a song for me.

MERI. Oh Sokol, don't make me sad.

DRITA. Okay Sokol, come with me. I can only take you so far, and then I'll leave you with a map. It isn't a long way but you'll have to be quick . . .

[*Sokol and Drita exit.*]

SARA. Oh God, I have a bad premonition. Did you notice how he didn't resist at all? He has always resisted me, but not this time. And he asked me to take care of Xheki, and he said Xheki, which is what I call him, not Xhevdet, which is what he always says. Oh, he's so romantic.

MERI. Don't be like that, Sara. He'll return. It will all be fine.

SARA. He said, *"Sing a song for me."* He said it as if he'll never hear you sing it. What will I do without him?!

ENKELA. Sara, there's no point thinking like this. He'll be back tonight.

SARA. He wished you luck, as if he'd never see you again. Oh God, protect my Sokol.

[*Ahmet and Gazi enter.*]

GAZI. What's going on? Why did you all go quiet? Where's Sokol?

AHMET. Enkela, you're still here?

ENKELA. Shut up, you dirty old man.

SARA. Sokol put himself on the line to save someone wounded. Ahmet, he asked me to tell you to take care of the café until he gets back.

AHMET. Sara, I don't have time for that. I have to check the lists and chase down documents.

SARA. Please Ahmet, perhaps he'll never return, and I know how much he respects you.

AHMET. Why are you talking like this? Okay, since Sokol asked, I'll stay.

[*Ahmet goes to the bar to work.*]

SARA. And you, Gazi, he asked that you try to send Xheki abroad. You know how much he wanted Xheki to be educated, not to remain a simple café owner who everyone knows but no one knows. Please, Gazi. Sokol and I love you like our own son.

GAZI. Sara, you don't need to ask me. I'll do it, I promise.

[*Gazi exits.*]

ENKELA. Sara, now I have to go.

MERI. And so do I.

SARA. You're leaving me alone.

MERI. I don't have any more time.

ENKELA. I don't either.

SARA. Okay, well then, goodbye, girls.

WAITRESSES. Goodbye!

[*The waitresses exit. Xhevdet and Betim enter dragging Mom, who is shouting.*]

MOM. Let me go, or I'll show you.

SARA. What's wrong, Mom? What's wrong?

XHEVDET. She tried to beat up an aid worker.

MOM. I was first, and she cut in front of me. Every day she steals my stipend. She thinks I'm crazy. I'll show her. From the time I was little, she wouldn't leave me alone. She never gave me anything to play with. She kept everything for herself.

SARA. Mom, don't shout, because no one can take your stipend. Come with me.

MOM. Why not? Didn't you see Hamide, that bitch? I'll show her!

SARA. No one will bother you. Sit and rest over there. Here, have some juice.

MOM. I did it the right way. I got in the line. That American pointed at me and said, *"Come,"* and nodded. She was saying it was my turn, then she made a fuss: *"Hamide,"* I said, *"Go away; let me pass because it's my turn."* She said. *"No, I'm next."* So, of course I got mad.

SARA. What are you saying, Mom? Hamide died twenty years ago.

MOM. What?! Go now, go to the aid line. See whether she's dead or not.

SARA. Why did you go there, Mom? Xhevdet, why did you let her go?

MOM. So what?

XHEVDET. I didn't. I was waiting in the line and Grandma was standing nearby and watching. The woman who works there gestured to me, and then I saw that there was a fuss around the woman who was first in line. She was pushing her and shouting, *"Hamide, Hamide!"*

SARA. Mom, let's go. If you carry on like this, they won't let you leave.

MOM. You still have a lot to learn. That's your problem. I know what I'm doing.

[*They exit.*]

Scene Three

[*On the mountain, in the darkness, Sokol walks slowly, looking around. He turns on the flashlight and looks at a map. Then he flashes twice toward the distance. We hear the sound of gun shots. Sokol drops the flashlight and falls to the ground.*]

SOKOL. Nightingale on the verandah, nightingale on the verandah.

Scene Four

[*The refreshment tent. Sara, Ahmet, and Xhevdet are there sitting around a table.*]

AHMET. Sara, don't worry. Nothing will happen. I trust Sokol. He'll come back alive and well.

SARA. Thank you, Ahmet, but I can't help myself. Somehow, I have a bad feeling. I feel sick.

AHMET. Shall I make you some coffee? You'll feel better.

SARA. Yes, thank you. Xheki, go and help Ahmet. You'll need to learn how to run a café.

XHEVDET. Don't worry, Mom. I'll do whatever you say.

SARA. [*Cries.*] Oh Xheki, you're all I have left.

AHMET. Oh don't, Sara, don't. Look at me. I've lived alone for years, and I never complain.

SARA. Sorry, Ahmet. It must be hard for you.

[*Gazi enters.*]

GAZI. Sara, good news! I've come to let you know that I've sorted everything out for Xhevdet. You're in luck! He's all processed and cleared to go, but you need to pack now because the group will be on their way to the airport soon.

SARA. Really?! Where will he go?

GAZI. To Austria.

SARA. Austria? Very good, they have great art schools there. Thank you so much, Gazi. We'll never forget this. Come on, Xheki, let's pack a suitcase. Hurry.

[*Sara and Xhevdet go to a corner of the tent.*]

AHMET. And what about me, Gazi?

GAZI. Later.

AHMET. How much later?

GAZI. I'll tell you when the time comes.

AHMET. But now is the time, Gazi. If you can't fix it now, when can you?

GAZI. Ahmet, trust me when I say this. I'll sort you out as well.

AHMET. Okay, but hurry. I told you, as soon as I get there, I'll draw my pension and pay you. Don't you believe me?

GAZI. I believe you. How can I not? But while you're waiting, keep looking around the camp, perhaps you'll meet your soulmate.

AHMET. Ah, you're teasing me!

GAZI. No, I'm not. Every day, people are getting married here. Who knows, it could happen to you.

AHMET. For old people like me, it's a bit harder.

[*Sara returns with a suitcase. Xhevdet follows with some clothes. They pack the case together.*]

XHEVDET. Do I need to take anything else?

SARA. We have nothing else, but they'll give you some things there.

GAZI. Faster, faster.

SARA. Wait, wait a minute. Did you take your toothbrush?

XHEVDET. Yes.

SARA. Take these biscuits for the journey.

GAZI. Sara, hurry up. There's no more time.

SARA. Okay, okay. We're done. Listen my son. Be polite and cultured. Try to go to school, learn the language, win a scholarship. If you don't get a scholarship, work. Work in a restaurant, greet people politely, smile. Let them see you were well brought up.

GAZI. Sara, hurry up. We'll be late.

SARA. Come and hug me, my sweetheart. Have a safe journey, study hard, make us proud.

[*Mom enters.*]

MOM. Where are you going, boy?

XHEVDET. Goodbye. Say hi to Dad. Good night, Grandma. Uncle Ahmet, goodbye.

AHMET. Goodbye, safe journey.

GAZI. Let's go.

[*Gazi and Xhevdet exit.*]

MOM. Where did you send the boy, Sara? Is the army taking him?

SARA. No, Mom, to school – to study. Come on, I'll put you to bed. [*Sara settles Mom in the tent and returns immediately.*] I'm all alone. Everyone's left. Just Sokol, if he returns.

AHMET. He'll come back. He doesn't give up easily.

SARA. Ah, if I only knew for sure.

AHMET. Like I said, Sara, don't worry. Sokol's a strong man. He knows how to look after himself.

SARA. Oh, if only he comes back safe and sound! That's all I ask for. [*A figure enters with an injury on his arm. The man in disguise drags Sokol, who has been wounded in the buttocks.*] Sokol, what's wrong? Are you okay?

SOKOL. Oh Drita, Drita, you gave me the worst flashlight in existence.

SARA. Sokol, what happened? What did Drita do to you? What happened?

SOKOL. What did she do to me? Nothing. That's just my way of cursing.

FIGHTER. Madam, we agreed that Sokol should flash three times, but he only flashed twice, and then I shot him by accident. I thought he was the enemy. I shot in self-defense.

SOKOL. The flashlight broke. I lit it twice, then the plastic snapped; something came apart. Then the shots . . .

AHMET. Thank God you're alive. We were so worried.

SARA. Ahmet, find the first aid kit. It's under the bar.

[*Ahmet brings the box. Sara binds Sokol's wounds and those of the fighter.*]

SARA. Thank God you're alive. Does it hurt a lot?

SOKOL. Not too much. I just can't walk normally.

SARA. Do you need an operation, to take the bullet out?

SOKOL. There isn't any bullet. It just grazed my leg . . . and went up . . . and out . . .

SARA. And you, sir, are you alright? Your wound doesn't look too bad.

FIGHTER. I'm fine. This bandage will do the trick.

SARA. Let's go to our room, and you can rest there.

SOKOL. No, let's stay here. It's a tent here and a tent there. Where is Xhevdet? Call him, so I can see him.

SARA. Xhevdet just left for the airport. He's going to Austria.

SOKOL. To Austria? Really? So fast?

SARA. Gazi fixed it. He's just left.

SOKOL. He did well. Now I feel better . . . my son . . . my boy . . .

[*Someone enters holding a bag, followed by seven others, also with bags.*]

MAN. Is this the refreshment tent?

AHMET. Yes, yes. Come in, come in.

MAN. At dinner, they said we could come here to drink something.

AHMET. Yes, what would you like to drink? Come and help yourselves.

[*Betim enters.*]

BETIM. Hey, haven't you heard the news?

SOKOL. Why, what's happened?

BETIM. What's wrong with him?

SOKOL. Leave me alone. I'm fine. Tell us the news.

BETIM. I'm about to tell you. Ahmet, turn on the radio. [*Ahmet turns it on.*] Do you hear them talking about Kosovo?

RADIO VOICE. NATO forces have begun to enter Kosovo. Serbian forces are withdrawing . . .

AHMET. Did I hear that, or am I imagining it?

BETIM. You're not imagining it. It's true.

SOKOL. Fantastic, fantastic . . .

ALL. Hooray!!

SOKOL. Put on the music, Ahmet.

[*They all start to dance, except Sokol and the fighter who are lying down, and Sara who is watching over them. Mom enters and begins to dance.*]

MOM. What's happening, Sokol? Is it a wedding?

SOKOL. It's more than a wedding.

MOM. Fantastic, fantastic! Why didn't you tell me there was a wedding? I'd have come earlier.

[*Drita enters.*]

DRITA. Sara, your organization is asking you to set off immediately for Kosovo along with the first group.

SARA. How can I leave Sokol, injured like this?

DRITA. Sokol is fine. I can see that it's nothing serious.

SOKOL. Go on, Sara. Don't worry about me.

SARA. Do you mean it?

SOKOL. Yes.

SARA. Alright, I'll go.

SOKOL. Sara, look after our home, if there's anything left of it, and don't forget to see if the safe is still in the cellar. If nothing remains, don't be sad. We'll build a new house. I'll make it beautiful. I'll build a hotel. We'll live well.

SARA. Of course, we will. Goodbye. Look after Mom.

SOKOL. Goodbye.

[*Drita and Sara exit. The dance continues.*]

MOM. I never saw such a huge wedding. Dad had to give me away too. Zadja was getting married, so I had to marry too. Thank God, I was lucky. Woo hoo . . .

THE END

BIOGRAPHIES

Fadil Bajraj is a well-known translator from English into Albanian, focusing in large part on American literature. He was solely responsible for introducing the Beat Generation to the Albanian-speaking world with his translations of Allen Ginsberg, Jack Kerouac, Lawrence Ferlinghetti, Amiri Baraka, Michael McClure, Philip Lamantia, Gregory Corso, Gary Snyder, Carl Solomon, Harold Norse, Peter Orlovsky, Bob Kaufman, etc. Likewise, through his efforts, Ezra Pound was translated and published for the first time in Albanian. Bajraj has rendered selected works by James Joyce, E. E. Cummings, Raymond Carver, John Fante, Dan Fante, Frank O'Hara, Marianne Moore, Charles Bukowski, Robert Frost, T. S. Eliot, William Carlos Williams, William Burroughs, and Ernest Hemingway, among others, as well as Gregory Pardlo and Lou Lipsitz most recently. Through the publication of the *Anthology of Rock Lyrics*, he introduced Albanian readers to such songwriters as Bob Dylan, Leonard Cohen, Nick Cave, Jim Morrison, Patty Smith, Tom Waits, Lou Reed, Tim Buckley, Jeff Buckley, Joy Division, Bruce Springsteen, and Robert Hunter. He has also published translations from Albanian into English, and from Albanian into Serbian and vice versa.

Xhevdet Bajraj is a poet, dramatist, translator, and professor. His works of poetry, which number more than 20 volumes, have been translated into English, German, Spanish, Danish, Serbian, Slovenian, Hungarian, Turkish, and Polish. He has been the recipient of many awards and honors. Among them are the prize for best book of poetry (both in 1993 and 2000), conferred by the Kosovo Writers' Society; the Goliardos International Prize for Poetry in 2004; the 2010 Katarina Josipi award for best original drama written in Albanian; first prize at the *Festival of Monodrama*, Vlorë, Albania, in 2013; and the award for the best book of poetry in 2015, presented at the *Prishtina International Book Fair*. In May of 1999, Bajraj and his family were deported from Kosovo. Through the International Parliament of Writers and their program for persecuted writers, he was granted asylum and a fellowship at the Casa Refugio Citlaltépetl in Mexico. In the years since, he has become a full professor of creative writing and literature at the Autonomous University of Mexico City and has been inducted into the Sistema Nacional de Creadores de Arte. In a parallel artistic universe, he appeared as a co-star of *Aro Tolbukhin, in the Mind of the Killer*, an Ariel award-winning film and Mexico's submission to the 2003 Oscars.

Doruntina Basha is a playwright and screenwriter from Prishtina. She is the author of five plays, including plays for children, and several short screenplays. In 2005, *Saved by the Stick* premiered in the Children's Theater Center in Skopje in a Macedonian translation. Doruntina is also the co-author of *Travels to Unmikistan* (2003), a Kosovar-French collaboration project that premiered in Kosovo and was subsequently shown in France and published in a bilingual edition by L'Espace d'un Instant in Paris. Her play *The Finger* (2011) was awarded the prize for Best Socially Engaged Contemporary Play (2011) in a competition organized by the Heartefact Fund in Belgrade, Serbia. It also won the Golden Laurel for Best Balkan Contemporary Play at the *MESS International Theater Festival* in Sarajevo, Bosnia and Herzegovina (2013), and the prize for Best National Play in the *Flaka e Janarit* theater festival in Gjilan, Kosovo (2015). It premiered at the Bitef Theater in Belgrade in 2012, followed by productions in the Albanian Theater in Skopje in 2013, the Sartr Theater in Sarajevo in 2014, as part of the triptych *Balkan Requiem* in the Hundsturm Theater in Vienna in 2014, at the National Theater of Kosovo in 2015, and at Kujtim Spahivogli Experimental Theater in Tirana, Albania, in 2018. It has been translated into Serbian, BHS (Bosnian, Croatian, and Serbian), English, French, German, Italian, and Turkish. Her screenplay for the forthcoming feature film, *Vera Dreams of the Sea*, is currently in production.

Alexandra Channer began translating in Kosovo in 2009 while conducting research for her doctoral thesis on Albanian national self-determination movements. Alex worked as a freelancer for four years in Kosovo, translating a variety of political and technical documents. Her collaboration with Jeton Neziraj began at this time, and she has since translated and edited many of Jeton's plays. She also translates a selection of prose and poetry for the annual *POLIP – International Literature Festival* held in Prishtina. Alex is a human rights expert, and she currently works for a consultancy based in the United Kingdom. Her professional background is in politics and human rights.

Anna Di Lellio is a professor of politics at the Milano School of International Affairs, Management, and Urban Policy, The New School, and the International Relations Program of New York University. She holds a Ph.D. in sociology from Columbia University and a master's degree in public policy from New York University. Her research and publications focus on memory, nationalism, and security in Kosovo, where she worked as an officer of the United Nations-led international administration. She is the author of several articles published in academic journals, the editor of *The Case for Kosova*: *Passage to Independence* (Anthem, 2006), and the author of *The Battle of Kosovo 1389*: *An Albanian Epic* (I.B. Tauris, 2009). Professor Di Lellio is the producer of the 2015 art installation "Thinking of You," by artist Alketa Xhafa Mripa, dedicated to survivors of wartime sexual violence, and the co-producer of the documentary *#MendojPërTy#ThinkingOfYou (The Making of)*. She is the co-founder of the Kosovo Oral History Initiative. In 2015 she was awarded the Kosovo Presidential Medal of Merits for her contribution in the field of freedom of speech.

Ariel Dorfman is an Argentine-Chilean-American novelist, playwright, essayist, academic, and human rights activist. He is the author of numerous works of fiction in Spanish and English, including *Hard Rain, The Last Song of Manuel Sendero, Widows, Konfidenz, Mascara, Blake's Therapy,* and *The Nanny and the Iceberg.* His dramatic works include *Death and the Maiden, Widows,* and *Purgatorio.* Among his collections of essays and memoirs are *How to Read Donald Duck; The Empire's Old Clothes; Exorcising Terror; Desert Memories; Heading South, Looking North; Feeding on Dreams; Other Septembers, Many Americas: Selected Provocations, 1980-2004;* and *Chile: The Other September 11: An Anthology of Reflections on the 1973 Coup.* His books have been published in more than 50 languages, and his plays have been performed in more than 100 countries. His awards include The Kennedy Center/American Express New Plays Award for *Widows* (1988); the Roger L. Stevens Award for Extraordinary Playwriting (1991); the Reader Time Out Award for best play in London for *Death and the Maiden* (1991); the Sir Laurence Olivier Award for best play in London for *Death and the Maiden* (1992); and the Literary Lion, New York Public Library (1992). He is the subject of the documentary *A Promise to the Dead: The Exile Journey of Ariel Dorfman.* On July 31, 2010, he delivered the Eighth Nelson Mandela Annual Lecture Address. His most recent books are a collection of essays, *Homeland Security Ate My Speech: Messages from the End of the World,* and the novel, *Darwin's Ghosts.* He contributes regularly to major newspapers and journals worldwide, including frequent contributions to The New York Times and the New York Review of Books. A citizen of the United States since 2004, he lives with his wife Angélica in Chile and in Durham, North Carolina, where he is the Walter Hines Page Emeritus Professor of Literature at Duke University.

Ani Gjika is an Albanian-born poet, writer, literary translator, and the author of *Bread on Running Waters* (Fenway Press, 2013), a finalist for the 2011 Anthony Hecht Poetry Prize and 2011 May Sarton New Hampshire Book Prize. She moved to the United States when she was 18, earning an M.A. in English at Simmons College and an M.F.A. in poetry at Boston University. Gjika is the translator from the Albanian of Luljeta Lleshanaku's *Negative Space* (New Directions/Bloodaxe Books, 2018) and Xhevdet Bajraj's *Slaying the Mosquito* (Laertes, 2017). Her honors include awards and fellowships from the National Endowment for the Arts, English PEN, the Robert Pinsky Global Fellowship, and the Robert Fitzgerald Translation Prize, among others. Her poetry appears in *Seneca Review*, *Salamander*, *Plume*, *From the Fishouse*, and elsewhere. Her translations from the Albanian appear in *World Literature Today*, *Ploughshares*, *AGNI Online*, *Catamaran Literary Reader*, *Two Lines*, *From the Fishouse*, and elsewhere.

Ilir Gjocaj is a playwright, screenwriter, dramaturg, librettist, director, and producer. Two of his plays have been staged, *The Basement*, which was performed at the National Theater of Kosovo (Prishtina) in 2009, and *The Kitchen*, performed at both the Dodona Theater (Prishtina) in 2009 and the Gjakova theater (Gjakova) in 2012. These have been translated into Serbian, English, German, and Turkish. One of his short films, *Denis the Prophet*, won first prize at the *Nine Eleven Prishtina Festival* in 2003. He has written and directed many television documentaries, among them *The Kurtaj Violins* (2001), *Why Me, A Documentary on AIDS* (2002), which has been broadcast over the years on three national television networks, and *Japanese People for the Children of Kosovo* (2002). Along with Visar Krusha and Artur Tahiraj, he wrote and directed the TV comedy *Tezga Alternative* (2002). He has co-written for the RTK public television sitcom, *Our Cafés* (2006–2009). As a dramaturg he has participated in *A Suspect Individual*, Albanian Theater (Skopje) 2013, *One Flew over the Kosovo Theater*, Qendra Multimedia, 2012, and *Tartuffe*, The National Theater of Kosovo, 2008. As a librettist, he has collaborated with the composer T. Dhomi on the musical *Arietta* (2012), and since 2003 he has been the production manager of Kosovafilm.

Saša Ilić is a writer, journalist, and social activist. He has published two short story collections, *The Prevision of the Civil War* (2000), and *Urchin Hunts* (2015), and two novels, *Berlin Window* (2005), and *Fall of the Space Shuttle, Columbia* (2010). Ilić was one of the founders and editors of the supplement for literary engagement, *Beton*, of *Danas*, a Belgrade newspaper. With Jeton Neziraj, he coordinated a series of two-way anthologies, as well as separate editions, of the new literature of Serbia and Kosovo (2011). His works of prose have been translated into Albanian, French, German, Macedonian, and Slovenian. In December 2013, with Alida Bremer, he founded *Beton International – a Newspaper for Literature and Society*. Ilić is a co-founder of *POLIP — International Literature Festival*, which takes place every year in Prishtina. As a journalist, he writes for the portal *Pescanik.net*. His research interests include literature, cultural policy, and peace-building in post-conflict societies. He is an editor of the website *Komunalinks.com* and lives and works in Belgrade.

Visar Krusha is a playwright, screenwriter, dramaturg, director, and producer. His plays have been translated into Serbian, French, German, English, and Turkish and performed in the Albanian Theater of Skopje (*The Crossroads Café*, 2003), and the Oda Theater in Prishtina (*The Key*, 2004). *The Key* was also published in the literary magazine, *Fjala*. His television work includes scriptwriting for the *Inside Justice* and the *Modern Family* series (the Radio and Television network of Kosovo). He has written, directed, and produced two short films: *Three Minutes of Solitude* (2009) and *Kaçanik Girl* (2011). In 2006 he founded Produksioni Krusha, a film production company that, in conjunction with Niko Film (Germany), Skopje Film Studio (Macedonia), and Eaux Vive Productions (France), produced the feature film *Babai* (2015), which won five separate prizes at the *Munich Film Festival* (2015), as well as awards from the *Karlovy Vary International Film Festival* (2015), the *Angers European First Film Festival* (2016), the *Crossing Europe Filmfestival* (2016), and the Prix Europe (2017), among others. He is a member of the European Film Academy, has won the Bosch Stiftung Co-production Prize (2011), and has taught in the Department of Dramaturgy at Prishtina University. He is the current artistic director of the Dodona Theater in Prishtina.

Janice Mathie-Heck is a Canadian teacher, poet, translator, editor, and literary critic. In 2000 she began to collaborate with Robert Elsie on translations of Albanian literature, producing English versions of numerous historical texts, two forewords, two novels, five volumes of poetry, and one drama. As a poet, translator, and essayist, she has contributed to various literary reviews and e-zines, including *Le Chinook*, *filling Station*, *Freefall*, the *Frontenac House website*, *The Gauntlet*, Illyria, *Jeta e re*, *Mehr Licht!*, *Phoenix*, *Tempulli*, *Transcript*, *TranscUlturAl*, *Translation Review*, *Wasafiri*, and *Wordweavers' Chapbook*. Individually, she has translated many of the poems of the Albanian writer Johan Vupa and worked with the Kosovar playwright, Doruntina Basha, on the translation of *The Finger*, her award-winning play which is published here.

Jeton Neziraj is a playwright and screenwriter. He has written more than 25 plays which have been translated into French, Italian, German, English, Spanish, Turkish, Kurdish, Polish, Romanian, Bulgarian, Serbian, Bosnian, Croatian, Slovenian, Macedonian, and Montenegrin. They have been presented at festivals and been performed by a great number of theaters and acting companies, such as Volkstheater (Vienna), L'Espace d'un Instant (Paris), Teater de Vill (Stockholm), *Festival Vie* (Modena), Schlachthaus Theater (Bern), Gerald W. Lynch Theater (New York), Gare du Théâtre (Paris), Heilbronn Theater (Heilbronn), Bitef Theater (Belgrade), Theater Nomad (London), Markus Zohner Theater Company (Lugano), Istanbul Municiple Theater (Istanbul), National Theater of Wales (Cardiff), Hessisches Staatstheater Wiesbaden (Wiesbaden), Yale Drama Coalition (New Haven), National Theater of Montenegro (Podgorica), and *International Theatre Festival MESS* (Sarajevo), as well as The National Theatre of Kosovo (Prishtina), of which he was for a time the artistic director. His screenplay for the film, *Donkeys of the Border*, has been an official selection at several film festivals. As a critic, his writings include a study of the celebrated Kosovar actor, Faruk Begolli. He is a member of the European Cultural Parliament, and one of the founders of *POLIP – International Literature Festival*, which takes place every year in Prishtina.

ACKNOWLEDGMENTS

From Saša Ilić

I thank these early translators from Albanian to Serbian: Shkelzen Maliqi, Anton Berishaj, and Qerim Ondozi — pioneers in this cultural adventure.

From Jeton Neziraj

I would like to thank Dr. Johann Brieger, the former Austrian ambassador to Kosovo; Levend Bicaku of the Palme Center office in Prishtina; Blerta Neziraj, Bajrush Mjaku, Ariel Dorfman, Alexandra Channer, Senem Cevher, Dominique Dolmieu, Shkelzen Maliqi, and Nina Kamberos.

From Ilir Gjocaj

I would like to thank Fadil Hysaj and Jeton Neziraj for their support, and Nina Kamberos especially for her hard work and persistence in the preparation of "Bodrumi" for publication.

From Doruntina Basha

My gratitude goes to Qerim Ondozi, my partner, always the first reader, as well as the first translator of my plays; my parents, Eqrem and Flutra, and my sister, Rozi, who are my most avid readers and harshest critics. I'd also like to thank Heartefact Fund in Belgrade, especially Andrej Nosov, for producing the first-ever production of my play. A big and special thank you goes to Sartr - Sarajevo War Theater.

From Visar Krusha

For the publication of my play in English by Laertes, I would like to thank Nina Kamberos, Alexandra Channer, and Jeton Neziraj.

From Janice Mathie-Heck

I am deeply indebted to my late colleague and mentor, Dr. Robert Elsie, for his inspiration, diligence, friendship, and kindness, and for so enthusiastically immersing me in the richness of Albanian literature! A special thanks goes to my dear friend, Besim Lumi of Calgary, who has always shown me the meaning of courage, perseverance, integrity, family, generosity, and hospitality — and how it is possible to cope with intense hardship, pain, and loss.

From Ani Gjika

I am grateful to my publisher, Nina Kamberos, for giving me the privilege to work with Xhevdet Bajraj's words. For that, your thoughtful edits, your kindness, thank you, Nina.

From Alexandra Channer

Thanks to Linda Meniku and Gazi Berlajolli, who taught me Albanian; Afrim Hyseni, who took a chance on me, giving me my first work as a translator; Jeton for trusting me with his writing; and Prishtina University, for letting me attend its 2002 annual seminar in the Albanian language.

From the Publisher

The shepherding of this book has been the honor of my life, and I have been blessed, to boot, by an association with Jeton Neziraj, Saša Ilić, Anna Di Lellio, Ilir Gjocaj, Fadil Bajraj, Doruntina Basha, Janice Mathie-Heck, Xhevdet Bajraj, Ani Gjika, Visar Krusha, and Alexandra Channer — all the most gracious of beings, all of whom I count now as friends. My very great thanks to Angelia Graf, who first spotted this anthology in its original Serbian version; to Gorancho Gjorgjievski for speaking on my behalf to Jeton Neziraj; to the extraordinary artists who grace this and all our projects: Maxine Mills, Biba Kayewich, and Ryan Dann; the sensitive, deft editors of this work: Moses Appleton, Elizabeth Gowing, Valerie Price, Erica Silberman, Garret Weyr, and Margaretta Yarborough; and to our directors: Heidi Madden, Wayne Pond, Sally Massengale, and Junius Chambers for giving me the basis to turn this dream into something actual.

For production rights information, please contact egret@laertesbooks.org.

See also, laertesbooks.org/egret-acting-editions/